# Working Girls in the West

# Working Girls in the West

## Representations of
## Wage-Earning Women

*Lindsey McMaster*

UBC Press • Vancouver • Toronto

17 16 15 14 13 12 11 10 09 08          5 4 3 2 1

Printed in Canada on ancient-forest-free paper (100% post-consumer recycled) that is processed chlorine- and acid-free, with vegetable-based inks.

**Library and Archives Canada Cataloguing in Publication**

McMaster, Lindsey, 1972-
   Working girls in the West : representations of wage-earning women / Lindsey McMaster.

   Includes bibliographical references and index.
   ISBN 978-0-7748-1455-3 (bound); ISBN 978-0-7748-1456-0 (pbk)

   1. Women employees in literature. 2. Women in literature. 3. Women employees – Canada, Western – Social conditions – 20th century. 4. Women – Canada, Western – Social conditions – 20th century. I. Title.

PS8103.W6M25 2007          C810.9'3553          C2007-905911-2

Canadä

UBC Press gratefully acknowledges the financial support for our publishing program of the Government of Canada through the Book Publishing Industry Development Program (BPIDP), and of the Canada Council for the Arts , and the British Columbia Arts Council.

This book has been published with the help of a grant from the Canadian Federation for the Humanities and Social Sciences, through the Aid to Scholarly Publications Programme, using funds provided by the Social Sciences and Humanities Research Council of Canada.

UBC Press
The University of British Columbia
2029 West Mall
Vancouver, BC V6T 1Z2
604-822-5959 / Fax: 604-822-6083
www.ubcpress.ca

For Rob

# Contents

Acknowledgments / ix

Introduction / 1

1 Working Women in the West at the Turn of the Century / 16

2 The Urban Working Girl in Turn-of-the-Century Canadian Literature / 44

3 White Slaves, Prostitutes, and Delinquents / 88

4 Girls on Strike / 121

5 White Working Girls and the Mixed-Race Workplace / 145

Conclusion: Just Girls / 169

Notes / 176

Bibliography / 190

Index / 199

# Acknowledgments

Writing a book is a daunting task, and I am immensely grateful to all those who advised, encouraged, and supported me in this undertaking. First to be singled out is my PhD supervisor, Richard Cavell, whose exquisite mentoring saw me through many of graduate school's dicey moments. He always told me, with all the authority of his wonderfully alive intellect, to keep going, so I did. I also give heartfelt thanks to Pamela Dalziel, whose kind encouragement and editor's eye make her an academic girl's best friend.

Many friends and colleagues have made the journey to authorship an intellectually and personally rewarding experience. I salute the contributors and editors of the University of British Columbia's (UBC) student publications the *Graduate* and *Babel* for creating the stimulating intellectual community that graduate school is all about. It was in editorial meetings for these that I met Anna Lehman, a force of nature and just the person to share a few of life's milestones with, and Maria Ticinovic, a true writer and intellectual, whose acerbic insight is a light to her friends. Thanks to Sharon Alker and Karen Selesky for organizing the work-in-progress meetings and staging the mock oral exams for UBC's English PhD students; the good fellowship and intellectual rigour of these meetings were an inspiration.

I was lucky to receive generous assistance in the form of graduate fellowships from the University of British Columbia and a grant from the Social Sciences and Humanities Research Council of Canada. The librarians of UBC's Koerner Library and the archivists at the Vancouver City Archives and the British Columbia Archives, in Victoria, were of great help in my research as I zoomed through miles of newspapers on microfilm and searched for rare and fascinating documents. I was also fortunate to spend a delightful afternoon with Irene Howard, talking about the inspiring life of labour activist Helena Gutteridge.

Finally, I come to the big inspirations. It's not every budding academic who can call up her mom and get not just the unqualified reassurance of a mother but also advice from one of Canada's smartest scholars of English. I'm that lucky. And I'm doubly lucky because a chat with my dad will delight and surprise like an intellectual version of eating chocolate. My husband, Rob, saw me through not only the creation of the book but, during the same time, the birth of our daughter, Liv, and I thank him for thoughtful intellectual discussion during the day and for perhaps equally thoughtful bath times and diaper changes at night. When you have a child while in the midst of revising a scholarly book, you also need a seriously understanding editor, so to Jean Wilson too, sincere thanks.

# Working Girls in the West

# Introduction

In 1891 Alice Barrett Parke went to visit her friends Lizzie and Mary Harding, who were living in Vancouver and working as school teachers. In her diary Parke recorded this singular evening of girl talk:

> We were all talking about marriage the other night, & Mary said so many people wondered why she had never married – how she had managed to withstand the opportunities and importunities of a new country, where so many men are walking about unattached. It seemed to me they are something like the little pigs in our old nursery rhyme who used to run about with knives & forks sticking in them, crying "Who'll take a piece of me" – only these self-sacrificing creatures are pleading to be allowed to give the whole of themselves. However, to return to our subject, Mary said she had so long earned her own money, and spent it as she pleased, not having to give account to any one, that she could not bear the idea of having someone else give it to her, & she added "To tell the truth I don't care to give up a sixty dollar school for a forty dollar man." It sounded so funny I had to laugh.[1]

This rare account of female conversation in turn-of-the-century Vancouver touches playfully on issues of work and marriage and suggests the pleasures as well as the pressures experienced by young women inhabiting this far shore of Canadian civilization. Parke refers to the large number of unattached men in the West who outnumbered unattached women and who, according to this account, dashed about in search of a woman who would take them. The expectation that all young women would indeed marry was strong, and twenty-five-year-old Mary attests to the curiosity surrounding her single status. Her answer is a striking assertion of female independence that places the labour market against the marriage market in the most rationalist of terms. Her words would have confirmed the fears of many social critics who believed that women's domestic roles as wives and mothers were put in jeopardy by the increasing entrance of women into paid employment, a dubious moral sphere where social and financial independence might weaken women's inclination to marry. My interest lies in the social discourse that surrounded the figure of the "working girl" in the West, where specific social and geographic conditions shaped the debate concerning women and work in the city. Parke's depiction of young women blithely setting men against paycheques was not the vision of womanhood that the fledgling nation espoused.

This book addresses representations of young wage-earning women in western Canada, who, in the early part of the twentieth century, became touchstones for judgments on city life, work, and morality. Young, single, wage-earning women were something new and troubling to the middle-class administrators and social critics of the time. The numerous single working men, with their overcrowded dwellings and tendencies to unionize, were considered somewhat disorderly, but the necessity of their presence in the rapidly expanding urban centres of the West was never questioned. Young working women, by comparison, seemed to embody all that was unnatural and unnerving about modern times: the disintegration of the family, the independence of women, and the promiscuity of city life. So serious was the moral danger surrounding these "working girls" that the very future of the nation, symbolized in these future mothers, appeared to be at stake. Indeed, the figure of the working girl gained increasing notoriety in her time and was the subject of intense public debate. These kinds of anxieties were not unique to the West: the issue of wage-earning women was deemed a social problem throughout Canada. But in the West these anxieties were exacerbated and amplified in particular ways. The West was known for its shortage of white women, and as a result the female minority and its pursuits were subject to a good deal of scrutiny. The West also continued to be popularly figured as a frontier space and as a colonial outskirt, long after the East was felt to be comfortably settled and urbanized, and ideals about women's roles in these liminal spaces – daughters of the British Empire, mothers of the nation – were carefully preserved. Also particular to the West was its extremely rapid industrialization and urbanization, which spurred equally rapid social change for both genders. Although the East was gradually coming into its own as an urban industrial setting, in the West conquering the wilderness was still the vivid theme – whereas urban peril was a troubling new horizon. The West also felt the pressures of immigration in ways distinct from the rest of Canada. The first two decades of the twentieth century saw rapid population growth in the cities of British Columbia and the Prairies, and the multiculturalism of the influx was cause for concern to a white middle class for whom the British Isles represented Canada's ideal roots. Hostility toward Asian immigrants was especially persistent in the West, and since women wage earners often filled the same kind of low-paying jobs as Asian workers, a specific kind of protectionism attached itself to white women in the workplace. A number of aspects of the western scene make it distinctive and deserving of independent analysis. I elaborate on them in this book.

Mine is not a broad overview but a focused attempt to examine how the working girl was depicted and characterized in this period of rapid growth and intense social change, and while I draw on texts that describe or originate in various parts of the West, I choose to highlight Vancouver for particular local detail because it exemplifies many of the characteristics important to the analysis of the working girl in the West. For one thing, it was one of the larger cities in the West throughout this period, second only to Winnipeg, and because the working girl really found her footing in the city, Vancouver offers a certain scope for analysis not available everywhere. Its position in the far West, meanwhile, gives it an almost liminal quality that is particularly interesting when it comes to the representation of women in a far-away frontier, hitherto known for its rugged culture of lone bachelors. And Vancouver too was highly preoccupied with the supposed problems of Asian immigration and its effects on the city's young white women. For these reasons, I use Vancouver as my local example of the issues that I also discuss with reference to the West as a whole.

As noted, it was a commonplace in the nineteenth and early twentieth centuries that western Canada suffered from a dearth of women. This concern referenced white women exclusively, for it was felt that white women had a key role to play as cultural carriers and agents of social uplift in Britain's colonial outposts, and this attitude persisted when it came to Canada's frontier space of the West. Promotional campaigns for British immigration to the West figured it as a land of lonely bachelors, hungry for wives. But behind the rhetoric was a more pragmatic and economic need that was no less pressing: women were in demand as workers in a range of female-identified jobs – domestic service predominated, but openings proliferated for waitresses, chambermaids, laundry workers, textile and retail workers, and telephone operators as well as for educated women, who were needed to fill positions as teachers, nurses, and stenographers. Yet despite this demand for women workers in a narrow but expanding range of jobs and industries, an emphasis on women's domestic roles persisted; middle-class social commentators and journalists represented domestic service as the best kind of work for women – as preparing them for their ultimate roles as wives and mothers while keeping them within the domestic sphere itself as a workplace. A preferred narrative had women working as domestics almost as a brief but productive apprenticeship before accepting one of the West's worthy bachelors. The idea of women entering the more public wage-earning arena did not make for such a reassuring narrative of marital and domestic completion. The working girl, living on her own in what persisted to be seen as a frontier space, away from family, earning her own paycheque in the morally dubious workplaces of Canada's newest cities, suggested whole new trajectories for women in the industrializing nation. These new developments were troubling to many, and a re-emphasis on domesticity often caused women's labour to be overlooked for its contribution to the economic development of the West. To some, however, particularly to writers of creative works, the working girl was a figure rich in representational possibility – a new inhabitant of a modern urban scene that suggested imminent transformation in gender roles and Canadian society.

This book focuses on the representation of women more than on the real women and what they actually did. It is not a history of the working girl in the West but a study of how she was imagined, represented, and constructed as a figure within the cultural narratives of Canada, the West, and the empire. Representations of people may, however, reflect and suggest the real people to an always shifting degree, and analyzing the representations means drawing on the actual history and connecting the rhetoric with the reality where possible. So with my eye always fixed mainly on the representational, I have tried to retain a sense of the real and the material as well, so that the importance of women's agency and experience is recognized. My primary concern has to do with the range of discourses produced by imperial idealism, reformist critique, and literary creativity; nevertheless, while these varied media sought to define her, the real working girl was out there, working her various jobs, living with family or without, socializing with co-workers, participating in new forms of leisure, managing her romantic life, and indeed perhaps pioneering new attitudes, new habits, and new ways of negotiating gender and work. Balancing the real and representational is a complicated process, but the working girl and the narratives that characterize her do lend themselves to a representational analysis, so I tailor my methodology to fit this important figure and to draw out what she can tell us about gender and work in the urbanizing Canadian West.

Most influential in guiding my approach has been Carolyn Strange's groundbreaking book *Toronto's Girl Problem: The Perils and Pleasures of the City, 1880-1930*.[2] Strange provides discourse analysis of accounts from city administrators, social reformers, and courthouse authorities to unearth the story of the working girl and her moral regulation in Toronto, and I take my cue from her in my focus on discourse and representation. However, where Strange focuses largely on crime and policing involving the working girl, I take a more literary approach to her story, placing her within the reigning narratives of settlement and urbanization in the West and seeing how she appeared in the creative literature as well as in the social documents of the day. Public debates used representational methods to make the working girl signify the perils of a swiftly changing society, and my analysis focuses on narrative and representation in order to examine and contextualize these debates as a way to understand the symbolic import of this figure. To do this, I examine a diverse collection of texts, including newspaper reports, reform and social-purity discourse, official reports on labour, women's travel accounts of Canada, and Canadian literature and poetry. I give some prominence to travel accounts because they seek to tell us about the Canadian West itself while also attempting to guide women entering the country; this urge to describe and prescribe women's place in a still new society is of particular interest because the situating of the working girl in the West is central to my field of inquiry. British journalist Ella Sykes, for instance, travelled western Canada in 1911 under cover as a working girl looking for work as a "home-help."[3] Her resulting book must be read with an awareness of the mediating factors of her discourse – that she wasn't a "real" working girl; that she was writing a form of immigrant advice literature bordering on promotion; and that with her she brought her own ideas about women and empire. Nevertheless, she does seek to foreground real experience, to document material conditions, and to give credit where credit is due when it comes to women and the work that they did. In my study I try to strike a balance in order both to appreciate how texts operate as they create meaning and shape the culture and to maintain a sense of the material past in which working women existed. I have also given special attention to literature and fiction about the working girl because these works imagine the working girl creatively and see her ability to act in a symbolic way – as a figure through whom important social themes of gender, work, and the city may be presented and explored. The literary representations of the working girl are also instructive insofar as they transcend the narrow view of the working girl that dominates the reform rhetoric about her. Although working-girl heroines in novels and stories grapple with issues familiar in reform literature about young women's embattled virtue in the morally exposed workplace, often in these fictional forms the struggles of the working girl are explored in narratives that render with sensitivity and prescience the upheavals of a society coping with industrialism, urban turmoil, and the trials of modernity for women; these texts also have the scope to explore the possible effects of the working experience on the individual psyche, suggesting how work might influence and affect women's individual choices, attitudes, and outlooks. These more complex representations are an important counterpoint to the depictions of the working girl in reform rhetoric and popular discourse of the day.

Throughout the book I place various kinds of texts into dialogue in order to examine the cultural contexts within which the figure of the working girl took on a range of meanings. I am particularly interested in how certain social narratives took hold of the popular imagination and how those narratives then began to explain and to influence women's roles in regard to work and domesticity in the West. Indeed, because the analysis of narrative is such an important part of my methodology, I will pause briefly here to discuss narrative style. I use the term "narrative" in the sense of "storytelling," and I look for stories that featured the working girl and made sense of her role through narrative elements like plot, dramatic conflict, romance, and moral endings. Narratives of female immigration to the Canadian West, for instance, often told stories not just of movement through space but of hardship rewarded with romantic fulfilment. More alarmist narratives of the white-slave trade, meanwhile, contained the implicit threat that women who left home for waged work in the city were placing themselves in dire sexual peril, from which they would require last-minute rescue if they were to escape a fate worse than death. This book examines these narratives for what they tell us about the working girl's symbolic import and about her lively setting in the provinces of western Canada. The working girl was a figure who seems to have ignited her society's imagination and its storytelling urges, so analyzing the narratives in which she appeared is a productive way to assess her cultural importance and social impact. These kinds of popular and media-based narratives constitute valuable social texts, providing insight into the cultural assumptions and social influences that followed women into their workplaces.

The ambivalence concerning women's new roles as wage earners was shaped by a complex set of ideologies concerning domesticity, female sexuality, and women's responsibilities as the bearers of empire. My analysis situates the working girl in a place that was not only a part of Canada but also an outpost of empire. As Anne McClintock has argued, women's entrance onto the imperial stage was largely choreographed by the "cult of domesticity."[4] This study focuses on imperialist rhetoric not in its official form as promulgated by policy makers or administrators but in its more popular guise as evinced in the enthusiasm of travel writers and promoters of western Canada. I am interested in how Canadians imagined themselves to be part of an imperial project and in how Canadian nationalism and imperialism worked partly together in the creation of a gender ideology that sanctified an ideal of "home" for women as the vessels of tradition, an ideal with which working girls were largely incompatible. In its more everyday popular forms – the poetry memorized in schools, celebrations of historical events – imperialism lasted well into the twentieth century. R.G. Moyles and Doug Owram study a wide array of literature produced in Canada and Britain that developed the tie between the two countries: "Canadians had been raised in the affirmation of their essential kinship with their transatlantic cousins ... Canada, pre-war children were taught, was heir to the most glorious tradition of freedom and adventure in the history of mankind."[5] In the context of this popular allegiance to the ideals of imperialism, women in Canada often embraced their roles as mothers and daughters in an imperial family drama. The Imperial Order Daughters of the Empire, for instance, was founded in 1900, and its speakers toured western Canada in 1909, recruiting philanthropically minded middle-class women whose loyalty to empire was a vital part of their patriotism for Canada. This kind of daily imperial enthusiasm was an important part of gender ideology in western Canada, which still felt itself to be a frontier, a colonial outpost, where women would play a vital role. Not all women were equally invested in this somewhat nostalgic depiction of the women of empire. The young women who filled the low-level, service-sector jobs in the West were not sought after as recruits to the Imperial Order Daughters of the Empire, and often their work was looked upon as a distressing departure from their true domestic functions. Placing the alarmingly modern working girl into the reigning narratives of nationhood and imperialism was sometimes a taxing undertaking.

In fact, the category of the "working girl" is still not always easily fixed or defined. The young women of my study include identifiably working-class women such as domestic servants and laundry workers, but also wage-earning women whose class position is less decided: teachers and stenographers, for instance, were often well-educated women of more middle-class background. Because this book centres on the politics of representation, my definition of the "working girl" does not depend so much on specific class or economic categories (although these are still relevant) as much as it does on the representational agendas that allowed a variety of wage-earning women to figure as "working girls" in the popular imagination and the texts of the time. Thus while a teacher would not think of herself as occupying the same class or social standing as a domestic servant, in the representational strategies of the popular press or of writers of fiction like Bertrand Sinclair and J.G. Sime, both could be figured as examples of the working girl. At the turn of the century it was becoming much more acceptable for young women of the middle class to think of entering the workforce at least for a while before marriage, and these women often looked to their working-class counterparts for cues on social behaviour, workplace culture, and wage-earning lifestyle. Telephone operators, or "hello girls," for instance, seem to have held a particular fascination for their middle-class contemporaries, and whenever they went on strike, young middle-class women seem to have jumped at the chance to try their hand at the switchboard. The image of the working girl thus took on a certain allure and a representational life of its own that could sometimes infiltrate the usually impervious boundaries of class and social position.

Social authorities of the day did not view the problems of wage-earning women as co-extensive with those of working men, who faced problems of wages, working conditions, and workers' rights; instead, they focused almost exclusively on the moral implications of women's entrance into the workplace, particularly insofar as it represented a break from traditional Victorian ideals of domestic femininity. The implications of this relentless reduction of women's work to issues of morality and social upheaval were far-reaching. Whereas men could easily, almost automatically, inhabit the part of the worker, with the rights and recognition that accompanied the

position, the roles of woman and worker were constructed in opposition –
almost as antithetical – to each other. Expected to inhabit a domestic realm
devoid of issues concerning capital, politics, or work, women were asked
to embody social tradition and family, to be mothers to the new nation.
When young women turned their backs on this sacred duty, they were
subject to intense moralistic badgering from the reform-minded elite, to
whom even the most far-fetched tales of white slavery seemed entirely
credible, given the grave moralistic peril to which wage-earning women
supposedly exposed themselves. Denied the recognition afforded male
workers as members of the labour force and economic agents, working
women suffered serious disadvantages in the workplace, their wages being
depressed and their rights as workers being ignored by employers and
union leaders alike. In fact, the conceptual apparatus that denied women
the identity of worker persisted well into the twentieth century, and even
now labour historians continue to rewrite and revise labour histories that
initially failed to mention women. This is why an analysis that focuses
on the politics of representation is especially important, for it is through
representational conventions that women were pressured to embody a
traditional domestic role, and likewise it is through a representational
agenda that women were denied recognition as valuable workers.

Who were the working girls in the West? What was the average working girl like (if an average can be said to have existed)? Before this study
launches more fully into the representations and narratives of her plight,
it may be useful to know a little about where the real working girls stood
relative to the rest of the population. As Linda Kealey puts it, "in the
contemporary mind and in the official census returns, the typical working woman was young, single, and in the labour force only until marriage
or family responsibilities precluded further wage work."[6] In the first two
decades of the twentieth century, women in the western provinces constituted roughly 7 to 12 percent of the workforce.[7] These numbers were
below the national average of 13 to 15 percent, but this is not surprising
given that women were outnumbered by men in the West by roughly two
to one. In terms of the percentages, the numbers rise gradually through
time; in Manitoba, for instance, the workforce was just under 10 percent
female in 1901 and almost 15 percent female in 1921. But in terms of the
actual numbers of women, the increase was significant because these
decades saw such dramatic population growth in the West. So Manitoba's
10 percent in 1901 represents 8,575 women, and its 15 percent in 1921
represents more than triple this figure at 31,682 women. And British

Columbia's female percentage of the workforce grew from just under 6 percent in 1901 to 11.6 percent in 1921, but this represents a more than five-fold increase in the number of women, from 4,762 to 25,513. So while the presence of women in the workforce was on the increase, the West's rapid population growth may have made it appear even more dramatic to witnesses on the ground. Apart from domestic service, which was available in rural homes as well as towns and cities, waged work for women was concentrated in urban areas, so women always formed a slightly larger proportion of the workforce in the cities than they did in the provinces overall. In 1931 in British Columbia, for instance, women accounted for 14 percent of the workforce in the province overall, but comprised 19 percent of the Vancouver workforce.[8] As for the women themselves, most of them were under twenty-five years old, and most – about three-quarters of them – were single. Melanie Buddle has shown that in British Columbia there was a higher proportion than in Canada overall of married women who continued to work, and these women were more likely to own their own businesses, such as boarding houses, so marriage did not always sever women from the working world.[9] Divorced and widowed women were also a small part of the female workforce, and in fact Buddle notes that despite the married status of many of the female boarding-house keepers whom she studied, the husbands in many cases were absent. Some working women were thus the sole providers in their households and supported themselves and their families through waged work and self-employment. Among the female workforce, however, young single women did dominate in numbers, and they were expected to fill their specific place in the labour market only for a limited time before they married – which in the West they were expected to do quickly. Buddle also notes that marriage rates were slightly higher for women in British Columbia than elsewhere in the country, supporting the idea that the West's numerous bachelors meant good marriage prospects for women, who seem to have taken advantage of their increased range of choice. Popular rhetoric of the day, however, certainly exaggerated these demographics; not all the West's bachelors were interested in marrying, nor did those who were interested always meet the standards of the female minority.

And what jobs did women take? The largest sector of female employment in the early twentieth century was domestic service, and western Canada was known for its voracious demand for servants; but these numbers were gradually declining.[10] With increasing industrialization and urbanization, other kinds of jobs became more available to women, and they fled the low-status drudgery of service as quickly as they could. On the rise was clerical work, but a woman needed a certain amount of education and training – language, shorthand, and typing skills – to be a stenographer, or "typewriter," so it wasn't a field available to all. In between the low-status unskilled arena of domestic service and the more educated professional fields of stenography, teaching, and nursing, then, fell a range of occupations for women, including work as chambermaids in hotels and boarding houses, as waitresses in restaurants, as workers in laundries and textiles, and as saleswomen in shops. Although there were some food-processing jobs in places like candy factories, bakeries, and fish-processing plants and salmon canneries, there weren't as many factory jobs for women in manufacturing in the West as in the East. This makes a difference because it meant that there were fewer workplaces where working girls congregated in numbers. Service jobs in hotels and restaurants and retail work in shops might bring a few women together, but often women's jobs – domestic service especially – could be isolating.

One important question to investigators of the time was whether the working girl lived at home. It is difficult to answer this question with statistical precision, but most studies suggest that the self-supporting working girl away from family was in a minority, though a significant one. The history of the YWCA is useful in this matter, for this organization focused its energies directly on young women living away from home; one history of the association records that in 1907 "there were at the time 15,000 wage-earning women in Winnipeg, of whom nearly half lived away from home," and that when new YWCA branches opened in western cities, "a residence was always the first and most pressing concern."[11] It was this independent working girl alone in the city who most interested her contemporaries: How did she live on her meagre wages? What did she do in her time off? What did she experience on the job? What did her work mean for her marriage prospects? The early part of the twentieth century saw the rapid settlement of the West, and as Paul Voisey notes, "one third of the pioneers who headed West before 1916 found themselves living, not on the farm, but in the country villages, the bustling rail towns, and the fast-rising cities that sprang from the prairie."[12] Working women living away from home were often involved in the country-to-city migration that was taking place as part of the West's rapid urbanization. In "The Log of a Calgary Stenographer," published in the *Morning Albertan* in 1914, a freshly trained stenographer recounts her arrival in the city and her search for employment, her rapid success suggesting that by this time cities had a relatively organized infrastructure for placing incoming female labour: "I was sent up to the office early on Monday morning by the Remington Typewriter Company and as I hunted up the place I decided it was the most wonderful institution in the world. Here was I, a green country girl, not a week in Calgary and without a friend, and yet I had a position all picked out for me and by night I would have earned some money."[13] The young working women who came to be known as working girls were thus a minority in the workforce and in the population, but they were a minority that made itself felt. Although restricted to a limited set of occupations and despite being expected to marry quickly and thereby leave their jobs, they nonetheless established their own place in the workforce and the urban scene.

I divide this book into chapters that engage women's imagined place in the West, the working girl in Canadian literature, the fears about prostitution, women's strikes and labour activism, and the issue of the mixed-race workplace. In Chapter 1 I explore the ways in which white women were represented as desirable civilizing agents in the colonial West. Given that white women were considered vital to the healthy growth of the community, while also being in such limited supply, those women who did take up residence in the West were under intense scrutiny and suffered from a degree of representational overkill. These women, moreover, were subject not only to the preconceptions born of colonial enthusiasm but also to yet another layer of administrative zeal – the moral panic over women's work. At the turn of the century, industrialism was rapidly changing Canada's urban landscape, and the new figure of the urban working girl – usually young and single and now in command of her own paycheque – challenged traditional notions of femininity.

In Chapter 2 I focus directly on literary representations of working girls in Canadian writing. In the United States the relatively new phenomenon of the independent urban working girl, sometimes referred to as the "woman adrift," represented for many writers the modern city – its opportunities but also its potential for immorality and cultural disruption. In Canada, however, writers were more hesitant to address social issues and urban ills in their fiction, and the influence of the historical-romance genre, dominant at the time, dampened demand for socially engaged fiction. Those works that did represent the working girl usually did so in the often marginalized forms of issue-oriented social realism or romantic melodrama. These texts are an important element of my study because they offer complex and sustained representations of this figure, illuminating her place within the literary and social discourse of the day. In this chapter I focus on five main texts: Marie Joussaye's poem "Only a Working Girl" (1886), Agnes Maule Machar's novel *Roland Graeme, Knight* (1892), Isabel Ecclestone Mackay's *House of Windows* (1912), Bertrand Sinclair's *North of Fifty-Three* (1914), and J.G. Sime's collection of stories, *Sister Woman* (1919). Because working women were considered a problematic social issue, much of the fiction that addresses them is strongly socially engaged; for this reason, part of my methodology involves reading works of literature as social documents. This approach, in turn, allows me to read literary works alongside social criticism of the day and to analyze the representational politics at work in both. Although the texts that I examine differ greatly from one another in style, genre, and content, they all use the figure of the working girl to raise questions about the renegotiation of gender in the context of urban industrialism. Female sexuality is of especial interest to these writers, signalling the unease – and sometimes the enthusiasm – regarding the new opportunities available to wage-earning women.

Chapter 3 picks up on the preoccupation with working women's sexual choices by examining the social discourse on prostitution. Sex work is one industry that, even today, tends to be judged in terms of sexual morality rather than as work. But in the first part of the twentieth century, all women's work was thought of in terms of morality, with prostitution as the worst-case scenario. This is one reason why it is important to include an analysis of sex work in discussions of women's labour, for the tendency to reduce the debate on women's labour to questions of sex alone finds its fullest articulation in the case of prostitution. One part of this chapter is an analysis of white-slave narratives and how they functioned to associate prostitution with mainstream working girls – as though to warn women of the dire results of challenging traditional gender norms. But I am also interested in prostitution as an example of women's work that, although constantly under siege by the moral majority, was in fact a significant – even vital – segment of the economy in western towns and cities. To balance out the alarmist quality of reform rhetoric, I examine at length the autobiography of a career prostitute and madam, Madeleine Blair (a pseudonym), who depicts the sex industry in turn-of-the-century western Canada in her own remarkably forthright prose.[14]

To what extent were working girls active in the organized labour movement, and how was their activism portrayed and represented? This is a question that I address in Chapter 4, where I single out two major examples of women on strike and examine how they were portrayed in the newspaper coverage of the day. The working girl's relationship to the organized labour movement was not without its tensions; the labour movement often perceived and represented itself as a brotherhood, and the labour market's new contingent of lively young women was not always deemed real membership material. Just as women's labour was downplayed as temporary, unskilled, and supposedly marginal to the economy, so was their activism sometimes disparaged by a labour movement that recognized protest only in highly masculine terms of militancy and fraternal solidarity. Despite these ambivalences, however, and especially where strong female leadership existed, working girls exhibited an enthusiastic spirit of resistance, forming their own unions, staging strikes, and proving the most capable of fundraisers, combining their union commitment with a genius for organizing dances. I single out two aspects that seem to recur in media coverage of striking women: fun and violence. Union women used their organizational skills and social acumen to organize highly profitable social events and dances, but they also gained a reputation for violence on the picket lines that was surprising to observers of the day. Moreover, reconciling these social and antisocial characteristics was difficult, and lends interesting complexity to the analysis of the working girl's labour politics.

The plight of the working girl often took on symbolic significance: the working girl's troubles, for instance, might be used to represent the hardships of the working class at large, or her moral fall might signify the heartless amorality of capitalism. In British Columbia, where the white elite felt their identity threatened by Asian immigration, the working girl sometimes came to represent the province's imperilled whiteness. Racist anxieties often coalesced around the mixed-race workplace, especially if it meant Asian men working alongside white women. When a white domestic worker was murdered in an upscale Vancouver home, with suspicion centring on her Asian co-worker, these fears exploded. In Chapter 5 I explore the racial discourse that drew on representations of young white working women in order to express deep-seated beliefs about racial and sexual purity in a multiracial society. A protectionist impulse to segregate white women from Asian men resulted in legislative agendas to ban white women from mixed-race workplaces, a policy that was highly unpopular among women workers, who didn't appreciate the kind of moral protectionism that deprived them of their income.

From our perspective at the beginning of a new century, it is clear that the steps taken by these early participants in women's waged labour were groundbreaking; in fact, many of the results feared by the reform-minded community – that women might concentrate on their work instead of seeking only marriage, that they might delay motherhood or reject it completely, that they might exercise the same sexual freedoms available to men – have indeed came about. However, rather than taking this as evidence of society's fallen condition, we congratulate a century of working women who changed society and the workplace. Some working women, like Vancouver's Helena Gutteridge, saw that wage-earning women were in effect redefining the parameters of womanhood, and in this book I draw out some of these moments of gender transgression and transformation.

## chapter 1

# Working Women in the West at the Turn of the Century

It is a great call for women. There must be some who
have the courage and the health to leave the ready-
made comforts of the old country, and come into this
wild beautiful West, giving their best of mind and body
for the race and for the Empire.

– MARION CRAN (MRS. GEORGE CRAN),
*A Woman in Canada*, 1908

At the turn of the last century, cultural narratives of gender in western Canada placed women between the highly traditional demands of home and family and the more material demands of the shifting nature of work. In the second half of the nineteenth century, the West was one of the distant outposts of empire, where a settler society primarily of British extraction sought to establish a stable and homogeneous settler culture amid the chaos of ethnic and cultural diversity. Women had a definite part to play in this setting, and campaigns to bring British women to the West were set in motion. It was hoped that women would bring a degree of civilization, permanence, and stability to the New World social scene: as wives and mothers they would reproduce British society both culturally and physically. This was a recognized ideal, born of imperial rhetoric and Victorian reverence for the home; but how seamless was this narrative once implemented? Were there contradictions that arose when the domestic and imperial ideals met the western Canadian setting? Women who came to the West through immigration campaigns were wanted, in part, to fill a labour shortage, yet the value of women's work was consistently downplayed, and a resistance to accepting women as workers would persist well into the twentieth century. In fact, the idea of "work" itself tends to shift as soon as women become the workers under discussion. As Keith Grint argues, concepts or definitions of work "are symbols of cultures and especially mirrors of power: if what counts as work is glorified or despised or gender-related, then the language and practice of work allows us to read embodied fragments of wider social power."[1] Waged labour is one area where gender difference forcefully asserts itself as a major organizing principle, such that male workers and female workers occupy utterly different conceptual spaces. In Canada the kinds of paid work involving women were often devalued or disregarded, signalling in part that women's primary function was thought to lie elsewhere. But economic demand and the initiative of women themselves told a different story of women's place in the young nation. A reluctance to represent and acknowledge women as workers was persistent, but the jobs did exist and women were willing to adapt to the new demands made of them, even if this meant cultivating very different behaviours from those they knew in the home. This redefinition of gender had to take place on a representational level even as it was being worked out on the job and in the workplace, so exploring how working women were positioned in the West is a demanding conceptual task.

This chapter focuses on the representational work that took place during two highly influential social movements: imperialism and industrialism. In the second part of the nineteenth century and continuing into the early twentieth century, imperialism set out specific functions for women as representatives of culture and empire. At the same time, industrialism, which came very rapidly to the West, was restructuring ideas of gender in the workplace. The working girl thus became the locus for many anxieties about the rapidly changing social environment, but she also embodied a certain romance about the young nation's ability to rise to new challenges. These forces of imperialism and industrialism were, of course, operative throughout Canada, but in the West there were certain key differences that enhanced the interest in the figure of the working girl: the sense that the West was still a frontier space of empire and thus in need of the kind of civilization and cultivation that "girls of a high stamp"[2] could bring; the ubiquitous concern about the shortage of women, which cast the West as a marital destination for young women; and the rapidity of industrialization, which created a demand for new kinds of workers – including female workers – especially in the quickly expanding urban centres.

## WOMEN WANTED IN THE WEST

In late-nineteenth-century western Canada and continuing through to the early twentieth century, single white women were considered a scarce and highly desirable commodity. Elsewhere in Canada this was not the case.

In Toronto, for instance, women outnumbered men, and the discrepancy increased as young women left rural areas for work in the city.[3] By comparison, British Columbia's gold rush attracted large numbers of male settlers early on, and with an economy based on logging, fishing, and mining, the province remained slow to draw women immigrants. Despite British Columbia's rapidly growing population, men still outnumbered women by two to one in 1911.[4] The prairie provinces, meanwhile, were also known for their lonely bachelor farmers and hired hands, who reportedly longed for wives to put their homes in order. Jessie M. Saxby wrote a travel account of western Canada in 1890 and entitled one chapter "Women Wanted":

> The want of home life is keenly felt as a very great calamity by those western settlers. They envy such of their number as have been fortunate enough to induce sister, wife or mother to come and "keep house." All would gladly do likewise. There seems about one woman to every fifty men, and I believe the old country could confer no greater boon upon this fine young nation than by sending it thousands of our girls to soften and sweeten life in the Wild West. The want of feminine influence tends to make the men (so they acknowledge) restless, dissatisfied, reckless, and godless. A Canadian gentleman of influence and education said: "Better even than money – and goodness knows, we need capital badly – should be a cargo of home-loving girls."[5]

Saxby implies a direct relationship here between female scarcity and male dissipation, with the arrival of women – specifically home-loving ones – being immediately restorative. The West's gender imbalance gave rise to campaigns to bring women to the West, and one promotional poster read, "Urgent! Thousands of nice girls are wanted in The Canadian West. Over 20,000 men are sighing for what they cannot get – wives!"[6] But the rhetoric of these projects, and even the notion of a gender imbalance itself, depended on a number of conceptual paradigms and assumptions, themselves productive of specific cultural narratives concerning gender in the New World.

Despite representations of a Canadian West devoid of the gentler sex, it is not as though there were no women in the West. Campaigns to attract white women to the West may have depicted a society of bachelors clamouring for wives, but Sylvia Van Kirk has found that throughout the history of the fur trade, marriages between European trappers and Native or Métis women were customary: "Such interracial unions were, in fact, the basis for a fur trade society and were sanctioned by an indigenous rite known as *mariage à la façon du pays* – according to the custom of the country."[7] That such unions were common and accepted long before the shortage of white women became an issue suggests that the discourse of female shortage was itself shaped by changing social systems. In the mid-nineteenth century, with the establishment of a settler society, a shift in colonial and national thinking took hold, whereby mixed-race unions were increasingly frowned upon and white women became essential to the notion of civilized society. Cynthia Comacchio describes the effects of this important shift in attitudes, which was reflected in the marriage laws of the time: "The arrival of white women effectively ended the long-standing practice of intermarriage according to the 'custom of the country,' as white men began to leave their Aboriginal families for new unions with white women. Previously upheld in Canadian courts, the validity of these mixed marriages was negated in 1886, when it was decided that the 'cohabitation of a civilized man and a savage woman,' for no matter how long, was not a legal marriage."[8] The so-called "shortage" of women in the West, then – although it did exist numerically – was actually a carefully constructed and deliberately promoted way of representing and shaping the West according to ideologies of empire and nation that held specific roles for women and families in a white settler society. Even the popular representation of Canadian men as lonely bachelors longing for wives proves suspect when one learns that many longstanding marriages were effectively being nullified to make way for new white wives.

The degree of energy devoted to attracting white women to the West is testimony to the significance ascribed to these women and to the roles that they were expected to fill. One early effort set the stage for ongoing immigration campaigns that caught the popular imagination by foregrounding the romance of colonial Canada as a matrimonial destination – it was aptly called the "Bride Ship" initiative of the 1860s. In this instance, the Columbia Female Emigration Society was founded for the express purpose of bringing women to the province by collaborating with the London Female Middle-Class Emigration Society, whose mandate was to send women from England out to the colonies.[9] This partnership was readily established because, while women in British Columbia were considered painfully scarce, Britain, by comparison, suffered from a female surplus. An 1851 survey in the United Kingdom concluded that, due in part to the departure of men to the colonies, in a total population of 27 million there existed a surplus of 650,000 women.

By the 1860s the number had reached 800,000, and by the early twentieth century 1 million.[10]

Like the notion of a female shortage, the idea of a female surplus rests on specific assumptions about women's place in society. The impossibility of the extra women in Britain finding husbands was a primary reason for their being labelled as "excess" or "redundant"; thus women's roles as wives and mothers were considered so important that, failing marriage, women were judged obsolete, even anomalous, and hence part of a surplus. A 1908 travel narrative by Marion Cran examining the position of women in Canada is expressive of this attitude toward Canada's female shortage and Britain's surplus:

> Whatever may be urged to the contrary by the enforced bachelor women of my own land, I know that in their secret hearts most of them think of marriage as the ultimate goal. An honourable wish, by no means to be hidden with shame. Every healthy normal woman has it ... Our little Island on the edge of Europe is overcrowded with people, chiefly women, and a vast Continent in North America is at its wits' end for inhabitants, especially women. Now why does not plus go over to minus and level things up a little, in order to make both countries more comfortable.[11]

Concern over Britain's surplus women and the mathematically satisfying plan of having "plus go over to minus" through Canadian immigration was thus persistent, lasting from the nineteenth century into the twentieth. And women's role as wives – their secret desire to marry no matter what they may say to the contrary – was given prominence, even though the arguably more pressing issue was a lack of employment for women in England and an increasing demand for women workers in Canada. The latter issue was discussed, but the romantic ending for women emigrants almost always framed the debate. A compelling and persistent narrative thus emerged, wherein Britain's surplus women, unable to marry and so fulfill the requirements of their gender at home, would be siphoned off to the colonial margins of western Canada, where an excess of bachelors was desperate for wives and families: unruly bachelors would turn sober husbands by joining with redundant-women-turned-happy-brides. The promises of this imperial romance were undoubtedly seductive – hence the christening of the two convoys of women to British Columbia as "Bride Ships."

Although little is known directly of the experience of the women who came to British Columbia on the Bride Ships, especially before they left, one account of the voyage survives in the work of Frederick Whymper, a travel writer who recounts his 1862 voyage to Canada aboard the *Tynemouth*, the first of the Bride Ships:

> Our most noticeable living freight was, however, an "invoice" of sixty young ladies, destined for the colonial and matrimonial market. They had been sent out by a home society, under the watchful care of a clergyman and matron; and they must have passed the dreariest three months of their existence on board, for they were isolated from the rest of the passengers, and could only look on at the fun and amusements in which everyone else could take a part. Every benevolent effort deserves respect; but, from personal observation, I can not honestly recommend such a mode of supplying the demands of a colony. Half of them married soon after arrival or went into service, but a large proportion quickly went to the bad, and, from appearances, had been there before.[12]

Frederick Whymper's writing is a lovely blend of colonial and romantic rhetoric, indicative of the interwoven narratives surrounding the Bride Ship initiative. Referring to the "invoice" of women as "living freight" that will "supply the demands" of the "colonial and matrimonial market," Whymper objectifies them through the vocabulary of capitalist enterprise – as cargo or marketable goods – thus revealing the degree to which these women, and the Bride Ship initiative itself, were embedded in the terms and dictates of mercantile imperialism. Whymper's rhetoric, in addition to the detail about the women's confinement on the ship, conjures images of imperial slave ships, similarly engaged in a colonial mercantile enterprise where humans were the "living freight." Such a comparison may seem extreme, but it is nevertheless worthwhile to note such connections, even if only rhetorical, because they are signals of the inexorable power of the colonial enterprise, which did, after all, choreograph these more and less voluntary migrations.

One assumes that the Bride Ship women, however driven by circumstance to emigrating, were relatively willing passengers, yet their confinement, coupled with Whymper's own view of them as cargo, suggests a sinister edge to this "benevolent effort." In her 1928 history, *The Pioneer Women of Vancouver Island*, N. de Bertrand Lugrin notes that "the first contingent of wives-to-be" (the precursor to those onboard the *Tynemouth*), who numbered about twenty, were drawn from orphan asylums,[13] and it seems doubtful that such young women (most of them between ages twelve and eighteen) would have been in a position to make free and informed choices about emigration.

Whymper relates how, shortly following the *Tynemouth's* disembarkation, a brief mutiny resulted in the confinement of a number of the crew, creating a labour shortage that he and the young male passengers made up for by volunteering their services: "All the younger men came forward readily, were solemnly enrolled, and set to work at once ... We found it good exercise, and worked with a will. Did we not know that the eyes of sixty maidens were looking on approvingly as we helped them on to the consummation of their dearest wishes? We did, and even our parson creditably proved his 'muscular Christianity.'"[14] Whymper casts himself as an agent of chivalry and object of desire for the now fully romanticized, even fetishized, young maidens. The voyage to Canada, previously characterized as "the dreariest three months of their existence," has now become the passage "to the consummation of their dearest wishes." The juxtaposition of this highly romantic perspective with the earlier mercantile imperialist rhetoric is telling. The promotional material that was used to encourage British female emigration depicted the Canadian West as a land of romantic adventure, where an overabundance of single men guaranteed marital bliss for the unemployed single women of Britain's female surplus, and here Whymper exploits this romance narrative, casting himself in a supporting role.

Shipped over by the boatload, these women were clearly being commodified, but it is not always readily apparent what the primary intent of this commodification was. Both Marion Cran's belief that "in their secret hearts" most potential emigrants from Britain "think of marriage as the ultimate goal" and Whymper's designation of the Bride Ship women as destined for the "matrimonial market" suggest that romance is the ruling narrative and that marriages will mark the happy ending. But part of the British anxiety about "surplus" women did arise from there being no adequate employment in Britain for the extra women. And the middle-class women of the Canadian Emigration Society were not motivated merely by a desire to plan weddings. They wanted domestic servants, and Lugrin mentions that many of the Bride Ship women had positions waiting for them where they would start work immediately upon their arrival. As Marilyn Barber points out, "Class interests as well as imperial enthusiasms shaped the work of emigration promoters [who] ... most warmly welcomed trained British domestic servants whom they and their friends could employ while advancing the cause of the Empire, but not educated women who would compete with their daughters for jobs and husbands."[15] In the minds of the middle-class promoters of emigration, those brought to British Columbia through the Emigration Society would enter domestic service and then at a later time move on to marriage and motherhood. Their immediate roles as workers, however, rested on specific assumptions regarding their class position and designated place in society. As Adele Perry explains, from the mid-nineteenth century onward, "It became axiomatic to argue that British Columbia lacked a sufficient number of domestic servants. Without an adequate supply of white women to labour in the colony's households, supposedly normal gender, racial, and class relations were disrupted."[16] This class-specific and labour-related agenda underlying female immigration efforts belies the narrative of high romance employed by the promotional material and echoed by Whymper. Tales of colonial romance may be alluring, but more material incentives for the emigration societies included the labour shortage in domestic workers in British Columbia and the problem of unemployed women in Britain. In other words, it was not just women-as-wives who were wanted for the colony, but quite specifically women-as-workers.

British journalist Ella Sykes travelled through western Canada in 1911 posing as a female immigrant in need of work and taking a number of jobs in homes there, in order to write a description and advice manual for prospective women immigrants. She acknowledges Canada's specific need for women workers and points out that it was often overlooked: "Canada is eminently the Land of Youth and Optimism, but it is also in very truth the Land of Work, and English people sometimes are apt to lose sight of this side of the shield."[17] She urged women to come to Canada only if they had training and skill in a specific field of work needed in Canada, and she noticed that too many young women lacked such preparation: "Some of the inmates of the [Calgary] hostel had no right to be in Canada at all, and had come out after reading the alluring literature, in which things are, to say the least of it, seen through rose-coloured glasses."[18] A certain ambivalence thus characterized the demand for female immigration to the West; women workers were wanted in private homes as domestics and in a number of female-defined fields such as the service industry, and a strictly pragmatic approach would simply have communicated the existence of the labour shortage. But the appeal of the colonial romance – when joined to the mathematical satisfaction of remedying the female "shortage" in

Canada by drawing on the "surplus" in England – was irresistible, and a characteristic conflict emerged between representing women as useful, necessary, and valued workers and perceiving them instead as icons of romance and domesticity.

In its day, the Bride Ship initiative was given a great deal of media coverage, and onlookers swarmed the dockside as the women arrived. Lugrin relates how one man supposedly made his way to the waterfront as the young women disembarked and seized one of them by the hand, then whisked her away to a hasty backwoods wedding to live happily ever after.[19] The project clearly caught people's imagination, and even forty years later, the same story was still active in the minds of young female immigrants. Ella Sykes describes her voyage to Canada in 1911 aboard the *Empress*: "Nearly every girl on board had her mind set on matrimony. Some acquaintance confided to me their hope of being married in Canada, where husbands were said to be a drug in the market."[20] In fact, Sykes finds out in a Women's Welcome Home in Winnipeg that by this time women may have been taking things one step further: "One of the inmates of the Home interested me by giving me details of the way in which many of the British girls hurl themselves, as it were, into marriage. They were in the habit of frequenting a matrimonial agency in the town, and some had actually gone all the way to Vancouver to marry men whom they had never seen; while others told her, without any appearance of shame, that they had left unsatisfactory husbands behind them in England, and intended to take fresh ones out here."[21] This was clearly not the intended outcome of campaigns to bring women to the West – the official narrative did not feature the possibility of trading in a British husband for a Canadian one – but it does show women, at this later date, rather shrewdly taking matters into their own hands and putting their own spin on the colonial romance narrative. Sykes does not follow up on the story, but the way that it is relayed to her by a fellow traveller as a savoury piece of local gossip, which Sykes herself passes along in her book, suggests the interest that people took in the working girl's behaviour and pursuits, particularly in how she managed her love life. The western Canadian setting, moreover, proves central to the story: it is Winnipeg where a matrimonial agency can apparently do thriving business, and Vancouver where bachelors will take a British wife, sight unseen; and more generally it is "out here" where even a married woman can find herself a new husband and consign the previous one to her best-forgotten Old World past. Working girls were the object of interest and debate throughout North America, but in the Canadian West their story took intriguing new turns. Although

Sykes only offers us a fleeting glimpse into their stories here, one senses why these young women may have drawn the interest and captured the imagination of the culture around them.

Sykes also relates a more pathetic tale of the disappointing results of swallowing the romance narrative whole: as a girl at the hostel complains, "'Before I came out to Canada, I read that I should find a number of men on Winnipeg platform waiting to propose to us girls, but, would you believe it, when I got out of the train not a single man even spoke to me?' and her voice trembled with mortification."[22] Though comic, this anecdote suggests that women attracted to the West through immigration campaigns likely struggled to reconcile the romantic ideal that cast them as the West's happy brides-to-be with the stark reality that replaced the marriage proposal with a job in domestic service. Reconciling the romantic and prosaic in westward immigration may have been a bitter struggle for women who arrived in this time when heady romantic mythology sometimes veiled a reality of necessary drudgery and toil.

## WOMEN AND CULTURAL REPRODUCTION

With the completion of the Canadian Pacific Railway (CPR) in 1885, settlement of the West moved into high gear. Whereas the East had been settled and urbanized in a gradual, arguably more organic way, the West was poised for rapid growth, and there was a sense that the growth might be planned and shaped. The prairie provinces in particular were represented as a cradle of incipient nationhood, where the ideal of a white, rural settler society could be fostered. And British Columbia was perhaps even more single-minded in its dedication to a British ethos. As Jean Barman has documented, British Columbia attracted a larger proportion of British immigrants than did other provinces, doubling its British-born population in the first decade of the twentieth century, and the social elite thus formed was eager to reproduce the culture most familiar to them, which they believed to be the most advanced in the world: "Whatever the locale, middle-class Britons sought to re-create familiar class-based institutions, ranging from social clubs to private schools on the British model. Underlying their actions was the same assumption of superiority over the host society that had half a century earlier been exhibited by many colonial Victorians towards Canadians."[23] Realizing this goal of cultural continuity, however, would not prove easy in the multicultural setting of British Columbia. Cole Harris describes the setting that the Bride Ship women and their successors would have entered, where the preferred representation of settlement as primarily British and white with a few peripheral minorities belied a much more chaotic cultural field: "Immigrants came from many different cultural backgrounds in widely different parts of the world. No individual culture could be replicated in British Columbia."[24] In his novel *The Eternal Forest*, set in turn-of-the century Vancouver, George Godwin describes entering Vancouver by train, as thousands of immigrants would have who journeyed West on the CPR: "Through the window the long low platform made a picture of teeming humanity, a motley throng: smart townsmen, drummers with big grips, overalled loggers with fat, canvas-covered packs, white-turbanned Sikhs, negroes, Klootchmans, Chinese and Japanese. Vancouver in miniature. Vancouver, city of all nationalities, the West's racial melting-pot."[25] Instituting a dominant white majority in this context required a deliberate strategy, wherein constructs of gender, race, and nation figured largely. Such negotiations are not uncommon in settler societies: "Immigration and settlement in Canada were considerably more ethnically and racially diverse than the white British settler agenda suggested. Indeed it was this diversity which compelled the conscious construction of a racial/ethnic hierarchy."[26] Constantly confronted by differences of culture and ethnicity, settlers clung fiercely to the vestiges of their cultures, creating icons and symbols out of every detail. Women were important figures in these struggles to solidify contested social norms because cultural continuity and cohesion had everything to do with family, morality, and respectability, and women as representatives of these ideals were indispensable.

How did women figure into the establishment of a cultural and ethnic hierarchy in the New World setting of western Canada? It would seem that in addition to their maternal roles as the physical reproducers of the population, not only did they take up the day-to-day work of cultural reiteration, but they also came to symbolize, in their very bodies, the essence and purity of the original culture. Adele Perry explains the crucial role that women played in the imperial settler society of the late nineteenth century: "The ambiguities of settler colonialism had special resonance for women. Imperial rhetoric and policy bestowed a literally pregnant mission on settler women, defining them and their reproductive work as essential to, and constituent of, settler regimes."[27] White women were thus thought to be integral to forwarding a white British elite in the West – on a material level as members of and mothers to the collectivity and on a conceptual level as symbolic of a British cultural ethos. Ella Sykes expresses this when she muses on the need for British women to immigrate to the West: "The influx of Americans and foreigners is so great, that every British woman, worthy of the name, who settles in the Dominion is, as it were, a standard of Empire, and if as is probable, she marries, she will train her children to love the Union Jack."[28] Sykes captures the sense of a culturally diverse setting where the assertion of British culture can be achieved specifically by women in their roles as mothers, reproducing the culture and its subjects by bearing children who will "love the Union Jack." Sykes's book was addressed specifically to young female immigrants planning to find work in the West, and it is significant that she saw these working women as part of the empire-building process. One notes, however, that it is once they marry and have children that their imperial work really begins. The time before marriage, when women are single and working, is not as easily inserted into the narrative of imperial motherhood and nation building. The working girl did not reflect the womanly ideal familiar to the culture at large, and this was partly why she attracted an often anxious attention.

The colonial setting for men, meanwhile, was often depicted as a moral danger zone, where adventurers and frontiersmen might lose their moral compass. Frederick Whymper, for instance, characterizes the new country as subject to a "floating population" among whom there is "a large proportion of 'black sheep.'"[29] And Elizabeth Lewthwaite, who moved to British Columbia in 1896 to keep house for her brothers, writes that "it is too often forgotten that the Colonies are the 'dumping-ground' for the ne'er-do-wells of the Motherland; so, naturally, cut off from the only rock which might steady them, they too frequently merely go from bad to worse in the land to which they have been sent."[30] Especially in the West, known for its less-than-refined population of loggers, miners, farmhands, and migrant workers, images of rowdy frontier bachelors fuelled perceptions of a morally dubious social setting lacking a feminine principle. In fact, accounts of the time convey a palpable sense of domesticity in crisis. Strong emphasis was placed on the supposed inability of men to create a clean and comfortable home without a woman, "a 'bachelor's shack' being often synonymous with disorder if not dirt."[31] Narratives of the household makeover that took place upon the addition of a woman to a bachelor home told of a transformation from chaos and disarray to order and hygiene. When Elizabeth Lewthwaite joined her brothers she described her arrival at their farmhouse: "Here, indeed, my expectations were more than fulfilled. Lowly though my ideal had been, it was a world too high. The rubbish that was round about was amazing (and this is characteristic of most bachelor's establishments, all that is not wanted being simply pitched outside) ... And then – when I got inside – even now I can hardly look back without a feeling of horror."[32] By the end of an account like this, the woman establishes a clean and orderly household where before there was chaos and "horror"; at the same time, traditional gender roles are reaffirmed as the troubling all-male household is replaced by reassuringly familiar gender roles and the appropriate division of labour. Freed from domestic chores – the incompetent performance of which dramatized the unfitting nature of the all-male household – the men could immerse themselves more fully in the public sphere of paid work, while the woman turned to the representational work of signifying, by her presence in the home, a traditional vision of gender and culture. Men's supposed domestic ineptitude, when coupled with their alleged moral disorderliness, thus underlined the need for women in their domestic role.

In the Victorian imagination the family was the crucial staging ground for the construction of moral and sexual identity. As Barbara Roberts explains, "If the family were the cornerstone of the nation, the woman's role as wife and mother was the cornerstone of the family and thus the key to building the nation. On her shoulders rested not only the nation, but the empire and the future of the race – or so thought the Canadian reformers involved in female immigration work."[33] Seen as a microcosm of culture, the family was of critical importance in the quest to instill British values in Canadian society. This was especially true in the West. In *Prairie Women*, Carol Fairbanks analyzes representations of the female pioneer in the West, in whose honour statues have been raised in cities in both Canada and the United States. The statues all depict the prairie woman as mother, demonstrating the iconic value accorded to the western woman in her married and reproductive capacity.[34]

These expectations blend nicely with the romantic narrative in which women immigrants are instantly incorporated into the community through marriage, thus becoming the wives and mothers to the future nation. But other than the legendary girl seized upon disembarking and married on the spot, such instant immersion into an idealized private sphere was neither plausible nor ultimately desirable for a society experiencing a female labour shortage. On the contrary, many of the women who came to British Columbia to fill positions in domestic service or other, more public employment were unaccompanied and therefore devoid of the important familial connections necessary for this iconic womanly status. Indeed, the young women who flocked into Canadian cities across the country looking for work were conspicuously independent of family protection or support. Women's place in the new society was being negotiated, then, through narratives that were conceptually satisfying but not always wholly suited to the actual Canadian setting; the resulting attempts to blend a discourse of family romance devoid of women's work with the more material demands of settlement created a troubling discrepancy.

This conflict influenced the debate on female immigration, with some encouraging the immigration of educated middle-class women, who, by virtue of their culture and breeding, would exert the civilizing influence so dearly desired, while others held that working-class women were better equipped to take on the hard work of frontier living and to fill the urgent demand for domestic servants. In her 1908 book of advice to potential female settlers, Marion Cran took the former view: "The working-class woman does not bring the intelligence to bear on domestic emergencies which a cultured woman can, out of her ignorance how can she reduce disorder to comeliness and make the prairie home a beautiful thing? ... A woman of refinement and culture, of endurance, of healthy reasoning courage, is infinitely better equipped for the work of homemaking and race-making than the ignorant, often lazy, often slovenly lower-class woman."[35] Cran displays the Victorian urge to impose a hierarchy on the classes and races while also conflating them in such a way that the working classes come to be viewed as racially inferior and incapable of the kind of progress that the imperial mission represented. She stresses "culture" and "refinement" as the attributes that Canada needs most in women. And she emphasizes too the woman's place in the home. The trouble was that when educated middle-class women from Britain arrived in Canada, they were decidedly reluctant to fill the positions in domestic service that the Canadian labour market proffered – positions that they considered menial work. Unsatisfying compromises ensued. Ella Sykes reports on the tense atmosphere in many Canadian households, where what the mistress truly wanted was a servant whom she could treat as such but where, given the dearth of domestic workers, what she begrudgingly faced instead was a British gentlewoman who refused the moniker of servant in favour of "home-help" and who demanded other symbolic gestures of respect and equality like sitting down to eat with the family. Enthusiasts like Marion Cran had no easy answer for such scenes where the disconnect between the imperial ideal and the actual Canadian scene was sometimes uncomfortably clear.

Cran refuses to endorse the planned immigration of working-class women, depicting them instead as "ignorant, often lazy, often slovenly" and as undesirable in the task of "race-making." Her racist elitism was fairly typical of the time, however, and her words reflect the widely held attitude that independent wage-earning women, far from embodying the tradition of home and family, were a challenge to those very structures and thus posed a threat to the ideal of cultural reproduction. Because of their dubious class and race positioning, their frequent lack of familial connections, and their alignment with the public sphere of labour, industry, and capital, wage-earning women outside the home were antithetical to the cult of domesticity, the crucial arbiter of gender construction in the imperial context of western Canada.

In *Making Vancouver*, Robert A.J. McDonald comments on the reluctance to accept women in the workplace or to regard them as truly respectable: "Apart from an obvious desire to protect their jobs in a trade already threatened by cheap 'coloured' labour, two barbers expressed a widely perceived concern that working in a masculine environment outside the home would have a 'bad moral effect' upon women. As one of them commented rhetorically to the male commissioners [of the 1913 BC Commission on Labour]: 'I don't think you would choose a lady barber for a wife.'"[36] That such a comment is, as McDonald notes, entirely rhetorical signals the utter incompatibility, in the minds of both speaker and audience, of the idea of women as wives and the idea of women as workers. In the popular imagination, wage-earning women inhabited a realm so morally dubious as virtually to disqualify them from the sacred role of wife and mother. Women who took up paid work outside the home thus risked their very respectability.

One way to reconcile the ideal of domestic femininity with the fact of women's labour was to invoke the discourse of domestic service, emphasizing its value as the natural and proper sphere for women while downplaying its status as waged labour and hard work. Indeed, some regarded domestic service as a suitable training ground for young women, who would learn the domestic skills so important to their future roles as wives and mothers. But this set of attitudes was notoriously difficult to impose on Canadian working women, who consistently rejected domestic labour in favour of virtually anything else. In Britain domestic service was often thought of as a relatively good opportunity for young working-class women both to make a living and to take a step toward marriage. A similar trajectory was thought to apply in the New World, but both Canadian-born women and young immigrant women tended to resist domestic service whenever possible, and it became axiomatic in Canada that maintaining qualified domestic help was near impossible. It is difficult to accurately establish the degree of this discrepancy in attitudes toward domestic service on either side of the Atlantic. But Ella Sykes identifies a key difference between the nature of domestic service in England and in Canada: "British servants are usually specialists, and do not grasp that in Canada they must turn their hands to anything, and be cook, house-parlourmaid, washerwoman, and perhaps baker and dairymaid all in one."[37] In other words, domestic work in Canada was much more labourious and understandably unattractive compared to options in other expanding industries. One of the Bride Ship women, interviewed later in life, was severely disappointed with Canada and with the conditions under which she worked:

No, I was not happy, and I saw nothing beautiful about the new country. From the moment of landing I was disappointed, so was my sister ... the rain and mud were dreadful ... I used to cry myself to sleep every night. I slept in a garret room with big cracks that let in the rain. The houses were all very poorly built. I was supposed to be a sort of companion; but though they kept Chinese help, there were tasks to do which were distasteful to me.[38]

Domestic work in Canada could be extremely onerous, yet middle-class Canadians consistently bemoaned the reluctance of young women to enter domestic service, painting them as selfish, demanding, and misguided in their pursuit of other work. In 1886 Sara Jeannette Duncan commented in the *Globe* on this disfavour toward domestic service: "The safe, comfortable life of the valued domestic servant, with all the pleasant relations it involves, is neglected for other ways of living, more laborious and more exposed."[39] In fact, long hours, low wages, virtually no time to oneself, and the threat of sexual advances from employers consistently made domestic labour a last resort for working women with any choice in the matter. As Mrs. Mitchell of the Vancouver Local Council of Women explained, "people have so long looked down upon girls who do housework and subjected them to all kinds of indignities that young women of our day won't take these things. They would rather starve."[40] Vancouver labour activist Helena Gutteridge even claimed that "there is a greater percentage of insanity among domestic servants than any other class of workers, probably due to the long hours worked and the endless monotony of drudgery."[41] So the narrative of gender progress where domestic service in the colonies was one step in a woman's evolution toward wife and mother to the new nation was indicative of a set of social prescriptions that were not always successfully imposed on its chosen subjects. As a means of regulating the conceptual incongruity between women as workers and women as wives, the appeal to domestic service was thus tenuous at best. The cult of domesticity was powerful, but it had its limits.

Understanding women's roles as cultural carriers is important if we are to map their place within the physical and conceptual territories of empire, nation, and home. As emblematic of cultural continuity in the midst of intercultural turmoil, white women were subject to intense scrutiny as they entered the colonial Canadian West – a situation only exacerbated by their perceived scarcity. Essential to narratives of cultural and national identity, women were beset by colonial proscriptions and moral imperatives. But this cultural discourse of women as the custodians of tradition was highly monological in its location of women within a private domestic ideal. There was little latitude whereby working-class women could be integrated into this scheme, especially given their consistent resistance to domestic service. The romance narrative of "the colonial matrimonial market," together with the cult of domesticity, specified home and hearth as women's assigned station in the settler society of the West, but the figure of the working girl did not fit so easily into these conventional moulds, and the glimpses that we catch of her rejecting the maid's cap and leaving behind a British husband for a new one in Canada suggest a very different pioneer story.

## INDUSTRIALISM AND THE CITY

Industrial development in western cities was rapid and took place alongside a quickly growing population. Between 1901 and 1931, for instance, Vancouver's population grew from 29,000 to more than eight times that at 246,000. Winnipeg was a larger city in 1901 with a population of 45,000, and it too grew swiftly to a similar size in 1931 at 243,000. The cities in between were smaller but doing their best to catch up: Edmonton and Calgary each had about 5,000 people in 1901, but by 1916 both were more than ten times larger. Saskatchewan's cities were slightly smaller, but in 1916 both Regina and Saskatoon had over 20,000 people.[42] While the economies of western cities still depended in large part on resource industries such as forestry, fishing, and mining, and on construction work, all employing mostly men, service industries rapidly expanded to meet the needs of the quickly changing urban setting, and these increasingly drew on a female workforce. Ella Sykes notes that in her travels through Winnipeg, Edmonton, Calgary, Vancouver, and Victoria, she tried to stay at the YWCA boarding houses for young women but was never able to get in because they were always too full, and she was sent on to other boarding houses for women. Moreover, at one of these, in Winnipeg, she was given notice that she'd have to leave soon because "a big band of girl-immigrants was expected from England ... and fifty girls could be packed at a pinch into the big room at the top of the house."[43] This gives one a sense of how western cities were scrambling to accommodate the increasing numbers of young women streaming in and searching for employment. Industrialization and urbanization were taking place all at once, and one of the most obvious social repercussions was the sudden entrance of wage-earning women in numbers.

Suddenly more and more visible in the public spheres of work, wages, and city streets, the unfamiliar figure of the working girl was evidence of the fundamental shifts taking place in the social fabric. Women who entered the workforce, especially in nondomestic arenas such as factories, stores, restaurants, and offices, left the private confines of the home and family, a space associated with natural purity, and entered the public sphere of capital and industry, a realm suffused with metaphors of degeneration and contamination. In Vancouver an article in the *Province* on the need for domestic-science classes for girls linked industrialism to the decay of home values: "Economic pressure has burst open the doors of the home and its inmates, driven forth as outcasts and wanderers upon the streets of great cities, come to look upon the home as a mere lodging-house. Not only has man lost much of the domestic sense, but woman has lost pride in privacy and domestic seclusion."[44] The rhetoric here seems to suggest the expulsion from Eden, as though an industrial society is a fallen one, and most telling of this fall are the changed attitudes of women. Part of the comfort of having women in the home, especially in an ethnically mixed environment, involved the cordoning-off of their sexuality, but in the city such supervision was not feasible. Mary Ann Doane explains how certain anxieties concerning gender were often the product of modern urban change: "The conjunction of the woman and the city suggests the potential of an intolerable and dangerous sexuality, a sexuality which is out of bounds precisely as a result of the woman's revised relation to space, her new ability to 'wander' (and hence to 'err'). This was perceived as a peculiarly modern phenomenon."[45] Doane's analysis helps to explain the tendency in the early twentieth century to view urban working women in sexual terms and as particularly vulnerable to sexual downfall; working women were thought to be compromising their moral safety by moving so freely and independently through public streets and neighbourhoods.

Winnipeg reformer J.S. Woodsworth wrote about the problem of the city in his 1911 book, *My Neighbor*, which illustrates the deep suspicion of the city that was felt in this era of rapid urbanization in Canada:

> As we penetrate more deeply into its life, we discover evils of which we had hardly dreamed. Pitfalls abound on every side; dark crimes are being committed; dreadful tragedies are being enacted in real life. We get behind the scenes; we see the seamy side. We look beneath the glittering surface and shrink back from the hidden depths which the yawning darkness suggests.[46]

Woodsworth identifies working girls as a symptom of urban ills, particularly linked to the disintegration of home life:

> We come nearer to the home in the case of working girls, many of whom actually live in their own homes or with friends. Girls employed in domestic service form a class by themselves; it is to be greatly regretted that these girls, whose work brings them into such close association with homes, should be homeless, often having to resort to the street as the only place in which to meet a friend. With long hours and inferior social status it is little wonder that girls are glad to escape from housework to the more independent if worse-paid work in shops and factories. Here we find a life that is full of temptations, and only girls of fine instincts, high character and good training will escape a sad coarsening as the months go on.[47]

The population of western cities increased so rapidly in the years surrounding the turn of the century that housing was an ongoing problem, and with the special concerns about young women and domestic virtue, the housing of working girls was considered an especially urgent matter. The YWCA did its best to address this issue, and between 1897 and 1907 opened hostels in Winnipeg, Regina, Saskatoon, Moose Jaw, Prince Albert, Edmonton, Calgary, and Vancouver. But these hostels could seldom meet the demand of the many young women arriving in the city in search of work, and the perception that young working women were overflowing onto the city streets was not totally unfounded.

Vancouver in the early twentieth century consisted of specific sectors, or ghettos, identified with groups such as single working men, the Chinese community, and prostitutes, and the thought of young working women wandering through such danger zones was troubling to many. The Moral and Social Reform Council of British Columbia issued a report in 1912 on "Social Vice in Vancouver," which claimed that "there is a constant siege being laid to the morals of young girls here. No unprotected girl is safe. The committee has had numbers of complaints of such annoyances from all parts of the city. Young women of the best character have been thus molested constantly."[48] As white women, in their symbolic role, were regarded as the nation's future mothers, their morality, purity, and sexuality were felt to be in need of careful protection; but to many, working women seemed to be placing themselves in a position from which they could hardly uphold these expectations.

These kinds of concerns about women on their own in the city begin to explain why the entrance of wage-earning women into the rapidly growing public sphere of urban industry was so distressing to urban administrators and middle-class reformers of the time. In fact, western cities were certainly slower and arguably more reluctant than eastern Canadian cities to accept and facilitate the incorporation of women into nondomestic waged labour. Of the total number of working women in Vancouver, a higher ratio (42 percent in 1911) remained in domestic service much later into the century than was the case in eastern cities,[49] and this pattern was reflected to a lesser degree in Alberta and Saskatchewan as well.[50] This could be indicative of a number of different circumstances – there weren't as many other female-defined jobs in western cities as there were, for instance, in Toronto, where factory work for women was abundant. The work that was available – for instance, in hotels or laundries – was largely invisible to the public, so it went unrecognized. But certainly, the highly gender-segregated field of employment in the West influenced and was influenced by deeply held and longstanding ideologies about women's natural place and by strategies that might maintain this place. This disinclination to accept or recognize women's entry into nontraditional workplaces would have far-reaching effects. Because women's presence in new fields of labour was classified as an aberration to be reformed and restricted – or solved by marriage taking them out of the workforce altogether – the significance and value of the work that women performed was consistently disregarded.

Debates concerning working women differed according to the agendas of the parties involved, but what remained consistent was an inability to conceive of women simply as workers, with attendant needs concerning wages, working conditions, and so on; rather, working women might be represented as victims of capitalism, wilful and selfish girls wanting spending money, innocents in danger of corruption, "new women," "women adrift," and so forth. All of these were indicative of varying anxieties surrounding women and work in the city, but none were able to separate the idea of the worker from the gender status involved. This tendency to reduce a working woman to her gender indicates how vast was the conceptual divergence between the idea of the wage-earning man, an absolute given of society, and the notion of the wage-earning woman – a social problem and threat to the natural order.

One way that this conceptual divergence was managed involved the naturalization of the gendered division of labour; if women had to enter the public realm and thus upset the proper order of things, they could at least be confined to specific kinds of labour that, if not already coded as women's work, could soon be reformulated as such. A degree of order that reinscribed gender stereotypes would thus be restored, and traditional, supposedly natural, gender constructions would to some degree be upheld. In British Columbia the gendered division of labour was arguably more pronounced than elsewhere because the most prominent industries involved the heavy work of resource extraction, always associated with male physical strength and masculinity.

While stereotyped and restrictive, the narrative about men generously taking on all the heavy manual labour was also recognized by some as a deceiving fiction. Domestic work in particular, which involved heavy lifting, scrubbing floors, doing laundry manually, and working practically unlimited hours, was undoubtedly physically taxing. In British Columbia women were also the primary source of labour for the demanding but poorly paid work in the fish-processing industry. In her column for the Vancouver labour newspaper the *BC Federationist*, Helena Gutteridge objected explicitly to the hypocrisy of this notion about labour division:

> One of the pleasant conventions about women's work, still maintained by those who are unwilling to face the harsh reality, is the fiction that all the rough and disagreeable tasks are discharged by men ... If the world's work were divided on the principle of giving to men the heavier tasks and to women the lighter and more pleasant duties, the male clerk should at once change places with the housemaid and the ticket-collector with the laundress.[51]

Gutteridge might have gone on to point out that the male clerk and the ticket collector, despite their easy work, would likely both be paid more than the housemaid or the laundress. Playing on notions of male chivalry and feminine delicacy, the idea that men did the hard work conveniently ignored not only the physical demands of women's work but, more important, also its associated value. The gender stereotyping that had men doing the hard work on behalf of the weaker sex fed into the devaluation of women's paid labour and so provided justification for their lower wages. That Gutteridge identifies the gendered division of labour and the assumptions that underlie it as conventions and fictions demonstrates her recognition of the ways that society creates itself through these regulating narratives – narratives, moreover, that serve some more than others.

Wage-earning women, insofar as they represented the social changes brought about by modernity, were touchstones for judgments about urban transformation. The desire to maintain traditional gender divisions asserted itself in the popular belief that women did only lighter varieties of work, while men did the heavier, more important tasks, but the gendered division of labour was already being challenged by women who resisted the false chivalry of this narrative and who were eager for the opportunities of working life outside the home. What made this challenge to convention all the more disturbing to social critics of the day was that the women most conspicuous in this movement into the public sphere of work were young and single: at the exact moment when they should be taking up their all-important function as wives and mothers, they were instead delaying, even rejecting, this imperative by entering the very space most antithetical to true womanhood – the workplace.

## THE SINGLE WORKING GIRL

In addition to the idea that women's lower wages were in part justified by their doing lighter, less significant, or less skilled work than men, employers also argued that women's marginalization and devaluation in the working world were related to their status as temporary workers. At the turn of the century and in the first decades of the twentieth century, young women tended to enter the workforce for the few years prior to marriage. Many of them expected, as did society, that marriage would remove them from the labour force. Of course, in some cases the anticipated husband might not materialize, a woman might choose not to marry, or necessity might dictate that married or widowed women work outside the home. But insofar as a typical working woman existed at all, she would have been young and single – hence the creation of an identifiable group known as "working girls." Much of the controversy that surrounded this group of women was connected to their status as young and unmarried, conditions that contributed to representations of them as vulnerable and in need of protection. Employers exploited the women's youth by claiming that their inexperience justified their low wages, as did their familial status: since young girls were presumably still living at home with their families, they needn't be paid a living wage, only enough for "pin money" or to supplement the family's income. The following exchange took place during a meeting of British Columbia's Commission on Labour in 1912. Here, the commissioner questions a laundry owner on the fairness of his wages:

**Mr. Stoney:** What do you think would be a fair wage for women?
**Mr. Abrams:** Women might be able to earn much more if they would stay with their jobs and not run around from one to another.
**Mr. Stoney:** That hardly answers the question.
**Mr. Abrams:** Women in the laundry or any place else as far as I know, if they would stick at the work and become efficient, would run from $10 to $15 a week. But that doesn't figure the average woman.
**Mr. Stoney:** Figure the average woman. Have you any idea what it costs a young woman to live in a city like this, board, room, clothing, etc?
**Mr. Abrams:** I haven't any idea. I am not a young woman and haven't had any experience with any.
**Mr. Stoney:** With the minimum wage you pay a woman, $1.25 a day, if she were not living at home do you think she could live on that?
**Mr. Abrams:** No. I would not expect her to … They should not be away from home, those that get $1.25 a day.
**Mr. Stoney:** Suppose it was not their own fault? Suppose their parents were dead and they had to go to work?
**Mr. Abrams:** I don't expect they could live on that. But these girls that get $1.25 have homes and help to support the family by working in the laundry. That is the way I look at it.[52]

Young working women had a reputation for switching jobs frequently, a habit usually ascribed to the monotony of the repetitive, unskilled work open to them, the boredom of which might be slightly mitigated by moving from one to another. Here, the employer emphasizes this temporary status in addition to the women's inexperience and family situation to justify low wages. Despite his rationalizations, he seems noticeably evasive, needing to be told that his response "hardly answers the question," and after stating with authority what women should do to improve their wages, he subsequently denies having "had any experience with any" of them. The interviewer, meanwhile, seems to be searching for an admission that no woman could live independently on the wages offered. At another stage he asks, "What would she have to do?" – the implication being that she would have to turn to prostitution. So while employers emphasized young working women's unmarried status (which meant that they should be living at home) to justify low wages, reformers, too, cited their singleness (although without expectation of a family connection), but they did so to forecast young working women's exploitation and moral downfall. In both cases, the unmarried status of working women was a focus in defining the "problem" of the working girl. The assumption that single wage-earning women were destined for marriage and motherhood also contributed to their being regarded as temporary members of the workforce who didn't need a living wage because they should shortly fall under the care of a husband. But at this time women were beginning to delay marriage a little longer, and some of course would not marry at all. The single status of young working women was a category fraught with meaning, contributing perhaps more than anything else to the representation of working girls as a social problem and moral dilemma.

Given western Canada's legendary abundance of bachelors, single women were under significant pressure to marry, but the assumption that marriage was the immediate goal of all young women was somewhat undermined by their instead getting jobs and joining a working-class youth culture that in many ways validated a single lifestyle of dances, dating, and commercial amusements. Carolyn Strange argues that "female singlehood was a characteristic that brimmed with economic and cultural significance in the early decades of industrial urbanization."[53] That young female workers tended to be single and living on their own enhanced the degree to which they were looked upon in sexual terms. And the few years between childhood and marriage constituted an interim period in which the male control of either father or husband could not be guaranteed. It appeared that working girls were thus entering the morally dangerous world of industry at the precise time when they were most vulnerable to downfall; as Mrs. Mitchell of the Local Council of Women put it, "Take any girl full of life and romance and poetry and keep her at that drudgery and you can see what a brave girl she must be to remain a good girl, especially when there are temptations all around her."[54]

To be single and earning wages in the public sphere further suggested a degree of capability and independence that was uncharacteristic and even unfeminine in women. The workplace, it was thought, had a degrading effect on womanhood and unfitted women for marriage and motherhood. According to a paper presented by Mrs. Bayfield at the 1907 Meeting of the National Council of Women in Vancouver,

> No one will dispute that in its homes lies the true strength of a nation. That the home life gives the tone to political and social life, and that there souls must be trained for time and for eternity ... Yet at the present time it seems that our Canadian homes are in danger of slipping from us ... Our girls congregate in shops as clerks and in offices as stenographers, often underpaid, but they prefer this to helping in a home which their education has caused them to consider *menial work*. When they marry they make poor wives and mothers, and worse housekeepers, and so the evil goes round in a circle and gets worse.[55]

Here, the sacred space of the home is endangered by the attitudes of young working women who turn their backs on domestic duty and themselves make unfit for subsequent marriage. It is interesting to note that while the home is said to influence the public sphere, to "give the tone to political and social life," and to harbour the "true strength of a nation," the value of women's actual work in the public sphere of paid labour is carefully ignored; the girls don't *work* in shops and offices but "congregate" there, and their own estimation of domestic work as "*menial*" is italicized to highlight a supposedly corrupt logic.

Working girls were thought to be straying from the true path of femininity in other ways as well. For instance, they gained a reputation for using bad language, a trait judged to be inappropriate and unattractive in young women. A report about a number of young women working as waitresses at the Banff Springs Hotel criticized a work environment characterized by profane language and too much makeup:

> The girls are required to make themselves attractive looking, and with the thermometer in the kitchen, as it was one day recently, registering 114 degrees, the traces of fatigue can only be hidden by a liberal use of powder and rouge. Unless a girl is painted up like Jezebel, she will be sent away to make herself presentable.

Such a life does not tend to produce a high standard of ethics, and the only vent which the employees seem to find for their feelings is in a plentiful use of profane language. Any girl who cannot swear like a trooper finds herself very much out of place in these surroundings. This is perhaps scarcely to be wondered at in the circumstances.[56]

At stake here are the boundaries of appropriate gender behaviour. To this reporter, working women's use of makeup and profanity signals disturbing defeminization and moral degradation, but what the writer highlights are the kinds of transitions in gender construction that were under way in women's workplaces. Single working women were negotiating gender and identity as workers, experimenting, through makeup and language, with new styles of femininity that their experience in the working world made possible. Working women were also actively pushing the boundaries of respectability in their social lives.

Toronto journalist Maude Pettit (who used the pseudonym "Videre") wrote a series of articles on her experience posing as a regular working girl, living in lodgings, and taking on a variety of jobs. Upon asking one young woman how she spent her free time, the journalist received the following account:

"Here, says one girl, is how I spend my evenings: Monday night, an occasional (that means a man who just calls upon one sometimes); Tuesday, my steady; Wednesday, another occasional; Thursday, steady; Friday, another occasional; Saturday and Sunday, the steady. The steady worked three nights a week, so she filled up her program as above, according to her own words."[57]

This highly active and totally unchaperoned social life was of course much more available to young working women who lived on their own than to girls living at home, and this new kind of independence seemed to many observers a dangerous degree of social and sexual latitude to allow young women. Indeed, the important social shift that took place when women entered the urban industrial workforce and were able to rent their own rooms away from all family constraints had an undoubted effect on women's social and sexual freedom. As Kathy Peiss found in her research on working girls in turn-of-the-century New York, "The social and physical space of the tenement home and boarding house contributed to freer social and sexual practices."[58] It is no wonder, then, that discussions about working girls frequently alluded to the question of their lodgings; because they lived in single rooms and had no sitting room, they entertained their male guests in their bedrooms, a situation deemed most undesirable to some, although apparently not to the young women themselves, as Maude Pettit found: "'Do you shut your door when you have a gentleman in?' I asked of the girl in the next room. 'O-o-o-ooh yes!' she said expressively, 'shut it and lock it.'"[59]

The single status of young working women enhanced the tendency to view them in terms of their gender and to view their problems in moral terms rather than in practical ones that would address wages and working conditions. The report about the Banff Springs Hotel, for instance, does mention a problem with working conditions – the "114 degree" kitchen – but relates it to the moral issues of makeup and unladylike language. Elsewhere, when wage-earning women's working conditions were more carefully scrutinized, reformers used women's roles as future mothers to argue for better wages or shorter hours; sympathy for women in their traditional motherly roles was the keynote. The idea that women should simply have rights as workers seldom arose. The concern with maintaining gender norms could thus deflect attention away from women's roles as workers and from the social and economic value of their work. But their single and unsupervised status continued to be a focus of interest. A contradiction manifested itself between the idea that working girls were vulnerable to moral and economic victimization and the fear that they were uniquely positioned to discover a new sense of freedom that would allow them to play havoc with gender dictates.

Working women in turn-of-the-century western Canada were the subject of intense interest among groups with otherwise widely different agendas and concerns: for reformers and women's groups, they were objects for philanthropic projects; for travel writers, they were the most romantic of immigrants; for imperialists, they were daughters of empire and mothers of the nation; and for writers and journalists, they made excellent characters in tales of urban intrigue. On a number of different levels, working girls were in the vanguard of change both in gender constructions and in the culture of work in urban industrial settings. In their roles and behaviour as women workers, they pioneered new ways of enacting gender while challenging both the ingrained assumptions unique to Canada and the inherited traditions of a British elite. But breaching so many sets of interwoven assumptions and cultural narratives gave rise to many complications. Due to the social reluctance to accept women in the role of workers, ideologies of gender separation and hierarchy asserted themselves with force. The belief that women's natural place was in the home meant that domestic work was extolled not only as the best kind of work for women but also as a form of gender progress whereby lower-class and immigrant women could be incorporated into established society and made ready for their eventual roles as wives and mothers in their own homes. This narrative was especially attractive in the colonial view of the West, where the rhetoric of imperial progress suffused both public and domestic spheres and where women were considered invaluable as guarantors of civilization and family in the New World. Despite this glorification of women's indispensable domestic talents, women's work and labour in the home, as elsewhere, tended to be either ignored or devalued on the premise that women's work was easier, lighter, and less necessary than men's. That women were thought important enough to be brought over in ships or attracted through promotional campaigns belies this denigration of their importance, and part of this importance undoubtedly resided in their labour power, since the groups involved in such campaigns repeatedly specified their desire for working-class women to fill domestic-service positions. Moreover, that many women left or rejected such work to join the nondomestic workforce is testimony to the demand for their labour elsewhere as well. A serious contradiction is evident here concerning women's supposed place in the West, and it is in contradictions such as these that ideologies of gender construction and negotiation tend to manifest. In the popular imagination, women embodied tradition and family in the burgeoning nation, but more and more they instead refuted these romantic notions by becoming eager and willing social pioneers in urban culture and the world of work.

## chapter 2

# The Urban Working Girl in Turn-of-the-Century Canadian Literature

The eyes of the women met. They smiled at one
another. Fellow-workers – out in the world together.
That's what their eyes said: Free!

– J.G. SIME,
*Sister Woman,* 1919

At the turn of the century the relatively new figure of the independent urban working girl represented for many writers the modern city: its opportunities, but also its potential for immorality and cultural disruption. At a time when women, particularly young single women, were entering the paid workforce in unprecedented numbers, there emerged in social commentary and fictional narrative the recognized figure of the working girl – the representational counterpart of society's new female wage earners. It is to this culturally constructed figure that I refer in the following discussion of the working girl in Canadian literature. Many American writers seized upon the working girl as a heroine through which to explore the dubious social repercussions of modernity, but Canadian writers were hesitant to address this female harbinger of change. In a literary market dominated by historical romance, the texts of social realism more likely to depict the working class were often neglected, but a more specialized suppression seemed to apply to representations of the urban working girl. Subject to both economic and sexual exploitation, the working girl had the potential to take on universal meaning as the innocent working-class victim of unprincipled capital, and in some texts this is her role. But the confidence and enthusiasm with which young women entered the urban fray significantly undermined the appraisal of them as unwilling sacrifices to industrialism. The working girl was easily fixed in categories of innocence or corruption, and her absence from Canadian literature may in part reflect an unwillingness to face the complex social changes that she embodied. Notably, the few writers who did take up the figure of the working girl seem to fall into one of two distinct genres: issue-oriented social realism or light-hearted popular romance, both of which were often neglected in criticism. Although journalists and social reformers of the day voiced concern about the plight of working women, it would seem that literature directed at the middle-class literary audience was not expected to foreground social injustice too insistently, and it is this literature that entered the canon. There are, of course, myriad reasons for one text to be canonized and not another, but the coincidence that saw urban themes, working-class issues, and gender politics all frequently sidelined suggests a palpable resistance to acknowledging precisely those cultural conditions epitomized in the working girl. Those works that did address this figure were thus engaged in a politics of representation wherein even to depict the working girl was to invest meaning where it had long been denied. Just as working women contributed to the industrial economy in a whole new way, working girls in literature did cultural work in figuring social transformation and gender transgression, and given the momentous changes in gender expectations occurring in the twentieth century, the narratives that lent meaning to the wage-earning woman are social documents of great importance. In order to convey a wider sense of the working girl's place in Canadian literature, I temporarily broaden my focus in this chapter to examine texts from both eastern and western Canada, and I suggest along the way a few areas where comparisons can be made.

## "ONLY A WORKING GIRL"

In 1895 Marie Joussaye of Belleville, Ontario, published a collection of poetry entitled *The Songs that Quinte Sang*, perhaps the only work of Canadian literature written by a working girl and addressed to her peers. Joussaye's life story is difficult to piece together from the historical record, but Carole Gerson documents her family background in Ontario, where she was the youngest of five children in a working-class Catholic home.[1] At the age of seventeen she was working in domestic service, and after moving to Toronto she became an organizer of servant girls. She wished for a career in journalism but was apparently unable to overcome the sexism of the industry: "If I spoke to an editor or haunted a newspaper

office, there was an evil construction put upon it ... Young men pushed
themselves forward by sheer persistence and a little talent, but what was
permitted to them, was resented in my case."[2] She moved west shortly
after publishing *The Songs that Quinte Sang* and lived in Kamloops,
Dawson City, and Vancouver. After marrying in 1903 she was at times
plagued by legal disputes and even served two months of hard labour, but
she nevertheless kept writing and published one more volume of poetry,
entitled *Selections from Anglo-Saxon Songs* (1918), also concerned with
labour themes. It is in the earlier volume that her poem "Only a Working
Girl" appears, probably her best-known work to date because of its use
as a thematic touchstone for historians: Wayne Roberts quotes the phrase
"honest womanhood" from it in the title of his book *Honest Womanhood:
Feminism, Femininity and Class Consciousness among Toronto Working
Women, 1893-1914*, and Linda Kealey uses it to open her discussion of
women workers in *Enlisting Women for the Cause: Women, Labour, and the
Left in Canada, 1890-1920*.[3] For the working girl in Canadian literature,
it is an important piece because it comes from the pen of a working girl
herself. Though collected in *The Songs that Quinte Sang*, the poem was
published on its own earlier, in 1886, in the *Journal of United Labour*,
when servant-girl leader Joussaye was only twenty-two years old.

ONLY A WORKING GIRL[4]

I know I am only a working girl,
    And I am not ashamed to say
I belong to the ranks of those who toil
    For a living, day by day.
With willing feet I press along
    In the paths that I must tread,
Proud that I have the strength and skill
    To earn my daily bread.

I belong to the "lower classes";
    That's a phrase we often meet.
There are some who sneer at working girls;
    As they pass us on the street,
They stare at us in proud disdain
    And their lips in scorn will curl,
And oftentimes we hear them say:
    "She's only a working girl."

"Only a working girl!" Thank God,
  With willing hands and heart,
Able to earn my daily bread,
  And in Life's battle take my part.
You could offer me no title
  I would be more proud to own,
And I stand as high in the sight of God
  As the Queen upon her throne.

Those gentle folk who pride themselves
  Upon their wealth and birth,
And look with scorn on those who have
  Naught else but honest worth,
Your gentle birth we laugh to scorn,
  For we hold it as our creed
That none are gentle, save the one
  Who does a gentle deed.

We are only the "lower classes,"
  But the Holy Scriptures tell
How, when the King of Glory
  Came down on earth to dwell,
Not with the rich and mighty
  'Neath costly palace dome,
But with the poor and lowly
  He chose to make His home.

He was one of the "lower classes,"
  And had to toil for bread,
So poor that oftentimes He had
  No place to lay His head.
He knows what it is to labor
  And toil the long day thro',
He knows when we are weary
For He's been weary too.

O working girls! Remember,
  It is neither crime or shame
To work for honest wages,

Since Christ has done the same,
And wealth and high position
    Seem but of little worth
To us, whose fellow laborer
    Is King of Heaven and Earth.

So when you meet with scornful sneers,
    Just lift your heads in pride;
The shield of honest womanhood
    Can turn such sneers aside,
And some day they will realize
    That the purest, fairest pearls
'Mid the gems of noble womankind
    Are "only working girls."

Joussaye's poem became a kind of theme song in her labour activism, suggesting that it had real resonance for the women to whom it was written. It touches on issues of competence, status, purity, and pride, which held particular significance for the working girl, whose virtue was often impugned because of her experience in the public and exposed workplace. The poem speaks to the feeling of being looked down upon and having one's worth denigrated, suggesting that Joussaye felt the injustice of a society that refused to see the merit in women's work, denying them the status they deserved as workers and as women.

The poem explores the differences in meaning and resonance that the designation of "working girl" takes on in a class-interested society. Joussaye, who would clearly scoff at the idea of Canada as a classless society, depicts a world infected with class snobbery, where those who define themselves through "wealth and birth" show open disdain for the inherently "noble womankind" who "work for honest wages." The designation of "working girl" is used disparagingly by the former group – "she's only a working girl" – and Joussaye's project in the poem is to reclaim the "working girl" label as a term of pride and true female worth, making working girls "the purest, fairest pearls" of womankind. This struggle over meaning and connotation demonstrates the politics that were attached to the very term "working girl" – that it could be used as a form of denigration and belittlement or of pride and worth depending upon the speaker, context, and tone in which it was used. It is a battle over language and representation by a spokeswoman who refuses to internalize the denigration implicit in the language commonly used to categorize her group. Joussaye's poem is thus an important form of intervention in the representation of working girls, who saw themselves disparagingly depicted in the media and in reform language and who – according to Joussaye – heard themselves disparaged on the street yet refused to acquiesce to this portrayal. In the first stanza Joussaye asserts the central conflict between shame and pride; her working-girl speaker, "not ashamed" to claim her place in the "ranks of those who toil," counters the denigration she feels with an assertion of the competence required to earn a living through work: "Proud that I have the strength and skill / To earn my daily bread." This assertion of competence and ability is important, for not only does it suggest a contrast to a traditional nonworking ideal of womanhood, wherein women lack such skills in self-sufficiency, but it also implicitly counters the depiction of women's waged work as menial, unskilled, or "light" work that anyone could do. For this speaker, self-sufficiency depends on a "strength and skill" that one can be proud of.

The second stanza depicts the social depreciation that working women are subjected to by those who "sneer at working girls" and "stare at us in proud disdain." It is interesting that Joussaye depicts this conflict taking place "as they pass us on the streets." The public nature of women's waged work, which placed them outside the home in seemingly uncontrolled workplaces and saw them streaming unchaperoned onto the streets at the end of the day, was a key cause for the suspicion about their apparently compromised virtue. Here, there is a class antagonism that takes shape in the public arena of the city street, where working girls become the target for hostile stares and sneering remarks. To counter this derogatory attitude, Joussaye's following stanza once again emphasizes her speaker's pride in the competence and ability that it takes to earn a living, this time adding an almost combative element to the language: "Able to earn my daily bread, / And in Life's battle take my part."

To develop the idea of working girls' inherent worth and virtue and to inspire the sense of pride with which she wants to imbue the "working girl" label, Joussaye goes on to pair the working girl with Christ: "O working girls! Remember, / It is neither crime or shame / To work for honest wages, / Since Christ has done the same." Joussaye's portrayal of Christ stresses two main characteristics that are key to her figuration of the working girl as lowly in status but infinite in worth; on the one hand, she emphasizes Christ's identity as a "fellow laborer": "He was one of the 'lower classes,' / And had to toil for bread / ... He knows what it is to labor / And toil the long day thro'"; and on the other hand, she emphasizes his incontestable status as the "King of Glory" and the "King of Heaven and Earth." It is through this duality of the humble and the glorious that she seeks to redefine working girls, whose work "for honest wages" and whose "honest womanhood" are the true and Christly assurances of their status as "the purest, fairest pearls" of "noble womankind." Through the analogy that pairs the working girl with Christ, Joussaye strongly asserts working women's inherent and unassailable virtue, while also imbuing their labour itself with the value and dignity of Christ's labour. Joussaye's religious background was Roman Catholic, and she works shrewdly within Catholicism's familiar paradigms to assert a compelling definition of the working girl that stresses at once her virtue and competence in the face of a society that sought in many ways to deny both. The struggles that Joussaye dramatizes over competence, self-reliance, virtue, femininity, and status similarly permeate the literature that features the working girl as character and heroine, but few such texts have the rallying-cry quality of immediacy so prominent and so commanding in Joussaye's direct address to the working girl.

## SOCIAL REALISM AND WORKING WOMEN IN CANADIAN LITERATURE

And so, by force of cruel fate, as it seemed, this girl
was as truly chained by invisible fetters to her daily toil
among those relentless wheels and pulleys, as if she
were a galley-slave.

– AGNES MAULE MACHAR,
*Roland Graeme, Knight,* 1892

In 1919 J.G. Sime published *Sister Woman,* a collection of short stories that addressed the "woman question" by portraying, in stark realist mode, the struggles of Montreal's working-class women. Reviews of the work were not hostile, but they betray a marked ambivalence: "It is an attractive and clever book, but the constancy of the point of view in the tales gives a certain monotony. But one doesn't need to read them all at once."[5] More intriguing than mere dismissal, however, is the opening statement of the *Canadian Bookman* review, which situates its evaluation in the context of a national literature: "There are qualities about the collection of short sketches entitled 'Sister Woman,' by Miss J. B. Sime [sic], which make us hesitate to describe it as belonging to Canadian literature."[6] The reviewer admits that the writer has lived in Montreal for several years, and the setting is likewise Canadian, but "it is not a book for a young country. It is lacking in sentimentality and optimism, which we seem to demand from purveyors of fiction on this North American continent." Despite these reservations, the review is not otherwise negative; the reviewer describes the story "Munitions" as "one of the most effective presentations in modern literature of the desire of the modern woman for economic independence" and the whole volume as one "which should take rank among the best of the current work of English writers." The hesitation to embrace the text as part of Canadian literature, then, would seem to be based not on any lack of quality but on a feeling that, partly because of its dearth of optimism and sentimentality, the work was atypical of Canadian literature and unlikely to be appreciated by Canadian readers. The degree of ambivalence betrayed by these reviewers, particularly the articulation of this ambivalence in terms of the national literature, is indicative of the reluctance to accept social criticism as part of Canadian literature. But this nationalist bent further suggests a reluctance both to acknowledge current social problems in Canada and to see fiction as one part of the debate needed to address social inequity.

In her introduction to the 1992 edition of Agnes Maule Machar's book *Roland Graeme, Knight* (1892), Carole Gerson notes that "in nineteenth century Canada ... realistic social fiction was generally rejected in favour of historical romance inspired by the example of Sir Walter Scott. So rare was the literary acknowledgement of social problems that for *Roland Graeme*, one of the most sustained examinations of socio-economic issues to appear in Canadian fiction before the First World War, Machar chose an American setting."[7] Gerson explains that this may have been careful planning by Machar, who knew that America and Britain would likely hold the majority of her audience, and Canadian readers would more readily accept a social critique set outside of Canada. *Roland Graeme* appeared in 1892, but, as William H. New points out, the Canadian distaste for socially engaged fiction persisted into the twentieth century as "scores of writers produced lyrical tributes to place and youth ... or penned tender historical romances."[8] This predilection for historical romance was concomitant with a rejection of urban narrative. Despite the rapid expansion of Canadian cities, literature remained rural in setting and theme. Representing problems of social inequity may not demand an urban setting, but in literature of social critique, the city, as the spatial manifestation of modernity, often provides the milieu in which questions of social injustice are represented in most detail. Furthermore, the most sustained challenges to the social order of gender configuration were taking place in the city, as women's entrance into the paid workforce brought about fundamental shifts in gender relations. As New observes, there was also a gendered aspect to the taste for rural themes in Canadian literature: "The general resistance to 'city themes' was perhaps a refusal to recognize social inequities in Canada, perhaps part of a continuing rejection of women's newly visible role in literature and (urban) politics. The city was in some sense figuratively theirs, just as received versions of 'Nature' were extensions of male myths of control."[9] The rejection of urban social themes in Canadian literature was thus not merely a genre preference but also a refusal of those media that might allow for gender contestation. As one of the most visible and troubling figures of urban modernity, the working girl embodied precisely those conflicts that Canadian literature sought to avoid. It is not surprising, then, that Sime's *Sister Woman,* despite its acknowledged merit and its realist innovation, was excluded from established notions of what constituted Canadian literature, for it centred on the urban working girl.

Although contemporary feminist critics such as Sandra Campbell and Lorraine McMullen have brought to light writers like Sime who have often been neglected in the canonization of Canadian literature, novels of socially engaged fiction are still largely marginalized, meaning that narrative representations of Canada's urban working girls have been all but buried. In the United States the tale of the working girl is a much more recognized institution, with landmark texts such as Theodore Dreiser's *Sister Carrie* and Dorothy Richardson's *The Long Day* standing out from a crowd of lesser known popular works and serialized fiction. Indeed, at the end of the nineteenth century in America, the prolific serial fiction writer Laura Jean Libbey made the working-girl story into a formula romance and guaranteed best-seller, and her works may in some degree have influenced the Canadian writers who did portray the working girl in their fiction. In fact, the few texts that do revolve around this figure reveal a degree of class tension and social turbulence that is all the more fascinating for its Canadian context. One novel even has its working-girl heroine suddenly awaken to class hierarchy as she looks for work: "It had never before occurred to her that in applying for this place she had forfeited some of the rights of caste. Social distinctions had troubled Christine as little as they trouble most sensible Canadian girls. She had thought as little about her position as a duchess might: now, for the first time, she felt troubled and uneasy."[10] This passage draws on the Canadian myth of a classless society, a myth that often went unchallenged by mainstream literature, which curtailed class commentary by excluding social fiction. As Christine's troubling realization demonstrates, the struggles of the working girl are inextricably bound to class inequity, and the Canadian reader of working-girl fiction was likely, like Christine, to feel troubled when literature brought this conflict to light.

The four texts I discuss in detail here all feature themes of gender and labour, and although they differ greatly in their treatment of the social questions involved, the various depictions of the working girl suggest her representational power. Two of them, Sime's *Sister Woman* and Machar's *Roland Graeme, Knight,* are texts from eastern Canada, and two, Mackay's *House of Windows* and Sinclair's *North of Fifty-Three,* are from the West. Although it is impossible to draw any definite generalizations about eastern and western tendencies from so few texts, it is worth noting that the eastern writers, Sime and Machar, are strongly committed to realism in their style and portrayal of the social ills encountered by working women, whereas the western writers, Sinclair and Mackay, write in more popular modes that readily employ sensationalism and romance. As a result, the working girl appears somewhat differently in each. In the eastern texts her struggles and hardships strike one more forcibly, and her status as a "problem" figure takes precedence. In the western texts, she is more the lively heroine whose wit and spunk demand a properly romantic reward. One feels, when reading, that perhaps the popular narratives of pioneer adventure and unlikely romance that suffused travel accounts and promotional campaigns in the West may have subtly inspired the western authors as they fashioned the success stories of their fictional working-girl heroines. Since the texts are little read today, I briefly summarize the books to clarify the content and genre positions of each.

As with the Canadian working girl's realization of class in the quotation above, Agnes Maule Machar's *Roland Graeme, Knight* is a novel designed to elicit precisely this kind of awakening to social injustice. Machar was an author, poet, and historian who lived and wrote all her life in Kingston. She was deeply committed to the causes of temperance, labour reform, education for women, social justice, and the defence of Christianity, and her fiction reflects her profound social conscience. Writing under the pseudonym "Fidelis," she contributed articles, reviews, stories, and poems to the periodicals of her day, and she wrote fiction for children as well as historical stories of Canada and the British Empire. *Roland Graeme,*

*Knight* is one of her most highly regarded works, and in its representation of industrial conditions, its call for labour reform, and its concern for women's labour, it is decades ahead of its time.

Machar's novel and its labour hero, Roland, were inspired in part by the Knights of Labor, an early labour organization begun in 1869 by Philadelphia tailors. Open to male and female wage earners, both skilled and unskilled, the Knights of Labor expanded rapidly in the 1870s, reaching into Canada, Britain, Belgium, Australia, and New Zealand. It was committed to an eight-hour work day, the abolition of child labour, equal pay for equal work, and arbitration instead of strikes whenever possible. In 1888, four years before Machar published *Roland Graeme*, the Knights helped to organize a strike of factory workers in Gananoque, not far from Kingston; when the strike proved unsuccessful, the organization assisted workers in establishing their own co-operative factory in Merrickville. Machar thus wrote at a time when the Knights of Labor movement seemed full of promise – indeed, its membership peaked in 1886 at 702,000. Enrolment declined rapidly in the 1890s, however, and the Knights of Labor was partly replaced in the United States by the American Federation of Labor and in Canada by the Trades and Labour Congress and the National Trades and Labour Council.

*Roland Graeme, Knight* is set in a small industrial town and centres on a young middle-class woman, Nora Blanchard, who comes to sympathize with her working-class sisters and subsequently embarks on a number of philanthropic projects to help them, such as creating a space where the mill girls can meet, attend lectures, or read in their time off. The catalyst in her moral awakening is Roland Graeme, a member of the Knights of Labor and a Canadian, who introduces Nora to labour politics and thus educates the reader as well. With its focus on middle-class characters, the novel also clearly addresses a middle-class reader, urging sympathy for the working class in the form of maternal-feminist philanthropy for women and fair labour practices for men. Two minor characters are working girls employed at the town mill: Lizzie Mason, who supports an ailing mother and a wayward brother, is chronically overworked and on her way to an early grave by the end of the novel; Nelly Grove, the more spirited incarnation of the factory girl, displays the good looks and fancy dress that portend her fate as a fallen woman. These two versions of the working girl are recognizable tropes in both fiction and social commentary of the day, figures meant to evoke the pity and humanitarian impulses of a middle-class readership.

Although the novel remains largely conservative in that class hierarchy is not overtly challenged, the way that Machar executes her moral project along gender lines is interesting. The title character and ostensible hero is male, but the central character is undoubtedly Nora Blanchard, whose awakening to class inequity provides her character with the most development; Roland, by contrast, is virtuous but static. In this narrative of labour unrest, the presence of the Knights of Labor and the event of a strike suggest a male conflict, but the only working-class characters figured in any prominence are the working girls; meanwhile, what causes the major reforms for the mill workers are the complaints to the mill owner by his wife and daughter, who, like Nora, are appalled by the working conditions of the girls. The working girls would thus appear to stand in for the whole working class, as their exploitation is the most visible and the most likely to elicit middle-class moral indignation; and the middle-class women, albeit by pestering their men, are the primary agents of social change. The novel is thus very much about the role of women in labour politics, even though in 1892 a relation between these two would seldom have been thought to exist.

Novels aimed at a more popular audience represented the working girl differently. Both Bertrand Sinclair's most popular novel, *North of Fifty-Three*, and Isabel Ecclestone Mackay's *House of Windows* depict the working girl as adventurous and capable. *North of Fifty-Three*'s Hazel Weir is twice subject to unwanted physical advances by men, and both times she successfully slugs the offender and proves herself both physically and morally superior.

Bertrand Sinclair was born in Scotland and moved to Saskatchewan with his mother at the age of eight. He lived in Alberta's Peace River country and Saskatchewan's Qu'Appelle Valley but left at the age of fifteen to be a cowboy in Montana for seven seasons. In 1912 he moved to Vancouver, where he wrote *North of Fifty-Three*. He eventually settled in British Columbia's Pender Harbour, where he continued to write novels about western Canada, depicting its logging and fishing industries and espousing a socialist vision that valued the work and toil of the labourer. Few of these works feature female characters as prominently as does *North of Fifty-Three*, and none of them sold so well.

Published in 1914, *North of Fifty-Three* sold 340,000 copies and was made into a silent film in 1917. In many ways the novel depends on gender stereotypes, but a major part of Sinclair's project is a critique of urban industrialism, and it is significant that for this he chose the working girl as the pivotal figure. Hazel Weir starts the novel as a stenographer in an eastern city, engaged to a young man in real estate who breaks their engagement when he believes a false rumour that she had an affair with her boss. Disillusioned, Hazel moves to British Columbia to teach, where she gets lost in the woods and is found by Roaring Bill Wagstaff, who promptly kidnaps her and takes her to his isolated cabin to spend the winter with him. In many ways, this episode echoes the rumours of Bride Ship girls being whisked off by wilderness men to backwoods weddings, and indeed Sinclair is likely playing on the western Canadian folklore. Wagstaff, ever the gentleman, does not lay a finger on Hazel, and come spring he yields to her demand to be released, escorting her to Vancouver and leaving her there. Hazel plans to pick up where she left off by finding work as a stenographer, but the bustle of the city is now alien to her: "She had her trade at her finger ends, and the storied office buildings of Vancouver assured her that any efficient stenographer could find work. But she looked up as she walked the streets at the high, ugly walls of brick and steel and stone, and her heart misgave her."[11] Just when the city thus threatens to overwhelm her, she encounters, on the corner of Seymour and Hastings, her ex-fiancé, Jack Barrow, who is full of apology for his past behaviour and begs her to take him back and return to the East. Hazel cannot resist comparing him in her mind to Wagstaff: "And she could not conceive of Bill Wagstaff ever being humble or penitent for anything he had done. Barrow's attitude was that of a little boy who had broken some plaything in a fit of anger and was now woefully trying to put the pieces together again. It amused her."[12] Soon afterward Hazel makes her way back to Wagstaff's cabin, and they are married instantly. Hazel's moral choice between the rugged wilderness life – considered here to be more honest – and waged work in the city is represented as a romantic choice between the hyper-masculine mountain man of the West and the vacillating city boy of the East. In making money through mining, Wagstaff is willing to exploit nature via his own physical labour but not people: "I don't care to live fat and make someone else foot the bill. But I can exploit the resources of nature ... It won't be wealth created by shearing lambs in the market, by sweatshop labor, or adulterated food, or exorbitant rental of filthy tenements."[13] Wagstaff thus embodies the quintessential West Coast male, whose hard labour in resource extraction not only guarantees his undeniable masculinity but also sets him on industrialism's moral high-ground (environmentalism not being what it is today) and even assures his desirability to the opposite sex. However, this is also the figure who, when rendered as the quintessential agent of British Columbia's economic progress, relegates women workers to the background or overlooks their presence altogether. Sources of profit that Wagstaff rejects as exploitative include the stock market, sweatshop labour, and renting tenements, all industries set exclusively in cities, sweatshop labour often being associated with women workers. As a working girl engaged to a real estate man, Hazel begins the novel as a representative of this corrupt urban life: subject to harassment in the economically and sexually exploitative workplace and a victim of false innuendo, she is betrayed by her fiancé and ostracized by a hypocritical society. Here, the working-girl figure is clearly the touchstone for judgments on city life and the moral cesspool of urban industrialism. Her journey to the West is a moral one as well as a physical and romantic one. However, since redemption here is contingent on rejection of city and workplace hypocrisies and on valorization of the explicitly masculine resource industry, Hazel must renounce her role as a worker and become the devoted backwoods wife. The romance, of course, naturalizes this transition, but an extended section of the novel involves Hazel's reluctance to give up the pleasures of the urban social scene for the isolation of rural British Columbia. By positing Hazel's redemption, figured as romantic fulfilment with Wagstaff, as dependent on renunciation of city life, the novel demonstrates the tendency for moral arguments on urban life to coalesce around the working girl, whose independence in a setting of moral indeterminacy is considered unmanageable and thus thought to demand containment.

Also aimed at a popular audience, Isabel Ecclestone Mackay's *House of Windows* (1912) shares many attributes with the formulaic working-girl romance, including sinister plots and kidnappings, a hidden family lineage, an almost thwarted romance, and a heroine whose flawless beauty is exceeded only by her perfect virtue. Isabel Ecclestone Mackay (née MacPherson, 1875) grew up in Woodstock, Ontario, where she began writing at an early age, contributing stories and poems to periodicals from the age of fifteen. She moved permanently to Vancouver with her husband in 1895. There, she wrote all her major works, including a great deal of verse that she published in collected volumes and in numerous periodicals. *The Shining Ship and Other Verse for Children* (1918) was one of her most lasting publications, along with her novel *Blencarrow* (1926). She was the founding member of the Vancouver branch of the Canadian Women's Press Club, an important organization for early feminism and for bringing together women writers in Canada. Her verse was praised by critics, but her novels and stories garnered a wider audience. In the latter, she drew on the conventions of popular romance, though she also incorporated a degree of social realism in an often urban setting. *The House of Windows* was her first novel and was reasonably well received by critics but did not garner high praise.

The story goes like this. While still a baby, Christine is abandoned in the Angers & Son department store. One of the shop girls takes her home and, together with her blind sister, raises the child as though she were their younger sister. When she is sixteen Christine and her adoptive sisters fall on hard times, and Christine also becomes a shop girl at Angers & Son. Meanwhile, a fallen-woman subplot rises to prominence: before Christine appeared as a baby at Angers & Son, a shop girl there had turned to prostitution because of overwork, low wages, and the need to support an ailing mother. She died, but her mother swore vengeance on the owner of Angers & Son, Adam Torrance, whose indifference to the plight of his shop girls had indirectly caused the downfall of her daughter. The avenging mother, therefore, kidnapped Mr. Torrance's baby girl and left her in the department store, this being none other than our heroine Christine. Sixteen years later, with Christine a shop girl, the old woman fulfils her scheme of poetic justice by kidnapping Christine and imprisoning her in a brothel, where she is every moment in danger of experiencing the same fate as the hapless daughter. A letter from the old woman to Adam Torrance informs him that his long-lost daughter is not dead but likely soon will be or worse. The ensuing detective narrative has Christine finally rescued by Torrance's nephew, who has loved her all along. The novel concludes with a merging of upper and lower classes: Christine engaged to the nephew, the blind adoptive sister engaged to Torrance, and the other sister matched up as well. Although it is set in an unnamed city in eastern Canada, Mackay wrote the novel in Vancouver, and she includes a subplot that sends the shop owner's nephew to Vancouver, where he comments on the charm and sophistication of the city's young women. The romance formula tended to have the hero sent away as an obstacle to the eventual union with the heroine, and it is interesting that Mackay uses this convention to add a commentary on life in her own city of Vancouver, lending the tale a degree of West Coast character.

Undoubtedly, the most serious work of fiction regarding the working girl in early-twentieth-century Canada is J.G. Sime's *Sister Woman*, set in Montreal and published in 1919. Jessie Georgina Sime was born in Scotland in 1868 and grew up in London; she immigrated to Canada at the age of thirty-nine, and although she had already been writing in England, it was in Canada that her true success began. She wrote an advice manual on housekeeping addressed to single self-supporting women and entitled *The Mistress of All Work* (1916), and was commissioned to write a series of patriotic war-related stories called *Canada Chaps*, which was published in 1917. *Sister Woman* followed, and it also employed the form of short fiction. Her other major work of fiction is the novel *Our Little Life* (1921), which portrays the hardships of poverty in a city based on Montreal. Sime's personal life has aroused speculation and may have direct relevance to our understanding of her fiction. Never having married, she is believed to have had a longstanding relationship with a married man prominent in Montreal society circles, Walter William Chipman. As Sandra Campbell writes, "Given such a liaison with a prominent married man, and the constraints it would have placed on Sime, a middle-class woman, it seems probable that the vivid descriptions in such stories as 'Motherhood' and 'An Irregular Union' of a woman office worker's suffering and isolation in a clandestine love affair owe something to Sime's own life."[14] *Sister Woman* somewhat baffled the critics of its day, but it is currently receiving a wealth of new and undoubtedly long-deserved attention for its groundbreaking exploration of gender and work in the city.

Sandra Campbell points out that Sime intended the form of her writing to reflect the character of modern urban life, and for this reason she used the short story: "One feels in the cities, I think, the potentials of quite another kind of art – disjointed, disconnected art that finds its expression in thumb nail sketches, short stories, one-act scrappy plays and the like."[15] In *Sister Woman* the stories revolve around the many incarnations of the urban working woman: seamstresses, secretaries, munitions workers, domestic workers. Many of the narratives also explore female sexuality by representing the relationships of working women with men, drawing special attention to illicit relationships popularly known as irregular unions: a secretary's secret relationship with her boss, a housekeeper's relationship with her employer, an unwed couple faced with an unplanned pregnancy. All these are represented with a sympathetic and unapologetic candour very unusual for the time. Employing the fragmentary form of the short story, Sime carefully connects the tone of urban life with the struggles of the working woman, and by further focusing on gender relations in her fiction, she places the working girl at the forefront of cultural transformation.

All four of these texts depict the working girl in narratives of social unease, with economic exploitation and sexual danger everywhere immanent. In fact, as evidenced by the boss who gets socked in the teeth in *North of Fifty-Three* and by the mill owner's son who flirts with factory girls in *Roland Graeme*, the two are often conflated. In stories of the working girl, the alternating pressures of morality and money appear in infinitely variable permutations, and the attendant meanings shift with each new version. The working-girl narrative as the subplot for a middle-class morality tale in *Roland Graeme* works in a very different way than it does as the centre of popular romance in *The House of Windows*, where working-class virtue guarantees wealth and happiness. That the figure of the working girl could act as a recognizable trope in a variety of texts, yet a trope with many changing meanings, is indicative of the cultural significance of this neglected figure of Canadian literature.

## ESCAPING THE CULT OF DOMESTICITY

In 1903 *Canadian Magazine* published an illustrated article by Annie Merrill entitled "The Woman in Business," which both described the secretarial working woman and advised her on proper conduct. Instruction on workplace etiquette gives way to fashion dictates and dating advice, all of which signal the desire to clarify class and gender norms for the ambiguous new figure of the urban working girl. Although the first half of the article takes a fairly positive attitude toward "The Serious Woman in Business," assuring us that "she is not necessarily mannish,"[16] the second half displays a much more condemnatory tone: "Business is unlovely for a woman, and in many ways she were better out of it."[17] Where the unresolved ambivalence of the author becomes most obvious, however, is in her discussion of housekeeping and domestic work, as she castigates the businesswoman for neglecting the home, even though her own representation of housework seems ample reason to reject it:

> The fascinations of the constant excitement in a busy commercial life make the thought of house-keeping seem tame to the very young woman. Her immature judgement is not capable of giving correct values to the things of life. In common with the discontented "domestic," who has left the goodly, if monotonous, kitchen, for the doubtful factory, she likes the regularity of business hours, remembering that at home her work seemed never really to end.[18]

To today's reader, the discontented domestic and the woman who prefers paid employment to never-ending housework seem to be exactly capable of "giving correct value to the things of life." Merrill's implied chastisement of such women does not fully cohere in this passage, and the ambiguity is arguably symptomatic of the unresolved conflict between the cult of domesticity and the figure of the working girl. This conflict and the ensuing debate about women's renunciation of domestic work is an important part of the larger debate about women's place in society, a debate suffused with anxiety over the transformation in femininity that accompanied women's entrance into the public realm of work.

All four texts that I am examining make a point of explaining why their characters are not in domestic service. In *Roland Graeme* the factory girl Lizzie says, "I'd love, myself, to be in a good, quiet house, where one could sit down when one was tired, and not have to go out in the dark, all sorts of mornings, and have to be on the go all day! But, you see, if I live at home I can give mother my board, an' that's such a help to her."[19] Machar subscribes to the notion that domestic work is the best choice for the working-class woman, representing it as easier and healthier while also assuring the reader that Lizzie is all the more worthy of our sympathy: she is not like those "discontented domestics" who deliberately upset the social order by rejecting servitude for the morally dubious factory – her needy mother makes domestic work impossible. Lizzie thus represents a version of the working girl as an innocent victim of modern industry, forced into an unnatural role that will culminate in her early death. Her function in the text is to awaken our pity and moral indignation, and it is significant that for her to hold this function, her work in the mill has to be represented as a necessity, not a choice. Not only was the industrial workplace a morally questionable space in itself, but the mere choice to enter it could be read as a mark against you. Only once Lizzie has been cleared of this choice can she assume the mantle of innocence and go on to represent working-class victimization under capitalism.

In *North of Fifty-Three*, by comparison, the heroine has no intention of entering domestic work, and the socialist politics of the text are much more radical than those of Machar's narrative, with the heroine eventually refusing not only domestic work but all waged work as exploitative servitude to be refused along with the hypocrisy of class society. Initially a stenographer, Hazel already considers domestic service beneath her, demonstrating in her perusal of the "Help Wanted" column the subtle hierarchy of jobs for women. Sinclair also adds a geographic specificity to Hazel's job hunt by foregrounding the demand for domestic help characteristic of British Columbia:

Then she turned to the "Help Wanted" advertisements. The thing which impressed her quickly and most vividly was the dearth of demand for clerks and stenographers, and the repeated calls for domestic help and such. Domestic service she shrank from except as a last resort. And down near the bottom of the column she happened on an inquiry for a school-teacher, female preferred, in an out-of-the-way district in the interior of the province.

"Now that – " Hazel thought.[20]

Hazel takes the teaching job as a ticket out of a town where gossip and innuendo are pitted against her. Facing a degree of social ostracism because of a scandal caused by her boss, Hazel longs to turn her back on the hypocrisy of urban life: "She found herself hungering for change, for a measure of freedom from petty restraints ... 'What a country!' she whispered. 'It's wild; really, truly wild; and everything I've ever seen has been tamed and smoothed down, and made eminently respectable and conventional long ago.'"[21] "Tamed" is one of the root meanings of the word "domestic," and when Hazel couples this with the terminology of convention and respectability, her desire for wilderness adventure becomes a deliberate rejection of the domesticated East in favour of the rebel West. Rather than becoming demoralized by workplace harassment and unwarranted social censure, Hazel is galvanized by a pioneer spirit of adventure, and her movement through space reflects a transgression of traditional gender roles.

The most explicit representation of a young woman deliberately rejecting domestic service in favour of other work is J.G. Sime's "Munitions." Set on a streetcar packed full of female munitions workers on their way to work, the story relates the experience of one girl who left domestic work for the factory:

Just five weeks before and Bertha had been a well-trained servant in a well-kept, intensely self-respecting house – a house where no footfall was heard on the soft, long-piled rugs. ...

... Regret! Reconsider! Never again would she hear bells and have to answer them. Never again would someone say to her: "Take tea into the library, Martin." Never again need she say, "Yes, ma'am." Think of it! Bertha smiled ... The joy of being done with the cap and apron. The feeling that you could draw your breath – speak as you liked – wear overalls like men – curse if you wanted to.[22]

In this story, domestic work is drawn as a suffocating immersion in quiet, static respectability, set against which is the fast-moving streetcar, full of rowdy munitions women telling off-colour jokes. Freedom from restraint and respectability further allows the suggested gender transgression of trading in cap and apron – signs of female domestic servitude – for the working man's overalls and the licence to curse freely. It is doubtful that Canadian readers were ready to accept the idea of women being *that* relieved to escape housework for the unruly environment of waged work, as suggested by the reservations of one reviewer who described "Munitions" as "one of the most effective presentations in modern literature of the desire of the modern woman for economic independence – and the sometimes excessive reaction when that desire is gratified."[23] Reading a girl's enjoyment of a noisy streetcar ride with her co-workers as an "excessive reaction" to independence is likely more an index of the reviewer's anxiety than of Sime's intention here.

Annie Merrill's advice to working women in "The Woman in Business" outlines proper behaviour outside the workplace and suggests why the reviewer may have thought Sime's character excessive:

> Outside of the office the Serious Woman in Business takes life seriously … She commands respect by her demeanor on the street, and in her social circle, which, though it may not be a large nor a fashionable one, yet represents the world to her. She is careful to avoid being conspicuous in her manner.[24]

The preoccupation with working women's behaviour in public spaces demonstrates how new and troubling their presence there was. And the tendency of middle-class commentators to perceive their behaviour as excessive or conspicuous is further evidence of the feeling that they were thought to be out of bounds, beyond what was normal, acceptable, or perhaps even controllable. That working women were no longer in the domestic sphere was one thing, but once unleashed upon the sidewalks and the streetcars, their behaviour there suggested still other transgressions – of decorum, femininity, and sexuality. These connections between space, identity, and sexuality are addressed by Sime in a light-hearted tone, as though to reassure her reader:

> It wasn't in the least that they were what is known as "bad women." Oh

no – no! If you thought that, you would mistake them utterly. They were decent women, good, self-respecting girls, for the most part "straight girls" – with a black sheep here and there, to be sure, but where aren't there black sheep here and there? And the reason they shrieked with laughter and cracked an unseemly jest or two was simply that they were turned loose. They had spent most of their lives caged, most of them, in shop or house, and now they were drunk with the open air and the greater freedom and the sudden liberty to do as they liked and damn whoever stopped them.[25]

Although the tone here is very light and conversational, Sime does go out of her way to acknowledge that popular perception might mistake these girls for "bad women" or "black sheep" simply because "they made a row." Her need to clarify that girls being loud in public was not a necessary indicator of questionable morals makes clear the conceptual links that existed between public space, female identity, and the threat of uncontained sexuality.

Part of the controversy regarding women's rejection of domestic service in favour of work in the public arena undoubtedly involves the relative visibility of the two spheres of work. As Anne McClintock points out in her explanation of the cult of domesticity, the whole point of the realm of tasks involved in domestic work is to erase all signs of work or labour: "The striking difference between the rationalizing of the market and the rationalizing of housework is that the latter is rationalized so as to render women's work invisible and to thereby disavow its economic value."[26] Clearly, working women in the public sphere were visible in an entirely new way, but in addition, the work that they did was eminently visible as well – in a way that it never had been within the home, where, with kitchens, laundry rooms, and servants' quarters all pushed to the back, architecture itself suppressed the evidence of women's work. The social pressure to keep women in domestic service was thus part of the elision of the existence, visibility, and value of their labour. At the same time, the maintenance of women's traditional roles and the containment of female sexuality were both more readily secured through women's assignment to the domestic sphere.

I would argue, then, that a series of connections exists between the imperative to hide the evidence of women's work, the desire to curb changes in gender norms and female sexuality, and the suppression of representations of working women in Canadian literature. By representing urban wage-earning women, writers like Sime insisted on the materiality of women's labour as well as on the social, economic, and cultural repercussions that flowed from it. Indeed, at a time when women's roles lay mainly in the reproduction of tradition, the cultural work of wage-earning women in reinventing gender and sexuality cannot be underestimated, although it may not be as easily quantified as their paid labour. As the cult of domesticity demonstrates, the representation and implied acknowledgment of this labour was precisely what a traditional majority sought to avoid, thereby denying the material and cultural impact of wage-earning women.

## THE WORKING GIRL GOES WEST

She found herself wishing she were a man, so that she
could fare into the wilds with horses and a gun in this
capable man fashion, where routine went by the board
and the unexpected hovered always close at hand.

– BERTRAND SINCLAIR,
*North of Fifty-Three,* 1914

Bertrand Sinclair's *North of Fifty-Three* is the only text that I am examining in depth that takes the working girl west, and it is also the only one written by a male author. Without exaggerating the effects of the author's gender, it is fair to say that Sinclair doesn't have as subtle an approach to gender analysis as the women writers, but this doesn't make his work less fascinating to study. My reading of *North of Fifty-Three* goes partly with and partly against the grain of the text. For examining the working-girl narrative, it is the first part of the book, centred on Hazel Weir, that is most interesting; here, we see the dynamic heroine rise to several challenges with great competence, wit, and style. But once the male lead, Bill Wagstaff, enters the scene, his urge to dominate extends first to Hazel and then to the narrative itself. Indeed, in my estimation, Sinclair makes a mistake when he starts to think that his woodsman-miner is the hero. With his socialist ideals, Wagstaff hates to see Hazel as a wage earner because to him it renders her an instrument of corporate exploitation and a victim of moral corruption; but all he offers her instead is wifedom in the backwoods, and neither he nor Sinclair seems to be troubled by this. Wagstaff usurps the lead role, and Hazel as wife somewhat loses her edge. Before Wagstaff's take-over, however, Sinclair skilfully develops the working-girl narrative both as social critique and as female-pioneer story.

The novel begins with Hazel as a self-supporting single stenographer, engaged to a respectable real estate man. Her boss makes unwanted advances toward her, and for Sinclair this sexual harassment reflects the more general corruption inherent in the urban working scene, where the artificial and exploitative environment leads to both corporate and personal corruption. Sinclair's socialist politics hardly make him a feminist, however, for despite the boss's role as sexual aggressor, Sinclair seemingly cannot help but view his attraction to Hazel as a product of natural gender relations: "He admired her as a woman. She began to realize that. And no women ever blames a man for paying her that compliment, no matter what she may say to the contrary."[27] Here, once again, some reading against the grain proves necessary and undemanding, for Hazel not only says things to the contrary but physically resists these advances very capably, and in doing so she advances a model of the working girl who is more than equal to the challenges of the workplace and who can ably defend her own virtue, with force if necessary. Hazel punches her boss in the nose and even somewhat enjoys it:

> He kissed her; and Hazel, in blind rage, freed one arm, and struck at him man fashion, her hand doubled into a small fist. By the grace of chance, the blow landed on his nose. There was force enough behind it to draw blood. He stood back and fumbled for his handkerchief. Something that sounded like an oath escaped him.
>
> Hazel stared, aghast, astounded. She was not at all sorry; she was perhaps a trifle ashamed. It seemed unwomanly to strike. But the humour of the thing appealed to her most strongly of all. In spite of herself, she smiled as she reached once more for her hat. And this time Mr. Bush did not attempt to restrain her.[28]

Such an affirmation of the working girl's moral strength and self-sufficiency rejected the view that the workplace would destroy her purity or undermine her femininity. Hazel wavers for a moment at the thought that her actions were "unwomanly," but she dismisses the idea with a smile as she coolly collects her hat. By thus portraying Hazel as the capable heroine and placing her on the moral high ground, Sinclair advances a version of the working girl fully equipped to cope with the modern workplace.

Indeed, portraying the working girl as competent to handle the challenges of the workplace – the hours, the work itself, and any unwanted attention from co-workers, bosses, or clients – is a politically important feature in the representation of the figure. Middle-class analysts of the day often assumed that working girls – in need of help, guidance, and protection – were incapable of handling problems on their own. The YWCA, for instance, made it a priority in cities across Canada to have women placed in train stations in order to meet unchaperoned women and see them safely to respectable lodgings. While this was probably a helpful and welcome service to many women travellers, it does assume a certain incompetence in women who have, after all, made the bulk of their journey successfully and independently to that point. The presumption of incompetence, of course, also played a role in limiting the kinds of work women were thought to be capable of; so in the culture of gender and work, competence is a politically loaded attribute. The class politics regarding working girls' competence become more evident when we compare the novels and their heroines along these lines. In *Roland Graeme*, it is the middle-class heroine and her female friends who are invested with the social influence and individual ability to *help* the working girls; the girls themselves are nondeveloping characters, helpless victims in a workplace that is physically overwhelming and morally deadening. The novel suggests that it is middle-class women who can save their working-class sisters, who are incapable of helping themselves. Marie Joussaye, by contrast, places key emphasis on the value of the working girl's ability to work and support herself: "Proud that I have the strength and skill / To earn my daily bread." Sinclair, Mackay, and Sime perhaps follow this lead when they choose working girls for their heroines and, by making their embattled competence a key issue, invest them with the strength and skill to stand up to individual struggles as well as social adversity. By the time Sinclair was writing, the working girl had made great strides: far from the vulnerable workplace innocent of Machar's novel, she becomes in the twentieth century a force to be reckoned with, a heroine whose moral compass and self-reliance are more than equal to her modern environment.

Although Hazel ably defends herself from her boss's harassment, she cannot control the innuendo that follows the incident. Sinclair excoriates the scandal-mongering of a society that blames the victim for any moral infraction and destroys Hazel's social standing. Her fiancé fails to stand by her, signalling a crucial failure in his manhood, and her urge to go west thus arises as a desire to escape her suffocating social milieu for a place "where people were a little broader gauge, a little less prone to narrow, conventional judgements."[29]

Indeed, the thematically rewarding aspect of sending the working girl west is that her pioneer status is doubled; her work as a cultural pioneer in gender formation takes place through her job hunt, as she asserts women's newfound personal and economic independence in the working world, while in the same moment she expresses the pioneer enthusiasm for the freedom of fresh new spaces:

> But it was the huge background, the timbered mountains rising to snow-clad heights against a cloudless sky, that attracted her. She had never seen a greater height of land than the rolling hills of Ontario. Here was a frontier, big and new and raw, holding out to her as she stared at the print a promise – of what? She did not know. Adventure? If she desired adventure, it was purely a subconscious desire ... There was something in her nature that responded instantly when she contemplated journeying alone into a far country. She found herself hungering for change, for a measure of freedom from petty restraints, for elbow-room in the wide spaces, where one's neighbour might be ten or forty miles away.[30]

This story was a best-seller for Sinclair and was snapped up by filmmakers, something that occurred, I argue, precisely because of the appeal of this contentious new heroine who was both familiar and challenging to the readers and observers of her time. The figure of the working girl in the West – the pioneer on dual fronts – would have had a cultural resonance for readers who could see Hazel's counterparts crowding into the YWCAs and boarding houses of the West's new cities. Hazel is the independent working girl and the single woman traveller; both highly competent and decidedly nondomestic, she is a dual challenge to traditional gender roles. And rather than condemning her for this rejection of convention and domesticity, we are invited to admire her spirit of independence. Indeed, in the West more than elsewhere, competence and capability were considered determining factors for settler success. The independent working girl, accustomed to adversity and not nostalgic for the protected world of traditional society, was exactly the heroine for Sinclair's western adventure romance with a socialist bent.

Hazel experiences the social difference between East and West as a difference in its men. In the East her boss is both sexually aggressive and socially vindictive, her fiancé fails her, and a casual acquaintance also has to be physically repelled: "He caught her as she rose, and laughingly tried to kiss her. Whereupon he discovered that he had caught a tartar, for Hazel slapped him with all the force she could muster – which was considerable, judging by the flaming red spot which the smack of her palm left on his smooth-shaven cheek ... Being free of him, Hazel stood her ground long enough to tell him that he was a cad, a coward, an ill-bred nincompoop, and other epithets grievous to masculine vanity."[31] Eastern men are aggressive and untrustworthy, and Hazel must repeatedly fight them off. The Western man, Roaring Bill Wagstaff, is different, although perhaps not as different as Sinclair would have us believe. Wagstaff's key attributes are a rugged frontier manliness and a tell-it-like-it-is honesty. He also has a philosophical turn, blending socialism and primitivism while extolling the authenticity of a natural wilderness life over the artificial constraints of urban industrialism. Epitomizing the masculine West, he gradually wins Hazel over with his abrasive charm and anti-establishment appeal. His romantic approach is somewhat complicated, however: although he freely admits his attraction to Hazel, he is never physical in his advances. But he does essentially abduct her. Lost on a walk outside the village, Hazel stumbles upon Wagstaff's camp; he agrees to lead her back to town but instead leads her to his wilderness cabin, where her unfamiliarity with the landscape and the onset of winter confine her. Hazel expresses her outrage, but Sinclair makes it clear that these two were meant to be: "Even though she may decry what she is pleased to term the brute in man, whenever he discards the dominant, overmastering characteristics of the male she will have none of him. Miss Hazel Weir was no exception to her sex."[32] In the spring she demands to be set free, and Wagstaff capitulates, seeing her safely to Vancouver, where she could easily resume her life as a stenographer; but once free of him, she finds that she has lost her relish for city life, and when a chance meeting with her old fiancé confirms her rejection of the emasculated East, she quickly returns to marry Wagstaff.

The novel would have us believe that Hazel has made a choice between opposites – has found a true and loyal mate in the wilds of the West who eclipses the self-serving men of the stultifying East. But in her search "for a measure of freedom from petty restraints, for elbow-room in the wide spaces," what she in fact encounters is abduction, confinement, and then marriage. Although Wagstaff is a gentleman among kidnappers, his courtship is clearly on the predatory side, and Hazel's eventual surrender is a little like Stockholm Syndrome. This is not to exaggerate the sinister side of Hazel's marriage bonds: she does, in fact, enjoy a certain freedom with Wagstaff as they set out for a season of trapping and gold mining: "Hazel followed her man contentedly. They were together upon the big adventure, just as she had seen it set forth in books, and she found it good.

For her there was no more diverging of trails, no more problems looming fearsomely at the journey's end. To jog easily through the woods and over open meadows all day, and at night to lie with her head pillowed on Bill's arm, peering up through interlocked branches at a myriad of gleaming stars – that was sufficient to fill her days."[33] Marriage on the open trails allows the couple to leave behind the scene of Hazel's earlier captivity, but her ensuing domestic role in camp life is not without catastrophe. Though warned by Bill one winter morning to be careful of the sparks from the fire, which a northwest wind could carry to the vital winter hay stack, Hazel gets immersed in her domestic duties: "She piled on wood, and stirring the coals under it, fanned them with her husband's old felt hat, forgetful of sparks or aught but that she should be cooking against his hungry arrival."[34] The hay goes up in flames, and Bill grimly shoots their two horses to save them from starving to death. On one level, the episode demonstrates the unforgiving nature of the wilderness – only by respecting its rules can one survive and thrive in it. But it is significant that the catastrophe stems from Hazel's domestic exertions, for it suggests that the narrative has created a no-win situation for her. Having renounced her urban working life for marriage to a miner, Hazel attends faithfully to her domestic tasks with only disaster as the result. Meanwhile, Wagstaff – in whose arms she weeps for forgiveness about the horses – becomes the moral centre of the novel, and the plot repeats itself as Hazel drifts away from him (once more sampling city life) before making her way back again once she realizes that she cannot live without him. This Hazel is a far cry from the feisty stenographer with a mean left hook to whom we were first introduced. The heavily domesticated Hazel clinging thankfully to her man at the end of the novel doesn't satisfy our sense of what the spirited girl of the first chapters really deserves. A romance, of course, has to bring the protagonists together, but the formula ideally demands a degree of compromise and self-development on both sides. In this novel, Hazel is asked to capitulate wholly to Wagstaff's backwoods ideal. Sinclair's subsequent novels focus increasingly on men's pursuits in the West, valorizing an explicitly masculine ethos of work. With his own sympathies thus swept away by Wagstaff, Sinclair seems to neglect the heroine that so energetically launched the narrative, bringing his novel to a close that contains her into a too-smothering domestication.

The novel is fascinating, however, because it does play deliberately on the narrative so popularized in the cultural imagination of the day that had the working girl coming West in search of work only to be swiftly snapped up by one of the West's hungry bachelors. The book is in part a speculative work that imagines how the ensuing drama would unfold, as the working girl, used to a certain degree of social civility and urban convenience, tries to adapt to the rougher habits of an overtly masculine West. And all in all, she does well; valorized for her self-sufficiency, her indifference to convention, and her capable handling of adversity, she proves the right kind of woman to meet the challenges of the West. What Sinclair doesn't imagine is how the West might change itself to meet her – how her influence might be felt in this mutable environment, in men like Wagstaff, and in the society that the two of them embody.

## CLASS CROSS-DRESSING IN *THE HOUSE OF WINDOWS*

Again he took the small hand extended to him
and again it seemed to change miraculously from
the hand of Miss Brown into the hand of some
delectable princess.

– ISABEL ECCLESTONE MACKAY,
*House of Windows,* 1912

Isabel Ecclestone Mackay moved to Vancouver in 1909 and wrote a number of novels, primarily romantic in tone and aimed at a popular audience, but she was better known for her poetry, which was grouped with that of Pauline Johnson. Published in 1912, *The House of Windows* draws on the dime-novel tradition of the working-girl romance, a formula popularized in the late-nineteenth-century United States by Laura Jean Libbey, whose serialized narratives were devoured by the female working class. In Canada a writer of comparable popularity could be found in May Agnes Fleming, but her romances featured primarily middle-class characters, whereas the working-girl romance always had a working-class heroine. Although the works of Libbey and her counterparts were likely read in Canada, there was no equivalent trend in Canadian literature. *The House of Windows* was thus unusual for Canadian literature of the day; with its urban setting and shop-girl characters, it represented a side of Canadian life not usually addressed in literature. Far from Sime's direct realism, however, Mackay's novel mixes realist depictions of working women's hardships with romantic fantasies of danger, adventure, and wealth. Although beginning with detailed accounts of the everyday trials of shop girls, the novel progresses into an intrigue plot with the heroine kidnapped and almost raped before being rescued to claim her secret inheritance. Nan Enstad examines the genre of working-girl fiction in the US and notes that these plots of mystery, intrigue, and Cinderella romance characterized the working-girl formula popular in the US: "The stories invoked the difficulty of working-class women's lives – toiling at jobs that offered little hope for advancement – and offered them fabulous fantasies of wealth, fashion, success, and love."[35] In some ways, this popular-culture form, which closes with wealth and marriage and thus removal of the young heroine from the working sphere, would seem to reinscribe a traditional vision of female success. But as critics of the genre have pointed out, there is a noticeable current in such narratives that runs counter to readings that would thus circumscribe the meaning of these texts, especially as representations of class.

In *Roland Graeme* the factory girl, Nelly, engages in a flirtation with the mill owner's son, Harold Pomeroy, himself already engaged to another girl. This relationship is used to signify the moral degradation of both characters, but it is Nelly who fares worse in the end: although this relationship ends, it is implied that she becomes a fallen woman. Working-girl narratives often feature an involvement between the working girl and the boss's son, representing the latter sometimes as hero but more often as wicked seducer. As Michael Denning points out in *Mechanic Accents*, narratives like this render class conflict as the direct, personal confrontation of sexual intrigue or harassment,[36] but how this conflict unfolds may also indicate the social agenda of the writer: "Unlike the seduction novels that occasionally occur in middle-class fiction, which focus on the fallen woman, the Libbey stories [working-girl dime novels] are tales of the woman who does not fall, despite drugs, false marriage, physical violence, and disguise. Against middle-class sympathy for the fallen is set working-class virtue."[37] *Roland Graeme,* in which working girls are pitiable victims of industrial and sexual exploitation, is very much a novel of "middle-class sympathy"; middle-class philanthropy might ease their suffering, but there is no question of their class position changing or of the women themselves successfully resisting their treatment. By comparison, in the popular working-girl narrative established by Libbey and played on by Sinclair and Mackay, the sexually charged class confrontation of working girl and upper-class man unfolds quite differently. In *North of Fifty-Three* Hazel's able self-defence when she strikes her boss is a precursor to her ultimate rejection of class exploitation, represented through her relationship with the socialist hero. In *The House of Windows* the gentleman seducer hovers around the heroine's workplace, virtually stalking her, until she confronts him: "'I do not know you,' she said quietly, 'but if you are a gentleman you will annoy me no further. I do not wish to appeal to the police' ... It was a defeat as complete and unexpected as Waterloo!"[38] Christine is the embodiment of working-class virtue, and the introduction of this would-be seducer seems almost an off-hand way to highlight the impossibility of her being tempted. She does, however, strike up a romance with the boss's adopted son, the hero here, who must actually masquerade as a working-class piano salesman so that Christine's initial attraction to him will remain unsullied by questions of class aspiration. These popular depictions of the working girl appealed to a working-class readership, whose members might well have been insulted if the working girl were represented as morally weak. Whereas narratives aimed at the middle class may invite sympathy for the downtrodden working girl, her vulnerability to seduction and her exploitation in the workplace seeming to go hand in hand, they nevertheless leave class divisions intact. The moral and physical strength of the working girl who ably fights off her assailants, meanwhile, suggests a working-class resistance to exploitation, whether sexual or class-based. The endings of working-girl novels, in turn, reward their feisty heroines with secret inheritances and propitious marriages that defy class boundaries. What both the middle-class and dime-novel modes of fiction demonstrate is that in narratives of working-class womanhood, class identity and sexual purity are inextricably intertwined: in *Roland Graeme* Nelly's vulnerability to sexual degradation is a product of her class-specific environment, whereas in *The House of Windows* Christine's unassailable purity is, depending on your reading, a testimony to working-class virtue or evidence that she was really a "lady" all along. This connection between class and sexuality and the dual readings that arise from it are part of a debate central to the working-girl narrative. As Michael Denning points out, "in the rhetoric of the late nineteenth-century bourgeois culture, a working woman could not be virtuous, regardless of her virginity."[39] To contend, as working-girl novels did, that the working woman was indeed a figure of unquestionable virtue was to assert that she was as good as any "lady" – hence the central problematic in these narratives: "Key to the dime novel plot is the question: Can a worker be a lady? That is, does work indeed degrade, spoil one's virtue, make one coarse and masculine?"[40]

Concerned with the proper deportment in public of the working woman, Annie Merrill, writing for *Canadian Magazine,* dispensed the following fashion advice for the "Serious Woman in Business": "She is careful to avoid being conspicuous in her manner. Dresses plainly. Does not try to ape the 'lady,' with gaudy imitations in gowns and jewels."[41] Accompanying this admonition is an illustration of the modestly dressed working woman, with the caption reminding us, "She dresses plainly." This advice manifests the middle-class desire to clarify class divisions, especially when working-class women were at issue, and fashion was a major system of signification for female class hierarchy. In fact, the tendency of working-class women "to ape the lady," as Merrill puts it, was a common middle-class complaint about working girls. Nan Enstad examines the middle-class preoccupation with working women's supposedly inappropriate fashion choices. Through her analysis of working women's consumer culture, she suggests that implicit in working-class women's notorious fashion sense was a deliberate challenge to the conventional codes of ladyhood:

> Working women dressed in fashion, but they exaggerated elements of style that specifically coded femininity: high-heeled shoes, large or highly decorated hats, exceedingly long trains (if trains were in style) and fine undergarments ... By appropriating and exaggerating the accoutrements of ladyhood, working women invested the category of lady with great imaginative value, implicitly challenging dominant meanings and filling the category with their own flamboyant practices.[42]

Enstad draws a connection between this fantasy of ladyhood enacted through dress and the fantasies afforded working women in novels, where the working girl similarly becomes a lady. The heightened femininity of their attire, meanwhile, responded to the notion that work was masculinizing for women: class and gender definitions were clearly both at stake. Mackay describes the shop girls in *The House of Windows* engaging in this exaggerated and decorative femininity through their hair-dos:

> The fashion in hairdressing had also changed, and the young ladies behind the counters, who in Celia's day had been content with neatly coiled or braided tresses, were now resplendent in towering structures which held the eye with the fascination of the wonderful. It was all simple enough to one who understood the mysteries of rats and buns and turbans and puffs and curls, but to the uninitiated the result was little short of miraculous, for even supposing that Nature, in lavish mood, had supplied such hair – how did they get it to stick on?[43]

That the hair-dos here are extravagant, defy nature, and even include stick-on hair demonstrates the trend toward excess described by Enstad. A Calgary stenographer from a rural background described her struggle to live up to the fashion of the women whom she encountered at business school, demonstrating the importance placed on fashion and the effort that it took to acquire the working girl's fashion acumen: "The girls at Mortimer were pretty and petite. Their hair was wound in cunning little knobs over their ears; their skirts were short and narrowed daintily; there were fluffy ruffles around their necks and wrists and they were altogether so different from poor little countrified me that the tears came into my eyes in spite of all my efforts."[44] This speaker notes later that by the end of her course, "I had a diploma two feet by three" and "I knew how to dress." Interest in fashionable dress was something noted in working girls in general, but shop girls, whose work had everything to do with fashion and display, were thought to be particularly guilty of this kind of accessorizing overkill. In *Counter Cultures*, Susan Porter Benson describes how shop girls, working in the world of style and consumerism, often displayed their expertise through their dress, a practice that also narrowed the class gap between them and their customers, sometimes to the dismay of the latter.[45] For Christine in *The House of Windows*, it is interesting that even before she starts working in the Stores of Angers & Son, she is categorized with shop girls because of her appearance. Following her failed attempt to get work in a home reading to the lady of the house, the maid sums up her chances elsewhere:

> "She'll have some trouble getting anything respectable with that face, ... In her walk of life I always say that beauty is a drawback as often as not" ...
> "And what would you say Miss Brown's walk in life might be Martha?"
> The maid shook her head slowly. "Oh, she's got airs and graces enough! But you never can tell. Shopgirls are getting very dressy, these days, what with their false hair and all! And ladies don't go about looking for work."[46]

In other words, Christine resembles either a lady or a shop girl, according to her good looks (her hair in particular is often mentioned), her dress, and her demeanour; the only reason not to classify her as a lady is that ladies don't need work. Notably, it is the maid who makes these deductions; a working woman is highly versed in reading the subtleties of dress, deportment, and class, whereas the upper-class woman here is less astute, though equally curious. This scene has everything to do with identity and the class and gender markers that supposedly reveal this identity, but the working-girl figure poses a significant challenge to her interpreters. Undermining the maid's apparent accuracy here is the dramatic irony that – unbeknownst to the characters – Christine really is a lady. Mackay is thus deliberately playing on the class and fashion ambiguities that make the shop girl hard to distinguish from the lady.

Both in the maid's detective-like interpretation of Christine's walk of life and in the narrator's description of the shop girls' eye-popping hair-dos, there is an element of the indecipherable associated with working-girl fashion. To one of Sime's middle-class narrators, a shop girl's dress is baffling: "The way Altabelle dresses is one of the riddles of the universe – anything the Sphinx could possibly have to offer would be child's play compared with it. Altabelle has, you see, nothing whatever to spend, and no time to spend it in if she had, and yet she looks like the Countess of Malmesbury every time."[47] This kind of doubled vision, where the working girl appears both as herself and as an aristocratic version of herself – shop girl and countess, servant and "lady" – is a recurrent trope that signals an intense interest in the working girl's self-positioning along class lines but also along fashion lines that encode femininity, respectability, and virtue. Middle-class critics thought that the working woman was "aping the lady," but as Enstad points out, working-class women went above and beyond what middle-class women wore, purposely adorning themselves with an excess of feminine-coded accessories: imitation was not the point. Perhaps what middle-class observers of the time were slow to recognize was that, far from "aping the lady" or following upper-class trends, working women were engaging in their own sense of style – one that commented on the fashion dictates of class but that rejected these dictates in specific ways. The ability to draw on and innovate through an expertise in fashion is a skill not fully theorized but which clearly has immense power in the social negotiation of identity, class, and gender. That working girls developed their own expertise in fashion baffled and alienated many observers, yet by pioneering new trends to fit new versions of class and gender identity and by deliberately drawing attention to their presence as women and as workers in the public sphere, they exhibited their capacity as cultural innovators.

Turn-of-the-century social critics such as Annie Merrill not only judged fashionable working women's attire as tasteless but also predicted that it was the first step toward immorality: where class ambiguity led, aspersions of sexual impropriety followed. Mariana Valverde has documented the recurrence of the "finery-to-fall" narrative in late-nineteenth and early-twentieth-century texts, which connected working-class women's love of finery to an inevitable moral descent:

> "Finery" sometimes referred nonjudgmentally to "fine clothes," for instance among the aristocracy. A more common meaning, however, connoted moral flaws on the part of the wearer. Finery in this pejorative sense meant clothes that were too showy, clothes that looked elegant and striking but were in some unspecified way cheap, if only because the woman wearing them was herself a cheap imitation of upper-class womanhood. The same dress could be considered elegant and proper on a lady, but showy and dishonest on her maid … Finery in the pejorative sense meant the type of female dress that signified or brought about moral ruin.[48]

Working women's fashion begins to operate like a text of its own, decipherable to some but not all and read with an inevitable subtext of sex. At a 1901 meeting of the middle-class women's society the National Council of Women of Canada, one member gave a paper that lamented how young working-class women were leaving their country homes to work in the city and were thus losing their domestic skills; she uses fashion and dress to narrate this journey as one of moral decline:

> "M'amselle" has now gained other knowledge; she has come to the great city, wears a hat with feathers pointing to the four winds of heaven, a dress of shoddy material in many colours; has become an attachment of a machine in a factory, living with two or three other girls in one small room in the salubrious atmosphere of a close street! I think she was a healthier, happier, better educated and more useful member of the community as a member of that farm household. I say it is a pity, not only to lose her skill and knowledge, but that she should think it of 'no account', and so walk away from truth and beauty down the path of cheap imitation that leads to disaster.[49]

At the end of *Roland Graeme* the fate of the factory girl who flirted with the boss's son is rendered in a shorthand that the nineteenth-century reader would have instantly understood when Roland says, "I met that poor Nelly, the other day, very much overdressed. I don't think she works in the mill, now."[50] In *The House of Windows* the Stores of Angers & Son has a policy of "employing only such girls as have homes and other means of support."[51] When questioned on this, the owner explains: "Because long ago I investigated and found out that, as a matter of fact, a girl, entirely alone and dependent upon herself, would find it hard to get along comfortably upon her wage. This, in the cases of some girls more fond of display, etc., etc., led to a – ah – deplorable state of things. Things which I need not discuss."[52] Here, once more, a taste for clothes or a fondness for display essentially stands in for the less mentionable sexual downfall of the working woman. But in addition, this assumed connection between dress and sexuality influenced not only popular attitudes toward the working woman but labour policies as well. Mackay's is an informed depiction here, for in Vancouver and elsewhere it was common business practice to hire only girls who lived at home and had other means of support;[53] this reinforced the prevalent view that young women worked for "pin money" and thus did not deserve or require a living wage. This practically institutionalized preoccupation with working women's consumer habits, especially in the heavily symbolic area of dress, suggests the widespread anxiety over their potentially transgressive desires. The store owner in this scene is upbraided by his sister, who is lightly mocking of his euphemism – "fond of display, I think you said" – and his redemption in the novel involves a reformation of his labour practices. The way that working girls' fashion was considered an index of their morality signals the conceptual bond between class position and sexual purity: dressing above your station was a moral failing. With working women's dress signifying so much, it is no wonder that, like the novel, it became one terrain on which questions of ladyhood and respectability were repeatedly played out.

The store owner's desire to avoid hiring young women with the unfortunate fondness for display is ironic in an industry utterly predicated upon display. Such contradictions were bound to arise in the department-store setting, where the illusion of luxury and the glorification of the spectacle were often at odds with what was deemed appropriate for working-class women. Susan Porter Benson describes popular attitudes toward department-store work at the turn of the century as troubling to class and gender patterns: "Department-store selling had a thoroughly ambiguous status. On the one hand, it involved behaving as a servant to the customer, being exposed to the public in a way most distressing to those who believed that woman's place was in the home, and being tarred with the brush of immorality. On the other, it offered upward mobility, glamour, and white-collar respectability. There were as many viewpoints on the social status of selling as there were individuals passing the judgements."[54]

That Mackay's version of the working-girl Cinderella myth should take place in a department store is fitting, for this largely female line of work was known as "the Cinderella of occupations."[55] Unlike domestic or factory work, department stores offered working women the very public role of customer service, opening the door to fantasies of romance with wealthy customers. At the same time, store workers became experts on consumption, which was a defining element of class identity: "Basking in the reflected prestige of the goods over which she presided, located at the centre of action of a culture in which material goods increasingly defined personal and public fulfilment, the saleswoman became a minor priestess of consumption."[56] On the one hand, store workers blurred class boundaries in their stylish dress and consumer savvy, but on the other hand, no proper woman would do such visible work in the public sphere. One of the store clerks in *The House of Windows* warns Christine that her good looks may be a liability: "Many unpleasant little experiences will teach you. Of course, a girl can always take care of herself; still, it's annoying! Have you noticed that good-looking man who has been in several times to have you match ribbons for his sister? ... Did you notice the way he looked at you? ... Well, look out for him, that's all."[57] Suffused in the terminology of looks and display, these kinds of moral dangers were thought to make the visibility of store work unsuitable for women, despite this character's assurance that a girl can take care of herself. In fact, because the visibility of the department-store work troubled many, it made these stores important sites in the debate on women's work. *The House of Windows* stages a debate on labour conditions by referring to the stools provided for store workers, who worked for twelve hours or more constantly on their feet. Stools were supposedly provided for the women to rest on if necessary, but in fact, the stools were as much a part of the display for customers as anything else, as one ex-saleswoman in the novel points out: "'*What* do they have those stools for?' she asked. 'It seems to me that they do the customers far more good than they do you girls. Makes them feel better to see them there, I suppose, so that after they have kept you on your feet for an hour or two, matching ribbons that won't match, they can go home and talk comfortably about the conveniences provided for the comfort of shopgirls!'"[58] In the department store everything becomes display, including the workers and the workplace labour practices surrounding them. Although the stools here are merely cosmetic, the visibility of stores as workplaces would eventually make them the object of more serious scrutiny in women's working conditions.

Mackay enters into this scrutiny through her narrative; at times sounding like the undercover workplace-exposés popular at the turn of century, the novel details the common abuses of this highly visible line of female work. While the moral and sexual dangers faced by the store workers enter into the narrative, the major characters all prove equal to such challenges, supporting the clerk's assertion, voiced often by working-class women, that "a girl can always take care of herself."

In the class narrative of *The House of Windows*, Mackay seems at certain points to oscillate between extolling working-class virtue and reinscribing class essentialism by reminding us of Christine's hidden birthright. When Christine is kidnapped by an evil old woman who intends to make a fallen woman of her, the detective assures the girl's long-lost rich father that Christine will never fall because "blood tells. Don't you ever believe but that good blood tells."[59] Yet her goodness is elsewhere ascribed to the devoted upbringing given by her working-class adoptive sisters. She herself never thinks of her own class position until she looks for work, and the class indifference ascribed to Christine, who "thought as little about her position as a Duchess might,"[60] is also used to describe Vancouver girls, mentioned in a letter by the travelling hero, Mark: "One's notions of caste get a sharp knock out here ... These girls, for instance, whose mother waited at table and whose father worked as a navvy, would be quite undismayed in shaking hands with a princess. It would not occur to them that there was any reason for undue diffidence."[61] Mackay's repeated representation of young women whose self-respect defies class distinctions suggests her endorsement of this tendency ascribed to "most sensible Canadian girls."[62] Meanwhile, the upper-class characters like the store owner and his nephew have interactions with such women that shake their class-defined assumptions, and the store owner eventually marries one of Christine's poor sisters, thereby transcending class division.

Mackay seems to relish the moment where class distinctions are unexpectedly rendered visible and through this visibility shown to be unnatural and undesirable. By endorsing the views ascribed specifically to young Canadian women, even to shop girls, Mackay destabilizes class categories while also providing her novel with a Canadian specificity. To lend the working girl the voice of authority in matters of class was bold for Canadian literature, and perhaps the contradictions and inconsistencies in the class terminology of the novel indicate a hesitancy to fully challenge a conservative readership. Nevertheless, by situating the working-class woman at centre stage of her narrative, Mackay was already defying convention for Canadian literature, and her representation of the working girl demonstrates her familiarity with this figure and the debates surrounding her. By representing the working girl, Mackay contributed to the visibility of this figure (otherwise largely invisible in Canadian literature). Indeed, by choosing the highly visible shop girl as the heroine and by titling the novel *The House of Windows*, Mackay perhaps sought to lend greater recognition and social prominence to the working girl and her struggles. Given Annie Merrill's admonition to avoid being "conspicuous" and the moral imputations concerning those "fond of display" or "making a spectacle of themselves," to insist that women and especially working women deserve to have their presence felt, to be visible and recognized, was to protest codes of both gender and class. For this reason, the project of writers such as Mackay and Sime cannot be underestimated.

## SEX AND THE CITY

There was the Factory – the Factory, with its coarse,
strong, beckoning life – its noise – its dirt – its men.
Its men! And suddenly into Bertha Martin's cheek a
wave of colour surged.

– J.G. SIME,
*Sister Woman*, 1919

Literature that represented the urban working girl took a great interest in her social life, for despite long hours and low wages, young working women were known for their pursuit of leisure and amusement; and the city offered new kinds of pleasures, many targeted at the growing demographic of single working women. One area of leisure that underwent rapid change soon after the turn of the century was the practice of dating. Not surprisingly, Annie Merrill had advice on this activity as well:

> This Serious Woman in Business will not allow men to squander money upon her, remembering the admonition of her good old grandmother, that such a course would be vulgar. She insists upon bearing her share of the expense when going about with her men friends, and the nice man will appreciate her position, amiably permitting her to feel a comfortable independence which to-day is making real comradeship between men and women such a delightful possibility ... It proves to him that she values his friendship and companionship for its own worth; that she is not accepting his attentions

merely for the "good time" he is able to give her, in the way that the mercenary girl "makes use of" many a generous-hearted and blindly-devoted man.[63]

Two versions of the working girl appear here: the serious woman in business who listens to her grandmother's advice and the mercenary girl who uses men to have a good time. Meanwhile, the question over who pays for dinner was clearly as much an object of debate one hundred years ago as it is today. Merrill was reacting to the changing codes of dating, which may have been in part dictated by young women eager for amusement but low on spending money. Carolyn Strange and Kathy Peiss both document the leisure activities of poorly paid young working women, who often relied on men to pay their entrance to movies, dance halls, theatres, and restaurants in return for their company and a certain degree of sexual contact. These may have been the "mercenary girls" of which Merrill speaks, but whether exchanging a few favours with men or insisting on paying their own way, working women were playing an active role in changing the rules of dating and the associated rules of gender relations. Merrill even makes a utopian gesture in her assertion that women who pay for themselves will enable a "real comradeship" to exist between men and women. Merrill's advice signals the interest that was taken in the social practices of single working women and the dual vision that opposed the morally upright woman who shuns vulgarity to the mercenary vixen out for a good time – a contradiction that fuelled the imaginative fire surrounding the sex life of the working girl.

*North of Fifty-Three*'s Hazel Weir has no family in the novel, so she manages all her relationships on her own, without chaperones or advice. Working girls in literature tend to lack the traditional family and thus have to fend for themselves. Indeed, the popular perception of the working girl was that she lived on her own, away from family, and supported herself on her wages, and although this wasn't universally the case, it did reflect reality for a significant part of the female workforce in the early 1900s, when many women came from the countryside or from overseas to find work in the city. Signalling society's familiarity with the independent working girl as a romantic figure, Sime opens one of her stories with "A bachelor girl! What visions of cigarettes and latch-keys – and liberty!"[64] The reader here is expected to recognize the bachelor girl instantly, along with the accessories that symbolize her independence. The unconventional relationships made possible by this independence feature in many of Sime's stories, and the intentionality of the female characters in entering into these relationships is often reaffirmed – they are not innocents seduced but women whose social circumstances afforded them new choices: "And so they had – not drifted into it, not at all. They had entered perfectly open-eyed into an irregular union: into one of those unions with which our whole society is honeycombed to-day. Marion Drysdale had gone on working. She had taken nothing from David Winterford but his love."[65] In a literary context where the depiction of women engaging in illicit relationships was either completely absent or couched in the assertion of moral imperatives, to represent this choice in such an unflinching way was bold. But there are a series of choices represented here, the connections between them being noteworthy: Marion will engage in a socially unsanctioned sexual relationship, she will keep working, and she will remain financially independent. In a sense, then, the basis of the relationship and the suggested equality of Marion and David are posited on the economic independence of the woman, made possible by her work. Women's waged work was thus a determining factor in new types of relationships between men and women, and the immediate connection in this passage between work and sexual choices demonstrates the profound influence of women's work on the cultural handling of gender.

Sime elaborates on how working women conceived of their relationships and distinguished their behaviour from that of socially stigmatized mistresses, or "kept women," and the difference has everything to do with their position as workers. In "An Irregular Union" a secretary who has a secret relationship with her boss makes a point of continuing to work and taking nothing material from her lover:

> In plain words, she didn't take any money for the gift of herself.
>
> It is queer how a little practical fact like that can make an old episode seem new – a new thing in the history of the world … The little insignificant fact that she was able to "keep herself," as it is called, changed for her the whole complexion of her love episode. It gave her confidence and self-respect. She could feel with perfect accuracy that she was not a "kept woman."[66]

For this character, the fact of working colours her view of sexual relationships. Yet her need to justify her actions in her own mind and to separate herself from traditionally censured versions of female sexuality also demonstrates the difficulties faced by women who challenged social codes of gender and sexuality. Pioneering new kinds of personal relationships, working women may have readily rejected a certain degree of middle-class prudery, but enduring codes of female chastity and working-class honour still had influence, and in many cases contributed to working women's self-definition. Given that middle-class administrators were eager for evidence of moral degradation among working women, often the affirmation of purity was important not only to working women's pride but to their political activism as well. The niceties of an irregular union or the degree of supposed impropriety were thus considerations of some importance. Sime, though she often focuses on the sense of liberation and independence among working women, also represents some of the subtleties and contradictions that beset women who took advantage of newfound freedom. The secretary in "An Irregular Union," for instance, spends the story in her room waiting for the phone to ring because her lover is in the hospital, and, unable to visit him because of the nature of their relationship, she has to await news of his condition from a nurse who calls her. The new world of urban dating was an important manifestation of the desires of working women, but it was also a world of many pressures and constraints.

Both the freedom to enact new kinds of desire and the challenges involved in so breaking with tradition were linked in important ways to working women's residence in the city. In "An Irregular Union" the single working girl rents her own room and so is able to engage in her secret relationship unchaperoned and unnoticed; the narrative likewise depends on the telephone, a relatively new form of technology that came first to urban centres and that thus marks the urban setting of the story. As in "Munitions," which takes place on a streetcar carrying women to the factory, Sime's other stories also give prominence to urban technologies, suggesting the significance of these to her representation of modern women. In "A Woman of Business" the narrator repeatedly mentions the electric light beneath which she hears the life story of a woman who made a career of wealthy lovers:

Madame Sloyovska has led what we call a bad life. She is thoroughly disreputable from head to heel. She has walked in the shadiest paths, and there are few dirty tricks that her hands haven't dabbled in. The snatches of her life, as she gave them to me hurriedly in the glare of that unprotected light, sounded like something you might read in a dime novelette ... Madame Sloyovska had had lovers galore, and when she had had one lover's money she had gone on to the next one and she had had his money.[67]

Sime emphasizes the electric light here perhaps as a metaphor for the illumination of things usually kept dark and hidden. But it is striking that she specifically uses a modern technology to provide her metaphor, for in this way she links Madame Sloyovska's way of life to the conditions of modern urban settings. That her way of life depends on a type of sexual conduct wholly condemned by polite society thus suggests a link between urban life and illicit sexuality. The use of this illumination metaphor is another instance of a writer drawing attention to the existence of figures usually rendered invisible by both social custom and literary convention. In fact, the mention in this passage of the dime novelette is telling. The genre of the realist short story, in which Sime is working, is far from the dime novelette, yet by using this reference, she signals the only other literary milieu in which Madame Sloyovska might be encountered. This gestures in a subtle way to the exclusion of certain women – working-class women or in this case sexually suspect women – from mainstream representation. Sime was very aware of the form of her writing, choosing the short story for its ability to mimic the fragmentation of urban life, so her thematization of technology is perhaps part of her insight into her own technology of writing. In a sense, her story, like the electric light that figures in it, renders suddenly visible what was previously thought too sordid for exposure.

Sime's writing reveals the critical links between modern technology, urbanism, and women's work and, in this way, is highly sensitive to the social transformations that were taking place in part through the agency of working women. She could clearly imagine that the urban conditions that allowed working women a wholly new independence could lead to the creation of wholly new kinds of women. Although some of her characters fall into feminine stereotypes in their relationships, evincing a self-sacrificing devotion to their lovers that is somewhat essentialized by Sime as woman's nature, one story depicts a woman wholly separate from the heterosexual system. "The Bachelor Girl" focuses on a single working woman named Tryphena, whose way of life has always been free of men. Orphaned early, raised by a maiden relative, and educated in a convent, Tryphena now earns her own living as a masseuse for female clients only. The result, we are told, is a total indifference toward men:

Men for Tryphena really don't exist. She does not so much dislike them – she simply feels an absolute indifference for and about them. They don't exist for her … This liberty to look past men she buys with work – hard, honest work. Her work is, as she says herself, "just rubbing arms and legs" ... She knows her work and she is popular. Women like her quiet ways ... And they admire her too – Tryphena is emphatically a woman's woman.[68]

For this character, the ability to support herself and live on her own has made possible a way of life and perception of reality that renders traditional gender relations completely obsolete. The narrator points out that "Old Maid is what they would have called her fifty years ago," but old maids are usually thought of as women who have failed to find a husband; Tryphena, however, is not just indifferent to men but finds even the thought of marriage preposterous. Seeing her excited one day, the narrator wonders whether she has a suitor: "'Oh *no*,' she said. 'Not that.' She looked at me reproachfully. 'How *could* you think,' she said, 'I'd ever marry!' I felt a positive criminal."[69] The narrator's embarrassment here signals her feeling that she has blundered, her mistake consisting of the heterosexist assumption that Tryphena would ever be interested in men or marriage. Although the narrator does not draw further attention to it, this moment of realization that not all women want men takes place as Tryphena is giving her a massage, suggesting a more sensual level to this female dialogue. But the desire on which Sime elaborates in the remainder of the story is more maternal in nature; Tryphena is excited because she has bought a baby from the nuns, who were watching for an appropriate orphan for her to adopt. Now that they've found her a baby girl ("A *boy*! No, sir! What do you take me for?"[70]), Tryphena is engrossed in financial plans for single motherhood. Sime closes the story with Tryphena's intention to name the baby Tryphosa, alluding to twin sisters from the New Testament named Tryphena and Tryphosa. The reference is perhaps a suggestion that Tryphena will raise the child in her own image, relishing sisterly female bonds while dismissing heterosexual convention. Although many of Sime's stories address unconventional relationships of various kinds, this is the only one that suggests the possibility of rejecting heterosexuality outright, and it is striking how explicit the link is – almost cause and effect – between earning your own living and "this liberty to look past men." Here, work provides a degree of freedom that can influence women on fundamental levels of identity and sexuality. Moreover, in 1919 the idea that a woman might intentionally set out to become a single mother would certainly have been unfathomable to many people. By representing the many possible forms that the working girl might take, Sime shows an awareness of how subtle shifts in gender norms would give way to profound upheavals in the social fabric.

Carolyn Strange points out in her book on Toronto's working girls that "the issue of sexual morality loomed like a dark cloud over discussions of woman's work in the industrializing city, casting waged labour as a test of chastity rather than an economic or political issue."[71] Sime, however, resolutely sees the silver lining here, and in a society eager to condemn any increase in the sexual licence of women, she demonstrates in the tone of her writing a way to recognize women's sexual choices without castigating them. In a similarly utopian way, whereas many women virtually drew knives over who could be deemed a lady, Sime advocated a feminist sisterhood that would cross class boundaries. Although Mackay doesn't write with the same degree of political conviction, her working-class heroine similarly suggests the possibility of transcending class divisions. In fact, it would seem that where representations of the working girl lead, sexual transgression, class break-down, and gender instability soon follow. A denizen of factories, city streets, and department stores, the single wage-earning woman represented to her contemporaries everything that was unnatural and unnerving about modern life. Those who were watching closely could see her potential to unravel social codes and critically redefine what it meant to be a woman in Canadian society. This is where writers entered into the cultural work initiated by these women: by representing this often disregarded figure, they insisted on new distributions of social respect, and they validated the cultural innovations of independent women. Middle-class critics may have wished that Sime's characters were not quite so "extreme" in their reactions to economic freedom, but her unapologetic heroines were as striking in their realism as in their actions, making Sime's book as prescient a work of literature as it is a social document.

## chapter 3

# White Slaves, Prostitutes, and Delinquents

The men of this country exerted as great a fascination
over me as the whispering prairies, and I met them
with a glad response I had never known before. I
awakened to find myself the most sought-after girl in
town and I rejoiced in my popularity.

– MADELEINE BLAIR [PSEUD.],
*Madeleine: An Autobiography*, 1919

The reform era, during the first two decades of the twentieth century, was a period when intense effort went into improving a society thought to be in serious need of social uplift and purification. The reform movement set out to raise social standards by waging war on vice. With purity and vice thus antagonistically opposed, the representational project that accompanied reform rhetoric seized readily on imagery of light and dark, good and evil, uplift and downfall – an allegorical way of reading social conditions that pressed certain social members into set symbolic moulds. The defining vice for men was drink, and numerous temperance societies sought to purge society of the liquor trade and thus to combat the evils of drink that accompanied it. The defining vice for women, meanwhile, was sexual downfall, the limit case being prostitution; the tendency to interpret the figure of the prostitute as somehow symbolic of the community's fallen condition was persistent. In the Canadian West, moreover, the vices of prostitution and drink had found a friendly frontier. In a population consisting largely of young, single working men, prostitutes could do good business, and early on they established a recognized presence in western towns and cities. And if there was one consumer product that characterized the Canadian West, it was whiskey, with many towns and cities virtually founded by saloon owners – like Vancouver's "Gassy Jack" Deighton, for whom Vancouver's oldest neighbourhood, Gastown, is named. The two vices met in the brothel, where the sale of liquor accompanied the sexual services offered, and the complementary commercial interests of the two industries could make for remarkable profit. As the middle class established itself more permanently, however, reform efforts became more organized. The vice of drink had an obvious target in liquor, the production and distribution of which could be systematically attacked, but prostitution was a more complex industry, the components of which were human individuals whose motivations and practices were obscure and elusive.

Gender politics at the turn of the century were troubled by the effects of Canada's increasing urbanization and industrialization, and the female figures of both the prostitute and the working girl represented the changing moral landscape of the twentieth century. In the West prostitutes had been one of the most visible groups of women to populate the early frontier boomtowns, but with the establishment of a more settled urban society, the toleration of the sex industry was replaced with a more severe moral vigilance. Because the working girl was involved in the public sphere of commercial pursuit – traditionally considered inappropriate for women – interpretations of her place within urban industrial settings often paired her with the only other visibly independent woman of the city, the prostitute. These two figures were a challenge to conventional notions of femininity, and in an urge to fathom the dangers posed – both to the women themselves and to society – by rapidly shifting gender relations, reformers launched into analyses of female vice with all the enthusiasm of conspiracy theorists. The most remarkable product of these efforts was the supposed discovery of the white-slave trade, a vast international traffic in unwilling prostitutes. The narratives that illustrated the existence of this industry of sexual bondage soon congealed according to set conventions, but perhaps more intriguing still are the ways in which the narratives were put to use. As reformers agitated for increased suppression of prostitution, white-slave stories were invoked to further vilify the inhabitants of red-light districts. And the horror-movie quality of the narratives, which had terrible fates befalling young women who happened, even innocently, to defy convention, signal the possible function of these stories in policing female independence. Like young wage-earning women of the nineteenth century, who were often viewed as victims of industry, the white slave similarly represented an unwilling victim – this time of sexual predators; but as the twentieth century progressed, the increased association of mainstream working girls with both white slaves and regular prostitutes reflected a harsher attitude toward the supposed moral laxity of young working-class women.

In this chapter I look at the representational urge in the reform era to associate the working girl with her more pathological counterparts: the prostitute, the white slave, the delinquent, and the feebleminded girl. I start with the construction of the white-slave narrative, which represented working girls as the favourite targets of heartless procurers. I move on to the more scientific rhetoric of feeblemindedness and delinquency. But to counter the alarmist and diagnostic rhetoric that dominates these fields of discourse, I pause to examine the autobiography of a turn-of-the-century prostitute and madam who relates her experiences working in Manitoba and Alberta, providing us with a rare inside account of the sex industry so often demonized by analyses of this "social evil." The chapter thus covers a somewhat disparate range of material but focuses on two female figures – the working girl and the prostitute – who together played important symbolic roles in the rise of an urban West.

The white slave, as a narrative figure, has a close relative in the Victorian fallen woman. In both cases, the young woman's fall from innocence is due primarily to the machinations of others, who deliberately mislead, deceive, or even abduct her. She is not wholly to blame for her fall and can therefore be pitied, rescued, and perhaps redeemed by compassionate philanthropists – at least to a point, for the fallen-woman narrative is a complex one. It often asks its reader to sympathize with a highly virtuous but cruelly deceived victim; however, once her true inner virtue has been established beyond any doubt, she is nevertheless typically killed off by the end of the story, an implicit condemnation suggesting that even the most innocent victim of sexual downfall must be punished in the end. The fallen woman was a figure who provoked a highly ambivalent response in the Victorian mind: on the one hand, her passionless innocence and virtuous character protect her from direct blame for her sexual downfall; on the other hand, she can never be truly redeemed because true purity depends on virginity, the loss of which ultimately portends her death. The white slave is similarly innocent of any agency in her fall because she is a victim of kidnappers, yet the narratives often identify specifically working-class and wage-earning girls as those at risk of being taken, particularly when in search of employment. The innocent victim thus becomes slightly implicated in her own fall, and as with the fallen woman, the pity accorded to her is tempered with an oblique condemnation.

Analyzing these narratives in the reform era is further complicated by the changing attitudes toward female sexuality at this time. White-slave narratives were highly popular as one explanation for prostitution, but their Victorian underpinnings were giving way to the new rhetoric of social science. Barbara Meil Hobson and Mary Odem have analyzed the reform era and its theories of female sexuality. As Mary Odem explains in her book *Delinquent Daughters*, the fallen woman and white slave were being replaced by the juvenile delinquent:

> College-educated women involved in the Progressive movement disagreed with the Victorian assumption of girlhood sexual passivity and victimization. Instead, they acknowledged female sexual agency and thought of young women who engaged in illicit encounters as "delinquents" in need of guidance and control. These reformers did not blame evil men for young women's moral downfall, but rather, influenced by recent trends in the social sciences, they looked to societal and family environments to explain sexual delinquency among young working-class women.[1]

This change may at first appear to be a sensible modernizing of attitudes, but the application of the new theories consistently targeted working-class girls and women, castigating their lifestyles and pathologizing them with the new terminology of delinquency and feeblemindedness. Barbara Meil Hobson argues that the change was not necessarily a constructive one:

> Psychiatrists' analyses of prostitution as maladjustment or personality disorder differed little from earlier models of fallen women and female criminality. Scientific testing and new medical jargon were merely new wine in old bottles: the fallen woman was recast as the psychopathic, feebleminded, or moral defective. Sexual delinquency continued to be a barometer for criminality.[2]

While the rhetoric of female sexuality was thus changing – with fallen women and white slaves becoming delinquents – the ambivalence concerning female sexuality and the suspicion of working-class behaviours in particular remained constant. Joan Sangster has examined the Canadian scene, where leading Canadian eugenicists Helen MacMurchy and C.K. Clarke of the Toronto Psychiatric Clinic identified feeblemindedness as the root cause of sexual immorality, specifically among young female factory workers.[3] Anne McClintock explores the Victorian assumptions about the "promiscuous lower orders," and Sangster shows that even in the scientific rhetoric of twentieth-century Canadian doctors such as C.K. Clarke, "Suppositions about class and race informed most expert discourses on sexuality in the interwar period. It was assumed that those 'lingering at the bottom of the social ladder' were more promiscuous, contributing to the spread of venereal disease. Furthermore, because houses of prostitution were located in poor areas of the city, working-class children were exposed to this 'corruption' and were thus likely to adopt similar 'sexual behaviour.'"[4] Theories of female sexuality and the accompanying representations of prostitution and its causes were thus a site of intense concern and controversy in the decades following the turn of the century. The white-slave narrative had sensational appeal, whereas the diagnoses of delinquency and feeblemindedness had the sound of science on their side. But both looked expressly to young working-class women for their case reports, and the pairing of the working girl with the prostitute was thus established.

## WHITE-SLAVE NARRATIVES: ORIGINS AND CONVENTIONS

In 1885 William Thomas Stead reported a scandalous story of child prostitution in London entitled "The Maiden Tribute of Modern Babylon."[5] This instantly famous story of the purchase of a thirteen-year-old girl from her mother for the purpose of prostitution travelled quickly to Canada and stayed in the press thanks to Stead's subsequent trial on kidnapping charges; in order to prove how easy it was to buy a young girl for immoral purposes, Stead had done just that and was ultimately imprisoned for it. According to Stead's report, a child could easily be bought in the shady districts of London; once lured away from home, she would likely be chloroformed, later awaking to find herself imprisoned in a brothel, from which moment her fate was sealed. Stead not only reported on this but, to prove his point, enacted such a purchase himself, waking a terrified Eliza Armstrong from her drugged sleep, whereupon, the experiment complete, he sent her to the Salvation Army in Paris. This is far from the journalistic ideal of a distanced observer merely reporting the facts. Stead fully involved himself in the construction and enactment of the story, and in so doing he actually set out the conventions for what would become a genre unto itself: the white-slave narrative, the staples of which became the innocent girl of impoverished origins, the chloroform, and the prison-brothel. The white-slavery panic in Canada and the United States would peak some years later between 1910 and 1915, along with the social-reform movement, but Stead's report and the popular interest in the ensuing scandal would influence later depictions of female abduction in the press, which undoubtedly exploited the sensational appeal of such stories.

Cecily Devereux has documented the Canadian media's reaction to "The Maiden Tribute of Modern Babylon." From the colonial perspective of many Canadians, Stead's tale of sexual depravity at the very centre of imperial Britain was deeply upsetting to notions of progress and civilization: "At a time when the English Canadian nation was attempting to establish its own place within the British Empire and its own supposedly cohesive racial and cultural identity, 'The Maiden Tribute' played on a whole range of colonial insecurities and imperial sentiments."[6] Stead's exposé brought the problem of prostitution to the forefront of social-reform initiatives, and the idea of an international trade in women was especially alarming. Canadians, suspicious of cultural mixing and the supposed dubious morality of ethnic immigrants, were easily shaken by tales of unwitting girls caught in an international traffic run by vaguely "foreign" conspirators.

My analysis of white-slavery narratives turns not on whether they were true or false but on how they were constructed and deployed in the context of gender politics at the turn of the century. However, it is important to note that the white-slavery tales did have some basis in truth despite a good deal of sensationalism and exaggeration. To analyze them as a narrative genre does not mean to reduce them to wholly fictional status, and there is evidence that abductions of women into the sex trade did occur in some instances. In fact, the urge to deny this is interesting in itself. At the time when the panic was at its height, certain studies claimed to disprove that white slavery existed at all, and historians of today also frequently dismiss it as a hysteria that had no factual basis. As Ruth Rosen points out in *The Lost Sisterhood*, it was in the interest of certain groups to deny that sexual slavery existed: "Politicians, police, liquor interests, and property owners tried to convince the public that white slavery was simply a fantasy born of reformers' overactive imaginations ... Despite this mixed record, a careful review of the evidence documents a real traffic in women: a historical fact and experience that must be integrated into the record."[7] She estimates that white slavery was likely experienced by less than 10 percent of the prostitute population, making reformers' accounts exaggerated but not wholly erroneous.[8]

In 1921, at a time when anti-Asian sentiment in the West was especially virulent, Hilda Glynn Howard, writing under the pseudonym Hilda

Glynn-Ward, published her novel *The Writing on the Wall*. It is essentially a collection of racial stereotypes and alarmist narratives combined to elicit anti-Asian sentiment in the reader, and insofar as the novel thus draws on the recognized cultural anxieties of the day, it is not surprising that a white-slavery narrative is included. But Glynn-Ward's version of the story is revealing in that it both reproduces the familiar narrative and rewrites it in order to localize it for the West Coast context.

The tale starts in Vancouver with the broken-hearted parents desperate over the loss of their daughter, who has apparently eloped: "But there was an element of tragedy, of such utter hopeless despair in the attitude of these parents that even knowing nothing of the facts one would have realized there was something unusually sad about this particular elopement. And there was. Pretty Eileen Hart, the pride of her mother, the apple of her father's eye, and only eighteen years old, had run away and married – a Chinaman. The horror of it turned them sick. She had been better dead."[9] This depiction of the desolate parents is typical of the white-slave narrative, as is the sentiment that a woman's death is preferable to her sexual downfall. Procurers in the white-slave trade, meanwhile, tended to be portrayed as "foreigners" of some kind and marriage as one way that they lured girls away from their homes and families. Following an initial letter from Eileen, in which she boasts of the wealth and status of her new husband, the parents' worst fears are realized when they receive this hastily scrawled note: "Daddy, come and fetch me away quick, or I shall die. Wong has four other wives and they are beastly to me. They watch me every minute so I can't run away, and I'm never alone. I think I'm in Victoria, but not sure, and I don't know the street or the number, as I'm never allowed to go out. Please come as quick as you can Daddy dear!"[10] The multiple wives of the Chinese husband are a slight twist on the usual characters of the brothel madam and prostitutes who confine the victim, but the tale of imprisonment here is otherwise typical. The father departs immediately for Victoria, where he enlists the police and speaks to the premier, all to no avail because the premier is corrupt and the police no match for the labyrinths of Chinatown; hints toward the conspiratorial nature of the white-slave trade are thus established, and Eileen is never heard of again. Where the story diverges from the usual accounts of white slavery is that the character of the "foreign" procurer is not a stranger to the victim but a long-time friend and schoolmate (and presumably a Canadian citizen, although not recognized as such due to his racial positioning): "Wong Fu was an old schoolfellow ... he had always helped her with her sums and thus won her childish affection and admiration."[11] Typically, the "foreign" nature of the procurer is used in order to distance the criminal from the "true" members of the community, who can then direct their outrage toward the alien "other." But Glynn-Ward deliberately makes her villain both threateningly alien by virtue of his racial status and disturbingly familiar as an everyday associate and seemingly innocent schoolmate. She thus enlists a racism that assigned "foreign" status even to those born and raised in Canada, suggesting that even the most familiar faces and long-time members of the community are not to be trusted. She goes on to condemn co-education, a frequent focus for racist sentiment in British Columbia. This particular version of the white-slave narrative is thus tailor-made for a white Canadian audience, whose anxieties concerning mixed-race marriage and the association of Chinatown with prostitution would find realization in Glynn-Ward's lurid sensationalism. Her depiction of the white slave being kidnapped into Chinatown would have struck a chord with readers in the many western cities that contained Chinatown neighbourhoods. Victoria's is known as the oldest in Canada, but in Vancouver the red-light district, though periodically changing location due to fluctuating police activity, was often co-extensive with Chinatown, making for an easy conflation, in readers' minds, of sexual iniquity and racial otherness. The way that the international panic of the white-slave trade is thus modified and localized is worth noting because it reveals both the broad appeal of this cultural narrative and its ability to enlist specific regional tensions depending on the context. Perhaps this mobility explains part of its success as an urban legend that spawned major social-reform activity.

Mariana Valverde has examined the reform response to prostitution, and she explains that "for turn-of-the-century Canadians, the debates on public policy regarding prostitution constituted a key terrain within and through which the social was discussed and regulated: municipal reform, new ideas about sexuality and gender roles, class differences in culture, and ethnic/racial tensions did not only help to shape the prostitution debate but were also shaped by it."[12] Deborah Nilson has studied prostitution and the police response to it in early-twentieth-century Vancouver, and she notes the influence of urban development and women's entrance into the workforce on debates about the city's sex trade: "It was believed that the unstable social conditions resulting from urban and industrial development indicated a *moral* breakdown in society. The idea of the 'fallen woman' took on added force as women increasingly moved into employment outside the home."[13] This was the social context in which white-slave stories circulated, and they underwent further adjustments as they embedded themselves in their various Canadian settings. In John G. Shearer's 1912 tract, *Canada's War on the White-slave Trade*, explicit connections are drawn between sexual danger, urban development, and female employment, signalling specific social tensions of the day that found expression in this pliable narrative genre.

John G. Shearer was the head of the Presbyterian Church's moral-reform department and a leader in Canada's social-purity movement. Based in Toronto, Shearer brought his brand of reform rhetoric to the West when he toured the western provinces in 1910. He figured the West as a danger zone where prostitution was more tolerated than in eastern cities: "The White Slave Trade finds some of its victims on the prairies whence they are taken to Winnipeg, to British Columbia, or to American cities where prostitution is 'tolerated' in 'segregated' areas."[14] Misgivings about the rapid urbanization of Canada were embedded in these tales by inclusion of the country-to-city migration, a typical feature of the formula. The image of the wholesome country girl being thus ensnared and whisked off to the city of vice was powerful in a context where increased migration from country to city, especially by young working-class women, was visibly on the increase. And although a few tales had middle-class girls kidnapped by white slavers and rescued at the last minute, the more typical narrative addressed the "daughters of the working class," for whom the white-slavery narrative took on the aspect of cautionary tale, a warning for the girl who ventured far from home and into the dubious territories of city streets, train stations, boarding houses, factories, and dance halls – the landmarks of the fallen city:

> The first [of Shearer's cautionary tales] tells of an exceedingly narrow escape. An innocent looking advertisement appeared in the newspaper, for a domestic servant – work light – wages liberal. An unsuspecting country girl saw and took the gilded bait. She came to the Capital with no information but the street address of her future mistress. On arrival she found it necessary to inquire the way. The railway official happened to know that the address was of a house in the 'Red Light' district. The terrified girl was handed over to the S.P.C. officer and taken care of. One trembles to think how many similar lambs may not have thus escaped the slaughter.[15]

This story is essentially one of mobility but one that highlights only the danger, not the freedom, of mobility. The country-to-city journey is inspired by the "gilded bait" of an employment opportunity, suggesting that the increased employment offered to young women in urban centres was not a real opportunity but a trap laid for naive victims. The reality of women's growing presence in the workforce thus becomes a plot device in the stock narrative of sexual downfall, creating an impression that "innocent looking advertisements" for work – and perhaps by extension even innocent-looking work itself – are all just a cover for prostitution. In this way, white-slavery narratives were instrumental in furthering a prevailing social attitude that the entrance of young women into the paid workforce was a moral danger in that even the most innocent-seeming situations were fraught with inducements to prostitution.

A constellation of social fears and stereotypes thus entered into the construction of the white-slave myth; the sex trade, perhaps more than any other subculture, has always been little understood but much speculated about, and given the tendency to condemn prostitutes as irrevocably depraved, the narrative was somewhat recuperative in that it added the innocent victim to the regular cast of immoral reprobates. In fact, this aspect of the genre mirrors depictions of the working girl, who likewise fell either into the category of morally suspect mercenary vixens or helpless victims of industry. In many ways, then, the figure of the prostitute and that of the legitimate working girl came to be intimately related on a conceptual level, making it important to examine one with reference to the other.

## THE WHITE-SLAVE TRADE AND THE WORKING GIRL

White-slave narratives were directed at both working- and middle-class audiences, but the female victim in the story tended to be working-class and employed. Her fall from innocence was in subtle ways linked to the fact of employment, and while socialist critics pointed to low wages as the cause of prostitution, their arguments ostensibly did not apply to the white-slave scenario, in which the woman was forcibly kidnapped into the trade. Ruth Rosen argues that this was part of the middle-class appeal of the genre in that attention was directed away from real social and economic conditions leading to prostitution and deflected onto villainous foreign procurers.[16] Thus the pragmatic reasons why a link might in fact exist between working-class women and prostitution were removed, yet the association between the working girl and the white slave remained. Many felt that wage-earning women were exposing themselves to danger by entering the workplace, living independently, and engaging in a lively social life that appeared promiscuous to the older generation, but it is also worth noting that the middle class often tended to be suspicious of working-class sexuality; as Gary Kinsman points out, "Working-class and black women were seen as more 'sexual' than middle-class women, and there emerged a double standard separating male from female and middle-class 'ladies' from working-class women. This symbolic system affected the social organization of prostitution, and eroticism more generally."[17] Even though white-slave narratives often attributed the fall of the victim to country-girl naiveté or deceptive job ads, the relentless association of prostitution with working-class women betrays a bias regarding working-class women's sexuality that cannot be overlooked.

In the late nineteenth and early twentieth centuries, the West's rapid urbanization was cause for great social upheaval, and many historians link the white-slave panic to anxieties caused by this massive social change. Referring to the young woman who had a near escape when an ad for employment almost led her into the red-light district, John Shearer reminds his reader of "the need of faithfully warning all girls of the perils threatening them when they journey unchaperoned to any large city": "These dangers are many times greater when girls go to the city to remain and earn their living amid new surroundings, and are compelled to make their home in the less expensive boarding houses, and to find amusement on the streets or in the cheaper places of entertainment, as well as to be exposed to various insidious temptations from employers and work-mates."[18] It was not merely the city in general that was dangerous and morally suspect, but specifically those parts of it that constituted the daily terrain of the single working girl: boarding house, street, and workplace.

In 1912 Bessie Pullen-Burry wrote a travel account of her trip across Canada, entitled *From Halifax to Vancouver*, in which she took special account of conditions facing the female immigrant. She was very troubled by what she saw in the West, where affordable accommodation for independent women was scarce and where conditions at the YWCA were less than ideal. Leaving Cranbrook on her way to Vancouver, she worries about the dangers posed to young wage-earning women on their own:

> As I left this town early next morning, I observed from the train a number of small houses with lights in front of them of the colour of blood, and I thought of the perils the young of both sexes run in such places as these, where respectable housing for those who cannot pay hotel-rates is practically impossible to obtain.

> *The danger is for the women and girls of Canada* far more than for an
> occasional emigrant! ... History shows that no nation ever rises above the
> character of its women. In the West especially, the life of the girl wage-
> earner is hard. The lack of home, with its ties and its influences, means the
> weakening of restraint. The boarding-system, where girls, four in a room,
> often live and receive their visitors after business hours, is not ideal.[19]

Although Pullen-Burry begins with the very material observation that
affordable housing was limited, she adds emphasis by placing the home
in contrast to the boarding house, with the lack of a proper home resulting in the "weakening of restraint." In one sense, this is an interesting
acknowledgment that the domestic sphere places restraints on a woman.
But it also deflects the issue of prostitution from material circumstances to
moral laxity by suggesting that wage-earning women's living conditions
lend themselves to moral weakening. In fact, the independence of boarding-house living did allow women a new degree of sexual freedom, but as
Pullen-Burry's comments show, the middle class tended to interpret this
as promiscuity and prostitution.

The tone of dire warning used by Pullen-Burry also suffused the
narrative of the country-to-city move, so typical in white-slave stories. A
striking passage by Nellie McClung illustrates the tendency to render city
and country on a scale of morality as well as on a scale of appropriate
gender behaviour:

> The city offers so many dazzling, easy ways to wealth. It is so rich in
> promise, so treacherous in fulfilment. The city is a lenient, unfaithful nurse,
> pampering and pandering the child in her care not for his own good, but
> for her gain, soothing him with promises she never means to keep, a waster
> of time, a destroyer of ambition, a creator of envy, but dazzling gay with
> tinsel and redolent with perfume, covering poverty with cheap lace and
> showy ribbons, a hole in her stocking but a rose in her hair!
>
> The country is a stern nurse, hard but just, making large demands on
> the child in her care, but giving great rewards. She tells the truth, demands
> obedience, and does better than she promises. Though she sends her child
> on long cold journeys, and makes him face the bitter winds of winter, she
> rewards him with ruddy health, high purpose and clear vision.[20]

Although the city and country are represented here as two nurses, by the
end of the first paragraph the city nurse has clearly become a prostitute.

Given that the nurse was one of the most highly respected versions of the working woman, even though she is only a metaphor here, to thus change her into a prostitute within the space of one sentence demonstrates the conceptual trajectory that matched the city with inevitable female vice and even the most admired working girl with moral turpitude. Nellie McClung championed women's rights in law and in politics, but in her writings she extolled a domestic ideal for women. In her fiction centred on Pearl Watson, the daughter of an impoverished family of Irish descent living in rural Manitoba, she validates the expertise and value of the work that women performed in farm households, but women's wage-earning capabilities and career interests outside the home never rival marriage and motherhood as the goal of her female characters.[21]

Moving from the country to the city in search of work also meant for some Canadian women a move to the United States, which triggered further national anxieties. John Shearer depicts the danger of such a move, representing the success of working women abroad as little more than a convenient tale for wicked procurers to tell:

> Everyone knows that for many years a constant stream of Canadian girls have crossed the border to earn their living as writers, nurses, teachers, stenographers, ladies' companions, seamstresses, domestic helpers, etc. Success in unusual degree has crowned their effort. Their integrity and industry and ability have been rewarded with generous remuneration. Stories of their success are widely known. This makes the work of the procurer the easier. His promises of an easy life and otherwise incredibly large wages are believed. Deceptive advertisements are answered. The innocent victims go blindly into a bondage worse than Hell.[22]

This passage is unusual in that Shearer actually acknowledges the achievements of Canadian working women – that they were valued for their ability and paid accordingly – but rhetorically, this recognition is only a set-up for the dire warning that follows, a warning that reduces the success of wage-earning women to little more than a convenient lure cast by wicked procurers. By thus linking even the greatest achievements of working women to the white-slave trade, he undermines their subjectivity as workers and reinforces the tendency to subordinate the economic and social value of women's work to moral considerations. An interesting balance is maintained in these accounts, in which the victims of white slavers are repeatedly described as innocent and unwitting yet always depicted as working girls – looking for work, arriving in new cities, engaging in new and popular leisure activities. The singling-out of working girls as the ones most susceptible to becoming white slaves subtly impugns not only their ability to take care of themselves but also their very way of life and, by association, themselves; as members of the sole at-risk population for sexual exploitation, they are implicated in their own downfall – their status as innocent victims becomes suspect.

The distinction between the innocent victim of sexual entrapment and the potentially willing prostitute became especially strained when discussion of the working-girl "problem" turned to leisure activities. At the turn of the century the dance hall was rising to prominence as the major recreational venue for working-class youth. As the latest incarnation of youth recreation, dance halls mystified the adult elite, who could see only a dangerous style of abandon in the unfamiliar proceedings. It is worth noting here that the populations of western towns and cities were renowned for their youthfulness, young men being the major group drawn to the West in search of work, while young women, although fewer in number, visibly crowded the YWCAs and women's boarding houses; this young, single, working populace was becoming known for its hot pursuit of amusement in its limited time off, and movie theatres and dance halls both catered to working-class customers. The dance hall was routinely depicted as an enlisting ground for white slavers. Toronto reformer B.G. Jefferis describes the fatal combination of public balls and thoughtless young women in a point-by-point format:

1  **Public Balls.** – The church should turn its face like flint against the public balls. Its influence is evil, and nothing but evil. It is a well known fact that in all cities and large towns the ball room is the recruiting office for prostitution.
2  **Thoughtless Young Women.** – In cities public balls are given every night, and many thoughtless young women, mostly the daughters of small tradesmen and mechanics, or clerks or laborers, are induced to attend "just for fun." Scarcely one in a hundred of the girls attending these balls preserve their purity ...
3  **Working Girls.** – Thousands of innocent working girls enter innocently and unsuspectingly into the paths which lead them to the house of evil, or who wander the streets as miserable outcasts all through the influence of the dance. The low theatre and dance halls and other places of unselected gatherings are the milestones which

mark the working girl's downward path from virtue to vice, from modesty to shame.[23]

A degree of contradiction is evident here in that both the "thoughtless" young women and the working girls are engaged in the same activity, and both are working class, yet those of the first group seem more culpable for their own downfall – being thoughtless and out "just for fun" – whereas the working girls seem much less to blame, their innocence emphasized repeatedly. Jefferis himself seems confused, as though he would like to endorse the notion of the innocent victim, unwittingly lured into sin, but he can't quite convince himself because the girls are enjoying themselves so much. Kathy Peiss explains these dualistic conceptual tendencies as a product of Victorian ideals, which were beginning to weaken in the twentieth century but were still much in evidence: "The reformers who made working women's recreation a social issue drew upon a complex set of Victorian ideals and assumptions. Their gender and class position served as lenses through which they alternatively perceived working women as unwilling female victims and as enthusiastic members of the promiscuous lower orders."[24]

Prostitution did, of course, take place in dance halls on both professional and casual levels. And what became increasingly apparent to reformers, especially in the realm of leisure, was that casual or clandestine prostitutes were only one product of a swiftly changing culture where sexual dictates were ever more flexible and contingent. Some women would never exchange sex for money but did expect men to pay for drinks, entrance tickets, meals, gifts, and taxis in return for a woman's company and any favours that she saw fit to bestow. For working-class youth, the edict against premarital sex was weakening, while new standards to distinguish degrees of propriety and promiscuity were being established, but the dominant middle-class culture had difficulty recognizing these. To them, working-class youth and young women in particular – often looked to as symbols of traditional social mores – appeared dangerously profligate. The conceptual association between mainstream working girls and prostitutes was thus enhanced and inflamed by changing social patterns wherein the conventions of sexual propriety, dating, trading favours, premarital relationships, casual prostitution, and professional sex work were readily distinguished by working-class youth but were baffling to middle-class observers.

The supposed association between prostitution and working-class leisure venues was an expression of the middle-class tendency to generalize all sexual behaviour as tantamount to prostitution. Mariana Valverde notes that "in 1913, Toronto's leading moral reformers joined together to investigate 'social vice' in the city, and their 1915 report does not recognize a distinction between prostitution and going out on dates."[25] The venues where the white-slave trade was thought to be particularly threatening mark liminal spaces considered inappropriate for unchaperoned young women: the city in general, but more particularly the train station, the dance hall, the ethnic neighbourhood (which often overlapped with the red-light district), the street, and any workplace named in a deceptive ad for employment. But many of these spaces, such as the workplace and the dance hall, were precisely those arenas where wage-earning women were carving out new cultural territory and so travelling ever further away from middle-class norms and patriarchal control. Viewed in this light, positing the white-slave danger as prevalent in these exact locations appears to be both an expression of conservative paranoia and an urge to reassert control using dire warnings and scare tactics.

## PROSTITUTION IN THE WESTERN ECONOMY

Reformers who propagated white-slave narratives assumed the voice of authority in depicting the sex industry, and by virtue of their social position they had access to the mainstream media to disseminate their message. Less easy to locate are the voices of the women in question; lack of education, financial imperatives, and social ostracism are only a few reasons why writings by either working girls or sex workers themselves are few and difficult to locate. But in examining social attitudes toward prostitution, it is important to gain some sense of what everyday life was like in the sexual-service industry at the time. Prostitution in the West at the turn of the century was a significantly different industry from the one that exists today. Brothels owned and operated by women were the norm, and given the preponderance of young bachelors who populated the frontier, there was high demand for the services that they offered. Of course, the sex trade has always been a highly stratified industry, with different sectors of the trade catering to different classes of men. The life of a woman in a high-class brothel was very different from that of a street prostitute, and their earnings would differ accordingly. But until the militant suppression of the industry, which began in 1911 and peaked in the period 1914-16,[26] prostitution represented a female-dominated industry where real profit could be made and where wages were less influenced by the institutional sexism that depressed women's earnings in mainstream industries. Prostitutes-as-workers were treated as individual agents capable of supporting themselves, unlike in the more general economy, where women workers were viewed as dependants, whose wages were not expected to represent a living wage for a self-supporting person. For this reason alone, the sex trade would have held a strong appeal for women who, for whatever reason, had no other means of support. But it also provides a useful contrast to the mainstream economy, where the value of women's work was always subordinated through comparisons to men's ostensibly harder and more valuable work, a comparison not applicable in the context of the sex trade.

Social critics at the turn of the century wrote and speculated a great deal about women's motives for entering the sex trade, and the debate continues today as we try to calculate the degree of agency that prostitutes have in choosing an often emotionally gruelling and physically dangerous industry rather than accepting alternatives that entail their own degrees of hardship and exploitation. The financial necessity of the individual occupies an important part of this debate, though it is not the only determining factor. Debates about the causes of prostitution often turn on the motivations, financial or otherwise, of prostitutes themselves; what is addressed less often is the financial necessity or economic importance of the prostitute to the larger economy. The frequent claim that prostitution was a "necessary evil" referred to the supposed irrepressible sexual needs of men, but one wonders whether proponents of this argument might not have had an economic stake in the question as well – an undeniable consumer desire for something is bound to mean profit somewhere. In the historical context of the Canadian West the microeconomy of a hastily established small town was dependent on every financial transaction that took place. Charlene P. Smith has studied the brothel system at the turn of the century in the town of Rossland, British Columbia, where the sexual-service industry undoubtedly contributed to the town's economy: "In the early history of the boomtowns, prostitution was viewed not only as a 'necessary evil,' it was seen also as beneficial to economic development. As business owners, brothel madams provided what was viewed as an essential service, hired employees, paid taxes, and spent money within their communities. Their contributions to the city coffers through the payment of fines added significant amounts to the development of municipal economies."[27] In the brothel system, moreover, the sexual service component was invariably accompanied by the West's foremost consumer product – liquor. And this lucrative partnership was strong enough to have a profound impact on the prosperity – or lack thereof – of any community.

Greg Marquis writes about the attempted suppression of vice in Vancouver and points out that "Vancouver's vice industry fulfilled social needs and was as essential to the city's economic life as were its sawmills, railway facilities, and grain elevators."[28] While reformers regarded drinking and prostitution as questions of moral failure and possible reformation, those involved even peripherally in the vice industry knew that a small but thriving economy was at stake, the elimination of which would have serious economic consequences for many people on a variety of levels. In this sense, attitudes toward prostitution resemble in extreme form those toward women generally in the paid work force in that a persistent urge to regard women's work as a moral problem elided the significance of their contribution both to individual industries and to the economy as a whole.

As Lori Rotenberg points out in her study of prostitution in Toronto at the turn of the century, it is important to look at prostitution as one type of work within a range of female-defined employment: "The heavy emphasis on the 'sinful' nature of the prostitute's sexual activity has obscured her role as a worker. But the prostitute is indeed a worker, a service worker who provides her body for use in the sexual act in return for a fee from her clients. In selling her labour power in a capitalist society she is subject to considerable exploitation and alienation, as are other women workers."[29] In the larger context of women's work, it is therefore important to assess the role that prostitution played in influencing attitudes toward women and their relation to capital, work, and the city.

In her 1919 autobiography, Madeleine Blair (a pseudonym) confirms the importance of the sex industry within the local economies of western towns at the turn of the century. Having worked in a number of brothels in US cities, she writes of the refreshing change that she experiences in Canada, where the women are much more in demand and thus do very well for themselves; and when she decides to open her own establishment, she is welcomed by the police chief of an unnamed Alberta town that is suffering for lack of a local brothel. Whereas reformers who battled the "social evil" of prostitution depicted it as a social ill, Madeleine presents an alternate view of the industry as a vital part of a healthy economy, thus signalling the importance of women's work to economic growth:

I heard of a place in which the Mounted Police had closed the houses two years before because the women had made themselves so conspicuous that the citizens objected to their presence in the town ... After two years the business men had raised an objection to the 'closed town' because of the decrease in business. They attributed this to the fact that the town had no attraction for the hundreds of single men employed in various capacities in that section. They maintained that as soon as the men drew their money they went to one of the neighboring towns to spend it.

Partly because of this pressure from the business men, but mostly on account of matters that had come under his own observation, the commandant of the Mounted Police had decided to let one house open in the place, if the right woman applied for the privilege ... My informant was one of the leading professional men in this town, thoroughly familiar with the situation, and he gave me the full details.[30]

In Madeleine's experience, both the local police and the RCMP take a very tolerant attitude toward brothels, interfering only if they are pressured by complaints from other citizens. In this case, the officer in charge takes an active part not only in condoning the establishment of a brothel but also in interviewing prospective applicants for the position of madam. His candour in the ensuing discussion of terms is equally striking as he clearly and deliberately sets out for Madeleine her exact place within the town's society, economy, and legal system: "The O.C. warned me against investing too much money, because of the severe penalty for selling liquor without a license ... The police would not take official cognizance of any violation of the law unless a complaint was made by some citizen or hotel-man."[31] Despite the law, no one pretends that Madeleine's house will not sell liquor; instead, it is merely a matter of avoiding too many complaints since the third complaint would carry a prison sentence. Madeleine's description of the rules and conventions of her own house, as well as her accounts of those in which she has worked, establish that the sale of liquor was just as important as the sale of sex in the profitability of a brothel, and she remarks on the centrality of drinking, particularly in Canadian culture:

In the Canadian Northwest the sale of liquor and the profits therefrom were greater than I had ever seen elsewhere ... There were no amusements and in the winter few recreations, so that drinking was the greatest indoor pastime.

The bars closed at ten o'clock at night, and at six on Saturday nights. The sporting-houses remained open as long as they liked, usually until four o'clock in the morning. And Saturday nights and Sunday afternoons were the times when we did the big business.[32]

Even without the element of sexual service, then, Madeleine's house responded to demands that were not filled by the other sectors of the liquor trade, incorporating itself as a necessary component of the social and economic system. And as if this market were not enough, she inadvertently finds her house one of the most popular restaurants in town, thanks to the talent of her hired cook. Madeleine's business venture thus includes the furthering of liquor interests, the employment of some five prostitutes and two house workers, the financial support of the municipal authorities in the form of bribes, and the supply of food, drink, and sexual services much in demand. She thus not only provides employment but also facilitates the exchange of money necessary to the diversification and growth of the economy. The integration of her venture with local business interests is profitable to everyone involved and demonstrates that the sex trade, though often represented as a subculture to be suppressed or denied, played an invaluable economic role in opening the West. In this way, prostitution resembles other sectors of industry at the turn of century in which women were an important part of the workforce despite never being given credit by a society that would not recognize them as workers – as valuable economic agents – because of their gender status, which for sex workers especially, was always linked to their moral status.

## MADELEINE BLAIR: A PROSTITUTE'S STORY
## IN HER OWN WORDS

Born in the United States, Madeleine recounts her early experiences in a number of brothels in the urban Midwest. Her subsequent experiences in Canada, however, offer a rare first-person account of the sexual-service industry as it existed in the Canadian West at the turn of the century. It is important to treat the genre of autobiography carefully – not vesting too much in the seductive appearance of truth and authenticity in a text that is constructed to represent the author in a certain light – but I include it here to redress a certain imbalance in the critical discussion of prostitution during the reform era: because the voices of the women themselves (being much harder to locate) are sometimes neglected, I include Madeleine's first-hand account of her experience to serve as a useful counterpoint to the vice commissions and white-slave narratives that otherwise dominate. Madeleine's autobiography is a rare and valuable historical – and indeed, literary – document. It was published in 1919 by Harper and Brothers, and there followed an unsuccessful attempt by a US Society for the Prevention of Vice to have it suppressed as obscenity.[33] But since then, it has not received much attention, particularly in Canada. As the story of a prostitute, Madeleine's autobiography is a compelling representational project. Sidonie Smith has argued that for women the act of self-representation is fraught with difficulty because historically women have been denied access to the voice of authority in a male-defined culture and particularly in the male-defined genre of autobiography. As she explains,

> Primary among the ideological intentions inherent in forms and language, then, is the desire of culture to name and to sustain the difference of man's and woman's subjectivity and, by implication, man's and woman's self-representational possibilities. Thus, woman has remained culturally silenced, denied authority, most critically the authority to name herself and her own desires. Woman has remained unrepresented and unrepresentable.[34]

If women generally have found themselves marginalized and silenced by a masculinist culture, how much more difficult would it have been for a prostitute in 1919, utterly excluded from – indeed, condemned by – the society at large, to nevertheless tell her story and publish it. Madeleine's unusual situation does demand certain precautions and self-protective silences. The autobiography was published anonymously, Madeleine Blair is the assumed name that she took on as a prostitute, and the book is quite deliberately the story of the *prostitute* – we hear of "Madeleine's" life, not of the entire life of the person who lived as Madeleine for a time. She ends the autobiography with her exit from the sex trade at the age of thirty-four. She also holds back other details; she does not, for instance, "name names," protecting the identities of her clients and close acquaintances, and she does not name the Alberta town where she ran her own brothel. But the larger cities in which she worked – Kansas City, Chicago, Winnipeg – are named and described in some detail. Despite the deliberate silences, she clearly wants to convey her specialized knowledge of prostitution to a mainstream audience and to dispel certain myths and stereotypes. One common belief about prostitutes, for instance, was that they never lived more than seven years. Madeleine recounts how many of her co-workers had already been working over ten years and were hardly on death's doorstep, and she claims that "many of these women do leave the life, and many never return to it. Many make good marriages to men they really care for, and, contrary to the usual belief, these marriages are often happy, and few indeed are the wives who prove unfaithful."[35] In dispelling common stereotypes, Madeleine shows that she has her own agenda in writing, and as Smith cautions, one must read autobiography with this in mind: "When life narrators write to chronicle an event, to explore a certain time period, or to enshrine a community, they are making 'history' in a sense. But they are also performing several rhetorical acts: justifying their own perceptions, upholding their reputations, disputing the accounts of others, settling scores, conveying cultural information, and inventing desirable futures among others."[36] Madeleine does have a few scores to settle, but her forthright prose is nevertheless a welcome tonic after the sensational and alarmist qualities of white-slave stories and reform rhetoric.

Madeleine starts life in an apparently securely middle-class family, much respected in the Midwest town where she lives. She receives the beginnings of an excellent education, and she has a natural thirst for reading and a desire to pursue painting and the arts. Her father's alcoholism leads to financial ruin, whereupon the family takes up residence in a neighbourhood where the sex trade is much in evidence, and Madeleine indicates that this environment takes its toll. At seventeen Madeleine is sent to live with friends in St. Louis and work in a factory, but within a few months she finds herself pregnant. Deeply ashamed, she leaves her friends and finds a place in a very familial brothel in Kansas City, where her new co-workers help her to invent the name Madeleine Blair. Madeleine loses her baby and almost escapes the sex trade when she moves to Chicago to work in a department store, but the financial demands of her impoverished family lead her back to the more lucrative profession. Her story thus shows two different avenues that could lead a mainstream working woman into the sex trade: first, an unplanned pregnancy and the stigma attached result in her introduction to sex work; and later, financial need impels her return to it. Her account suggests that mainstream working women were well aware of the sex industry but were careful to avoid any association with it if they wanted to maintain their respectability in the community. Women who engaged in occasional prostitution were careful to keep their activity secret.

Madeleine's life, like that of many prostitutes of her day, was an itinerant one, and she travelled fairly widely. The brothels created an informal network for sex workers, and when Madeleine hears from a friend in Canada that there is a great deal of money to be made, particularly in the West, she makes her way to the new red-light district in Winnipeg:

At this period the bawdy-houses in Winnipeg occupied one short street, which stood alone in the midst of the prairie. It was more than two miles from town, but it was within the city limits; for the public men of that day had a vision of the great city which was to be built on those prairies, and the city limits extended out into the wheat-growing district ... Business was good for girls and for the houses and the profits were enormous, for "short" drinks were sold and everything from lemon-soda to Scotch whisky cost twenty-five cents a glass ... Champagne also was bought freely, and the men of this small city spent money with a grace and ease that I had never seen equalled.[37]

Madeleine finds Canada to be significantly different from the United States, and she much prefers Canadian men to American:

The men of this country exerted as great a fascination over me as the whispering prairies, and I met them with a glad response I had never before known. I awakened to find myself the most sought-after girl in town, and I rejoiced in my popularity. Time after time men came in from the outlying provinces of the Northwest who had heard about Madeleine from some friend in Medicine Hat, or Calgary, or Regina, or some other distant point ... Surely these men were as different from the men in Chicago as the prairies were different from State Street. Here were no blasé habitués of wine-rooms and bawdy-houses, seeking a new sensation by learning a new perversion. Here were men, fine and strong, courtly gentlemen such as I have never met anywhere else in the world.[38]

This is the first time in her narrative that Madeleine writes about finding pleasure and satisfaction in her work, and although she has her share of suffering – particularly regarding pregnancy and motherhood – she shows that the prostitute's life at the turn of the century could be reasonably livable and, under the right circumstances, even pleasurable.

Madeleine's experience of the brothel system reveals a great deal about working conditions for prostitutes at the turn of the century, and these differ significantly from the North American sex trade today. With the closing of red-light districts, which took place across the country between 1910 and 1920 in response to pressure from reformers, the working conditions of prostitutes declined significantly. The brothel provided women with a relatively safe working environment while at the same time assuring their food and lodging. Although the women paid rent and usually yielded half their earnings to the house, they would still make a decent income – more in the high-end houses. Brothels were also typically run by women, and although some madams were more mercenary than others, many took a maternal attitude toward the young women and fostered a caring and protective environment: a supportive female subculture. Madeleine works in one house where the madam takes an overtly motherly attitude toward her employees, and they in turn take the young, pregnant Madeleine in hand, sewing baby clothes for her and seeing to her medical care. Pimps, meanwhile, were frowned upon by madams and police alike. The only sector of prostitution in which they were prominent was the lowly "cribs," where prostitutes lived and worked out of a single room for little money, usually supporting boyfriends-turned-pimps as well as themselves. In a sense, the elimination of the brothel reduced the entire trade to this more suppressed and oppressive level, and with the industry no longer in the hands of women, it became a much more dangerous and destructive way of life, with fewer profits going to women.

One fascinating element of the book is that Madeleine's arrival in western Canada kindles a spiritual and aesthetic awakening; her writing takes on a more poetic tone, and we see the Canadian landscape inspiring the prostitute writer in just the way that it did other, more recognized immigrant authors. In the Canadian landscape, Madeleine sees possibilities for herself that have been elsewhere denied:

> I arose early and took long walks over the prairies, which soon came to exert a wonderful fascination over me. Often, if I were up late at night, I took a long walk before going to bed; for the dawn begins to break at two o'clock in midsummer, and every daybreak was a new revelation to me. I wanted to paint that first pink streak of dawn. I wanted to burst in poetry, and I did break into tuneless song as I tried to express to myself just what I felt was behind the rim of the prairies. Life became fuller and more beautiful than I had ever thought it could be … I began to dream again of art – to seek a medium for expressing the joy of life which thrilled me all through the day and made my nightly tasks so much less irksome than they had ever been; yes, and often made them a pleasure. Was it an awakening or a moral decay? I did not know. I only knew that I was changed in every way … my thwarted girlhood was behind me, and in my dawning womanhood I felt that somewhere and somehow I should demand from life the things that had been denied me.[39]

Madeleine is consistently confident and self-reliant in her narrative, but from this point on she becomes increasingly independent and ambitious.

We have seen how Canadians represented prostitutes as a social evil and blight on the community, but seeing Canada represented by the prostitute herself is a relatively new reading experience that bears some attention. Even though Madeleine comes to Canada already a seasoned prostitute with experience of many brothels, in the new setting she finds that her experience of prostitution itself changes: she likes the customers more, she feels better about herself, and she experiences the landscape as an artist would, with a feeling of awe and inspiration. Madeleine should not be taken as a wholly typical case (she worked mainly in high-end brothels and eventually became an owner and businesswoman, always avoiding the industry's more brutal side), but she nevertheless offers her story as partially representative of the prostitute's life, and through her eyes we see that even for the prostitute the Canadian West held a romantic allure as a land of opportunity whose physical beauty somehow promised personal fulfilment.

After a holiday in Banff, Madeleine decides to stay in Canada: "At the end of my month in Banff I had decided to remain in the Northwest Territory, for here was the land of opportunity. With a small capital I could open a house in some one of the busy towns, and in two years have a working capital of twenty thousand dollars. I would then be independent."[40] Madeleine was exceptional among prostitutes for her business acumen, her intellectual pursuits, and her remarkable independence. Nevertheless, for a single woman in her twenties supported only by her own earnings to thus calmly contemplate personal and financial independence is a significant accomplishment and speaks to the kind of opportunities available to prostitutes in the Canadian West. Having come from American cities where a more settled society and longstanding sex trade made for greater competition, Madeleine sizes up the women of Alberta's sex trade thus: "Not one of these women could have competed in the open market with the younger members of her profession, but here in this new country where hundreds of single men were hungering for feminine society they were making a great deal of money."[41]

Madeleine looks for the right place to open her own brothel and lights on a town in Alberta where, as mentioned earlier, the local economy is suffering for lack of a brothel and the economic benefits that accompanied a sexual-service industry. She buys an eight-room house a half-mile from any other dwelling but within the official town limits. Her opening night draws a virtual stampede of local men from all walks of life, and in true Canadian fashion the event coincides with the worst blizzard of the year:

"For three days we were marooned. I turned my house into a life-saving station and kept the lights burning all night. Four wayfarers lost on the prairie saw the light and came to us. It is certain they would have perished had they not seen it. One at a time they straggled in, and we nursed their frost-bitten feet and hands and shared our food with them."[42] Madeleine's house does stellar business. She quickly hires another woman, a pianist, and an assistant for the houseboy, and she builds additions onto the house to create two more rooms and a ballroom.

Madeleine runs her house successfully for about five years but eventually grows sickened by the life and develops a self-destructive bent – gambling away much of her capital and contracting a drinking habit. When she realizes that enough is enough, she abruptly leaves the house, turning it over to her housekeeper and friend, never to return. This is the conclusion of her narrative, but in an afterword she mentions the difficulty of exiting the sex trade:

> The woman who marries well has few difficulties placed in her path by society. A husband is a visible means of support and covers a multitude of dead sins. It is the woman who goes forth alone to fight for her soul who finds every hand against her and every door of opportunity closed in her face. She is cut off from the world she knew; and the larger world, outside the door of the brothel, seeks to drive her back, as if she were a wild beast who had strayed from her cage.[43]

Ultimately, we are left with the sense that Madeleine overcomes these difficulties, finds friends who don't judge her for her past, and gains enough security and stability to write her 300-page autobiography. The accusatory tone of her afterword is telling, however, for she also uses this space to openly critique the dominant representations of prostitution in her time, speaking directly to the construction of the white-slave narratives and providing an account of the prostitute's own view of the matter that is highly unusual and instructive. Although Madeleine says that when she was working – at the turn of the century – the white-slave myth was not in evidence, at the time when she is writing, presumably 1917-18, it is ubiquitous, its dominance challenged only by the new scientific and juridical discourses of juvenile delinquency and feeblemindedness. She strongly contests all of these, starting with white slavery: "I do not know anything about the so-called white-slave trade, for the simple reason that no such thing exists,"[44] and she continues, "It was left for the enlightened twentieth century to create the Great American Myth. 'White slavery is abroad in our land! Our daughters are being trapped and violated and held as prisoners and sold for fabulous sums (a flattering unction, this), and no woman is safe.'[45] This is a lovely moment where we hear a real prostitute playfully mimicking the dominant discourse about her in order to render this controlling voice ridiculous and undermine its authority using humour. Her parenthetical, as though *sotto voce*, note about the flattering aspect of being worth "fabulous sums" is presented with a wry humour particular to her experience as a prostitute well aware of her market value, and it simultaneously comments precisely on the sensational rhetoric and its absurdist tendencies. Through all her travels, Madeleine claims never to have encountered a real victim of white slavery, so based on her own experience she argues that it never existed. It is perhaps in her interest to suggest this, so the historical record remains contradictory, but she provides a certain amount of support for the argument that white slavery, if it existed at all, was marginal to most of the sex trade.

With a narrator as successful and articulate as Madeleine, it might be easy to romanticize the life of the frontier prostitute, but her accomplishments are balanced by a great deal of adversity and suffering. Venereal disease, alcoholism, pregnancy and abortion, social ostracism, police harassment, as well as her feelings of disgust toward the male customers all enter into her account. These were hazards that every sex worker faced; they may have made more money than women in other occupations, but their lives were certainly not easy. It is worth noting, however, that the terrible physical danger faced by present-day prostitutes in the West is not a part of Madeleine's story; nothing in her recounted experience could be described as life-threatening. So while her story may be taken as partly representative of the prostitute's life in 1900, her experience is nevertheless a highly particular one. Although her choices are severely influenced by financial necessity, she also has other more personal reasons for pursuing the life and career that she does. At one stage, Madeleine herself has the opportunity to marry a man who is loving, wealthy, willing to forgive her past life and be a father to the child she is carrying, but despite loving him in return, she refuses, demonstrating a spirit of independence impressive for a woman of her time: "His was a strong, dominant nature that would have molded the woman of his choice to his own will, and I was as unmoldable as any girl possibly could be. Young though I was, I sensed that indomitable will, and I had no desire to beat out my own individuality against it."[46] Madeleine's life as a prostitute and as a woman reflects the tenuous balance between the experience of intense suffering where bare survival is at stake and the exercise of a strong will that admits no compromise. For this reason, her story is a useful reminder that figures like the prostitute or the working girl cannot be reduced to either pathetic victim or invincible heroine, but occupy a range of positions not easily predictable.

## DELINQUENCY AND FEEBLE-MINDEDNESS: CONSTRUCTING THE BAD GIRL

As Victorian character-types like the fallen woman began to lose their cultural relevance in the self-consciously modern world of twentieth-century cities, a newly scientific tone began to dominate the rhetoric on young female sexuality. The white-slave stories were slowly replaced by studies of the "feebleminded" girl and the female delinquent; young women's morality and purity were still the central issues, but social scientists veiled their moralizing in scientific terminology. This type of reform effort particularly irritated Madeleine, who once again aptly summarized the situation by mimicking their discourse:

> Above the tumult of the white-slave myth promulgators the voice of pseudo-science is striving to make itself heard. "These poor creatures are feeble-minded, they are the ripe and noxious product of poverty and degeneracy; this is the fertile and only soil in which they are produced. We must build institutions, that they may neither contaminate our own pure offspring nor propagate their kind."[47]

As a child of poverty who became a long-time prostitute, Madeleine speaks from the category that these scientists were attempting to consolidate – a category that automatically disqualified its members from speaking for themselves as rational subjects. By so deftly assuming the institutional voice herself, she mocks its pretensions to authority. Her derision of the project and her contempt for those involved is clear, especially in her use of the term "pseudo-science," which gestures toward the partly unconscious habit in many reformers of cloaking class and gender bias in an aura of scientific objectivity. She also emphasizes their institutional agenda; by pathologizing young women, medical authorities could exert a degree of control not available in the disciplining of sane, law-abiding individuals. The white-slave panic provided a useful morality narrative for arguments connecting working girls and prostitution, and the rhetoric of

female feeble-mindedness took up where these stories left off, bringing
in the authority of science and, with the construction of the "juvenile
delinquent," the arm of the law.

In 1912 the Moral and Social Reform Council of British Columbia
issued a report entitled "Social Vice in Vancouver." The agenda of the
report was to describe the city's vice problem and prescribe a solution –
namely the wholesale suppression of prostitution as opposed to the quasi
toleration of the existing red-light district then located on Alexander
Street. The report was one part of the ongoing dispute in Vancouver over
police policy toward prostitution. Because the police knew that banning a
red-light district would result only in the scattering of the sex trade across
the city, and as they likely realized the important role of the sex industry in
the economic and social relations of a city with a disproportionate number
of single working-class men, they would have preferred to turn a blind
eye to activities in the Alexander Street area. As Greg Marquis argues,
"the police better than anyone knew that the tenements of Chinatown
and the rooming-houses, cheap hotels, beer parlours, and bawdy-houses
of the downtown core were essential to Vancouver's racial and class
relations. The 'underworld' not only catered to the needs of a large
part of the unskilled, seasonal working class and the city's largest racial
minority, it also provided employment for hundreds if not thousands."[48]
But increasingly organized reform groups in Vancouver and across the
continent were exerting pressure on lawmakers and police to suppress
the sex trade and to outlaw brothels. John McLaren has documented the
patterns of enforcement of Canada's prostitution laws, and he shows an
increase in arrests in the reform era, peaking in the period 1914-16.[49]

While Vancouver's moral-reform report advocated the increased
suppression of the sex industry – a project ostensibly focused on already-
practising prostitutes – a significant portion of the document addresses the
more general populace of young working-class women, representing the
whole category as dangerously close to (if not virtually interchangeable
with) prostitutes proper. In *Toronto's Girl Problem,* Carolyn Strange
attributes the social consternation over unruly young women in part to
the rapid increase in the number of single women who flocked to the
city for work, making Toronto's population more than half female.
Vancouver, by comparison, was always disproportionately male, so it is
somewhat surprising that girls were even numerous enough to constitute
a "problem," but as the report reveals, when it came to morality, girls
were trouble:

> Our detention officer says that there is an enormous amount of vice going
> on with young girls in the city ... Girls of the age of 14 to 16 years have
> been known to leave home and stay away for days. Their employers have
> no means of knowing where they are residing. They register their home
> address, and when there is no home control they go where they please. The
> ruin in which such a course must end is only too evident.[50]

The mention of employers identifies working girls as the specific problem
here, their freedom from "home control" tantamount to delinquency
and vice. The story of employers having home addresses for working
girls where they were not to be found is revealing of the pressure to
identify even the wage-earning woman with the home, but employers
often required addresses because they preferred to hire girls who lived
with family rather than independent women; they could then justify
not paying a living wage. Naturally, some independent women would
therefore supply a false address to secure employment. The working girls'
absence from these listed homes mentioned in the report could be due
to this or any number of reasons, but the reform literature consistently
reduced complexity or indeterminacy to a single conclusion: vice.

Working conditions, poor wages, and rooming houses for working girls
all come under attack in the report as "causes contributing to the Social
Evil," strengthening the assumption that young working-class women were
everywhere in moral peril, that their way of life was in itself tantamount
to vice, and that many were unable to resist temptation. This is why the
report states, as though with a sigh of relief, "A most valuable improvement
was made in the law when the government secured legislation for the new
Industrial School. A girl can now be taken into detention without having
gone to the length of actual crime."[51] The report refers here to the Juvenile
Delinquents Act, which was passed in 1908, allowing for a new kind of
legislative control over youth. Carolyn Strange and Tina Loo outline the
peculiarities of this Act designed especially for a select group: "With the
exception of the 1876 consolidated Indian Act, it was the first statute to
prescribe a distinct style of justice for a subgroup of Canadians ... Children
could be charged with ill-defined offences which, if committed by adults,
did not amount to criminal acts. Consequently, youngsters faced the
possibility of ending up in juvenile court for 'incorrigibility,' being beyond
parental control, and 'delinquency.'"[52] As Indiana Matters documents in
her article on Vancouver's Industrial Home for Girls, the rationalization for
incarcerating young, mostly working-class girls depended on their being

criminalized and pathologized for infractions that would never count as
real crimes if perpetrated by adult citizens: "It is quite evident that actual
crime had little or nothing to do with the reasons why most female juvenile
delinquents were imprisoned during this period."[53] Matters calculates that
of all the young women admitted to the Industrial Home, roughly 88 percent were charged with moral offences and "incorrigibility," an indefinite
term applied to any range of behaviour considered beyond the control
of the parents. As far as the authorities were concerned, as is evident in
the moral-reform report, most female offences related – or were made to
relate – to sexual misconduct and immorality. Staying out all night, for
instance, is frequently mentioned in literature on female delinquency
as something obviously synonymous with prostitution and vice. But as
Matters also points out, although some of the women may have engaged
in prostitution on some level and most had been sexually active, "many
of those charged with incorrigibility and immorality were sexually active
with only one partner and several had asked permission to marry the men
with whom they were involved."[54] Once again, there is an unwillingness
to distinguish between different degrees of sexual activity, so premarital
sex between partners willing to marry warranted the same punishment as
prostitution.

In fact, one expert on female delinquency created a special category of
delinquency that utterly conflates prostitution with regular consensual sex.
In her 1921 article in *Social Welfare*, Lucy Brooking, the superintendent of
an industrial school for girls in Toronto, identified three different kinds of
female delinquents: first, the feebleminded; second, "the girl who has not
been immoral, but who is virtually unmanageable"; and third, "the smart
bad. This type is growing more pronounced, and is usually a product of city
life. A few years ago, commercial prostitutes were found even among these
very young girls, but of late, promiscuous prostitution, with no end in view,
except a wild and lawless time, seems to be growing."[55] The "smart bad," in
other words, is a prostitute who takes no payment for her services – meaning
a woman who is sexually active by choice. Today, the difference between
being a sexually active single woman and a prostitute is obvious, nor does it
seem likely that the "smart bad" would have considered herself a prostitute,
but in the first two decades of the twentieth century, social critics almost
went out of their way to ignore and confuse variations in sexual conduct.
A militant urge to contain the shifting cultural norms of the working class
clearly motivated reform groups, who looked upon the young working-class
woman as symbolic of the promiscuous tendencies of urban working life.

As in the case of the white-slave trade and prostitution, female delinquency was consistently perceived to be a problem related primarily to working-class youth, who were habitually suspected of sexual promiscuity. Lucy Brooking demonstrates this class specificity when she identifies "Industrial conditions" as one of the main causes of female delinquency:

> In these days the young girl is more thrown out, more exposed, more dependent as a wage earner, than was the girl of a score years ago. In a case where a very young girl had been out at all hours of the night, and with very doubtful company, resulting in a ghastly downfall, I suggested to the mother, who was a decent woman, that she should have insisted on proper hours and right company. She replied that she could not say much to the young daughter, because "she brings in the rent."[56]

Under the heading of "Industrial conditions," one expects to find commentary on working conditions, long hours, poor wages, or the intermingling of men and women in the workplace, but here, the "industrial condition" posing a problem is the working girl herself; the young daughter's earning power directly undermines parental authority, suggesting a virtual cause-and-effect relationship between female employment and delinquency. And delinquency, for women, always meant sex.

White-slave narratives had warned girls against entering the danger zones of the city, the workplace, and the dance hall while recuperating a degree of innocence for the naive working girl and the unwilling prostitute inveigled into the trade by deceptive procurers. But women's continued entrance into urban workplaces, accompanied by their decidedly independent approach to leisure pursuits and sexual activity, offended a conservative middle class, whose members developed newly modern forms of discourse to condemn women's apparently wilful defiance of feminine convention. The young women admitted to institutions such as Vancouver's Industrial Home for Girls suffered the consequences of this class, age, and gender conflict, but for every one of those unlucky enough to get caught, several more would have eluded authorities and cheerfully pursued cultural and sexual alternatives unthinkable to the previous generation.

The conceptual association between working-class women and prostitutes reinforced the tendency to treat wage-earning women as a moral problem, a tendency that denied their function as economic players. In western cities such as Vancouver, moreover, a thriving population of prostitutes among proportionally few women likely enhanced the association between working-class women and sexual misconduct. Yet it was precisely the frontier culture and economy of the city that made prostitution a crucial part of economic growth and social relations. Nevertheless, attempts to denigrate both mainstream women's work and sexual-service work were deliberate and sustained. Both white-slave narratives and the rhetoric of delinquency invoked the symbolic figure of the prostitute as the limit case of female vice, and both tied prostitution to the working girl. But these efforts to police female independence could not wholly inhibit women whose paid labour and cultural pursuits were transforming gender relations and sexual norms.

## chapter 4

# Girls on Strike

I n 1918 a protracted strike by laundry workers was in the news in Vancouver. The laundry workers had formed a union shortly before the strike with the help of Helena Gutteridge, and they struck for better wages and union recognition at a time of significant labour unrest in British Columbia. Only a month before the strike, labour leader Albert "Ginger" Goodwin was shot and killed, having fled to Vancouver Island to avoid the draft. The police officer who shot him claimed it was self-defence, but many thought Goodwin had been murdered for his labour politics, and a spontaneous twenty-four-hour strike by organized labour ensued.[1] Helena Gutteridge was on the scene when Vancouver's returned soldiers, deeming the strike unpatriotic, stormed the Labour Temple and attempted to push one of its occupants out the window. While a stenographer bravely stood before the window to block the soldiers' attack, Gutteridge reflected with some fear on the three hundred dollars in her purse – the union dues of the recently organized laundry workers.[2] The laundry strike thus took place in a context of tense labour politics, only months before the Winnipeg General Strike would spread across the West to ignite already bitter animosities between business and labour.

For the young, newly unionized laundry women in this era of high-spirited protest, the strike had its hardships and its triumphs, many of them typical of the struggles of working women involved in labour disputes in this period. This chapter looks at working girls involved in labour activism and examines how they were portrayed in the newspaper accounts of the day. The history of women's involvement in the labour movement was, for a time, overlooked by historians, who were swayed by the assumption that the labour movement was a male effort and that women were difficult to organize and hardly ever participated in unions or strikes. Happily, these oversights have been rectified. The study of women's labour activism in Canada is a thriving area of scholarship, and the participation of women in unions in the West is a recognized part of the story, with its major leaders, such as Helen Armstrong of Winnipeg and Helena Gutteridge of Vancouver, deservedly profiled and biographized.[3] This chapter draws on this important scholarship but does not seek to do the same thing. Rather, I focus on certain aspects of the working girl's labour activism that were of particular interest to observers of her time and that perhaps tell us something about the representational politics that surrounded her. Two aspects in particular seem to stand out from the newspaper coverage of the unionized working girl: fun and violence. Young, single, and often new to the culture of organized labour, working girls seem to have expressed their solidarity and "spirit" in ways that reflected the active youth culture most familiar to them: they organized dances. Press coverage highlighted the many social events organized by union women, and in the process it often romanticized these dancing strikers. What the media found more surprising in women on strike was the species of fervour with which they joined demonstrations and even became violent on the picket lines. Press coverage reported physical violence such as damaging property and intimidating or attacking strike-breakers, as well as less physical but still violent conduct such as jeering, cursing, and throwing eggs. On the one hand, there is the more traditional and stereotypically feminine expression of support in the organization of socials and dances and, on the other, the ostensibly unfeminine violence of raucous female strikers. This chapter explores this unlikely mixture as a way to address the representational and perhaps even the real complexity of the working girl's political activism.

My analysis centres on two cities known for their intense labour activism: Winnipeg and Vancouver. And I focus in particular on 1918 and 1919, when tensions were at a peak.

Joining a union was unusual for members of the female workforce, for many things made the labour movement and the female gender somewhat allergic to one another. It is telling, for example, that Vancouver laundry women had only just been unionized when they first went on strike. Women workers confined to a limited set of unskilled occupations didn't have contact with the kind of longstanding, established unions of skilled male workers. For skilled craftsmen, union belonging and loyalty had a long history and an established culture, so for those within the trade, as Todd McCallum notes, "entry into the craft fraternity was seen as marking the transition from youth to manhood."[4] Women had no such tradition to draw upon, and entry into unions was not this natural initiation but was, in many cases, something novel, unfamiliar, and perhaps even unfeminine. In contrast to the male experience, where union membership was paired so easily with the acquisition of manliness, for women a tradition of female acquiescence to male authority made conflict with male employers that much more challenging. Added to this were other deterrents. Unskilled women often found themselves in job ghettos involving work that was gruelling and monotonous, and as a result they often didn't stay in one job for very long, opting instead to "vote with their feet" and try something else. This kind of rapid turnover made unionization difficult. Many of these monotonous jobs also took place in isolation from one another; domestic servants, for instance, all working in their separate houses, had no automatic meeting ground, so joining together as an organization was highly unlikely. Another major impediment to female unionization were women's domestic responsibilities. These would be particularly onerous for women who were married or had children to support with or without a husband, for finding time to attend meetings would be next to impossible; needless to say, the opposite was true for the married union man, whose wife's domestic work enabled his union activity. Most working women of the time were young and single, but the idea that their workplace experience was a temporary stage ending with marriage also mitigated against their union involvement, for it meant that they weren't taken seriously as committed and permanent members of the workforce, and they themselves often expected (perhaps a little too optimistically) that they would leave work upon marriage, so they didn't see union membership as a priority. As if these obstacles weren't enough to seriously dampen women's labour activism, the problem was compounded by the male labour movement's deep ambivalence about adding women to their ranks. As Ruth Frager puts it, "In their struggles against employers, many female workers were faced with much less than total solidarity from their 'fellow' workers and 'brother' unionists."[5]

Frager aptly notes the language of male unionism here; suffused in terminology of brotherhood and militancy, the male labour movement was consciously and unconsciously exclusive in its cultivated men's-club atmosphere. Even when granted entry into men's organizations, women were often denied the same members' voting privileges, and less formal aspects of the culture excluded them too. Union meetings were typically conducted in an atmosphere figuratively thick with male bonding and literally thick with smoke. Convention of the day deemed it largely inappropriate for men to smoke in the presence of women, and women thus felt unwelcome and uncomfortable in this scene. Janice Newton documents the controversy that ensued when women pressed men to ban smoking at meetings; their requests were seldom attended to.[6]

This is not to say that men were uniformly hostile to the unionization of women workers. Often, they recognized the need to recruit women into existing male unions so that strikes would be more effective; the male electrical workers at a telephone company, for instance, could strike with much greater effect if the telephone operators joined them and thus paralyzed a city's communications. And where a union was created by and consisted predominantly of women, as was the case with the Vancouver laundry workers, the labour movement and its press could be very supportive, collecting donations from other unions and publicizing the strikers' demands. As Gillian Creese has shown, women employed in traditionally female-defined jobs were more easily accepted by trade unionists than those in male-defined fields.[7] But where women threatened to take men's jobs, for example by doing the same work for lower wages, things were less friendly, and in such cases the labour movement did not hesitate to mobilize the domestic ideology that women's true place was in the home. Helena Gutteridge was incensed when she saw the male labour movement – which often cast itself as the chivalrous protector of vulnerable girls "forced" into industry – turning on women out of blatant self-interest, and she aptly summarizes the back-and-forth quality of the male labour movement's attitude toward women: "First she shall not join the union as in early days, then she must, because his interests are at stake, then, finding that does not keep him top dog, she must leave the trade entirely alone – it belongs by divine right to him, Oh, Chivalry, thy name is man!"[8] Even when women were encouraged to join an existing male union to ensure solidarity within an industry, they were often relegated to "auxiliary" status and denied access to positions of real authority. Thus a profound ambivalence toward women's labour activism existed within the labour movement, and as Ruth Frager writes, "male craft unionists who shared this fundamental ambivalence often gave only half-hearted support to women workers' struggles."[9]

But remarkably, women did become involved in labour politics throughout Canada, and in the West they were galvanized by an often radical movement. Star Rosenthal documents women's labour activism in Vancouver, where women joined the unions of telephone operators, retail clerks, bookbinders, tailors, laundry workers, waiters and waitresses, candy-factory workers, and impressively, domestic workers, all before 1915.[10] With the arrival of Helena Gutteridge in 1911, Vancouver's women workers gained a remarkable leader, and as in the case of Helen Armstrong in Winnipeg, this kind of female leadership seems to have made a major difference for women's participation in unions and labour activism. Other parts of the West saw less union involvement. Christine Smillie examines women workers in Saskatchewan, and here, given the province's smaller population and its less developed labour movement, women's participation was more hampered. But she does document strikes by telephone operators in 1918, by teachers in 1921, and by waiters and waitresses in 1918, 1919, and 1927.[11] Winnipeg is another matter. Mary Horodyski documents women's involvement in the Winnipeg General Strike of 1919, where, led by Helen Armstrong, women played an invaluable role providing meals for needy strikers, both male and female, and where they also seem to have divided their time between organizing social events and participating in violent picket-line protest.[12]

## THE VANCOUVER LAUNDRY WORKERS' STRIKE, 1918

The laundry workers' strike in Vancouver arose during a time of great activity in women's unionism, led by Helena Gutteridge. A tailor who had come to Vancouver in 1911, Gutteridge was deeply committed to the labour movement and to women's inclusion within it. She involved herself in the middle-class suffrage movement too, for she saw female suffrage and female unionism as two connected projects: "The political organization of women and the organization of women into trade unions, although two separate and independent movements, are nevertheless supplementary and necessary to each other, if the economic freedom of women is to be obtained."[13] But not everyone saw the connection that she did, especially when it meant seeing across class lines, and as her biographer Irene Howard notes, "the ubiquitous Miss Gutteridge was never fully accepted socially by the middle-class women she worked with.

She was, after all, a wage worker, a tailor."[14] Once women gained the vote in 1916, Gutteridge turned her efforts more fully to women's labour activism, with great effect. While organizing the laundry workers into a union and aiding them in their subsequent strike, she had various other projects underway: she aided in a strike of waiters and chambermaids employed by the Hotel Vancouver, organized a union for office workers, and worked on the creation of minimum-wage legislation, which would ultimately be implemented in the laundry workers' favour.[15] The laundry workers had only just unionized when their employers demanded that they leave the union or be fired. In defiance, they went on strike for an increase in wages and union recognition. The strike had the support of the city's labour movement, and many unions from across the city contributed to the strike fund so that they wouldn't be pressured to end the action for lack of income. Since members of the Laundry Workers' Union were mostly women working in an unskilled, female-defined industry, they weren't considered to be taking jobs away from men, and with the element of competition removed, organized labour could be generous.

The raucous behaviour of the Vancouver laundry workers on the picket lines would be matched only by the clamorous festivities of their dances. One week into the strike, the *Vancouver Daily World* reported that "pickets were out at all the laundries and in one or two instances, where drivers not in the union left their laundries to make their usual calls, they were followed in autos by girl strikers who occupied their time hurling jeers and catcalls at the non-union members."[16] The picket lines were a clearly marked space for protest, and young female strikers seem to have relished the opportunity to forsake conventional codes of feminine restraint to carry out a sometimes violent vengeance against employers and "scabs." Early on, both the *Vancouver Province* and the *Vancouver Daily World* reported on requests from laundry owners for increased police presence: "Inasmuch as damage to person and property had resulted, according to the reports presented, the laundry proprietors wanted official assurance of strengthened police protection."[17] The owners had reported that, among other things, strike-breakers had been threatened, and a person "who drove up intending to leave his bundle of 'washing' at the plant, was jeered and 'booed,' and hustled back to his machine by a throng, and his bundle of laundry was scattered and kicked about the street."[18] As well, "a fireman was said to have been pursued to a street car, when the conductor was advised to 'throw that scab off.'"[19] At the same time, there were also accounts of more light-hearted picket-line action: "Some householder, tired of using his old collars and shirts, drove down to the Cascade in his auto with the laundry parcel aboard. A number of girls climbed on his car to urge him to go away and take his belongings with him. 'They climbed all over him,' said Mr. McArthur. He went. He took the girls too. Hitting it up at thirty miles an hour he bowled off downtown, giving the young women a regular joyride."[20] Interestingly, the story in the *Daily World* that reported this same joyride began on a much more sinister note: "'You are flirting with death,' a striker or strike sympathizer was alleged to have told a laundry employee who persisted in staying at his work." We aren't told the gender of the speaker here, but the media coverage of this mainly female-identified strike nevertheless demonstrates the uneasy combination of potentially serious violence and markedly less serious aspect of fun, both of which were also evident in other coverage of young women on strike. Reporters are of course motivated by the desire to tell a good story and to sell newspapers, so their dwelling on the sensational aspect of female violence is not surprising, but there seems to have been a genuine curiosity about the girl striker and how she conducted herself on the picket line – and the stories produced highlighted not only the violent but also the more playful side of this youthful female protest.

In fact, female violence didn't always come from the strikers alone. The day following the reports of scuffles and joyrides, the labour newspaper the *BC Federationist* reported rather gleefully on female violence coming from the employers' side; a laundry owner's wife had struck a union driver: "First blood was drawn during the week, when a driver was struck over the head by Mrs. Morrow, of the Star Laundry." The report moves on quickly, however: "This case has been aired in the police court, and is recorded in another place in this issue. Many local unions are contributing to the strike fund raised by the Trades and Labour Council on behalf of the employees on strike, and a whist drive has been arranged for Monday evening; tickets for which can be obtained at the Labor Temple, and all members of organized labor should take one or more tickets and assist the striking Laundry Workers in their efforts to secure decent conditions."[21] The labour press tended not to report on violence by striking women, and here, after such stories appear in other papers, it counters with female violence by the employers' class. It seems that Mrs. Morrow came to the aid of her husband, a laundry owner, in a scuffle between him and a male picketer. The politics of representation are clearly different in the labour press compared to the mainstream press; the *BC Federationist* covered the laundry workers' demands, publicized the poor wages that they received, and advertised the social events with which the union supplemented the strike fund. The mainstream press covered the strike less regularly and was more interested in violent conflict or in picket-line high jinks like the swarming of the car and the joyride. But the labour press was also interested in showing the striking women having fun, so while attending to the seriousness of the union's demands, it underlined the innocent amusements of the strike – the social events and dances put on by the women's union. Both kinds of media thus showed an interest in observing and portraying the striking women, and both paid their own kinds of attention to the aspects of fun and violence involved in the strike. An overall view suggests that although both things were taking place, and although both had a political component, they seldom received coverage in the same place or in the same way, as though putting two such disparate forms of female political expression together was a conceptual challenge not easily approached. Yet when one reads the different papers together, one gets the sense that women were jeering and cursing from the picket lines all day and dancing all night. Although these are presented in separate accounts, there is an uneasy combination of socially disturbing female violence on the one hand, and socially appropriate event organizing on the other, both of which entered into women's labour politics.

Because violence by strikers, though perhaps somewhat more surprising in women, is a common feature of labour protests, one might be tempted to read the violence as political and the social events as an "auxiliary" aspect. But there is evidence that for women unionists, social events were important to their political expression and to their demonstration of solidarity. Linda Kealey comments on how women's labour activism often involved a "redefinition of 'political' activity": "women's mobilization in the early twentieth century resulted in a mixture of political expressions, some of which have not been recognized and legitimized as 'political.'"[22] I am interested in how women's political and labour activism was expressed through less formal, more social avenues – through dances, whist drives, gatherings, and events that blended politics with leisure in ways that may not always have been intelligible to a male labour movement with its own tradition of militancy.

Helena Gutteridge seems to have known that the social side of women's labour activism was essential. Whereas male unionists gathered in the smoky settings congenial to them, the suffrage organizing of middle-class women's groups took place at parlour meetings followed by afternoon tea; both settings blended the social and the political, involving and including some while subtly excluding others; the afternoon teas appealed to the society women of the middle class, but they totally shut out wage-earning women, who were at work during these hours. Gutteridge saw that working women needed their own kind of meeting ground, and she deliberately broke ranks with the middle-class suffrage movement when she organized the Evening Work Committee, a gathering for working-class and wage-earning women interested in suffrage and unionism, which met in the downtown Labor Temple on Wednesday nights.[23] This meeting venue was remarkably productive; with average attendance of well over a hundred, it formed its own suffrage league and spawned union initiatives among women whose workplaces often isolated them from one another.

It was at this time that the Domestic Employees Union was started; reporting an initial membership of fifty after only one month, the union sought to expand: "Owing to the long hours of domestic employment and the tiring nature of the work it is by no means an easy matter for the girls to come in to register. The union however, intends to establish a 'walking bureau' to meet the exigencies of the case."[24] Star Rosenthal writes about this unusual female union, which wanted to reorganize domestic work along industrial lines by limiting the hours and demanding better working conditions and a minimum wage, and which had even more innovative long-term plans: the union imagined creating a boarding house for its members so that they could live together away from their workplaces and "further proposed that the union shall keep on record the nature of every situation in which any of its members are working, or have worked."[25] In other words, a record would be kept of how Vancouver's middle-class society wives treated their help. One can only imagine the goldmine that such files would have been in the historical record of Vancouver's business class, but sadly the union did not survive long enough to implement its plan. The union's leader, Lillian Coote, however, suggests the likely tenor of such a report when she remarks that often enough, when a domestic worker secured a position, "she may find that what the woman wants is not a human being, but a machine that will scrub floors and clean windows from early morn till dewy eve and at the same time tolerate the persistent bull-dosing which only some women are capable of handing out to their help."[26] That Gutteridge's Evening Work Committee helped to spawn this lively union of workers so characteristically difficult to organize demonstrates its political efficacy, and when you consider that the women whom Lillian Coote singled out as bulldozers were of the same class as

Gutteridge's erstwhile sister suffragettes, you realize how simple attention to the social detail of meeting times could lead to radically different kinds of politics. That Gutteridge both recognized and acted upon this to great political effect demonstrates how important the social side of things could be to women's feminist and labour activism.

Gutteridge continued on this path by creating in 1915 the Union Women's Social Club "to promote social intercourse between the members of organized labor and interest self-supporting women in the principles of unionism." This organization was initiated with a St. Patrick's Day dance followed by a meeting, and its mandate was explicitly social and political: "The labor movement will never be a great success unless the women workers are actively engaged therein, as well as the men, and it is the hope of the committee that the formation of the Social Club will tend in the direction of bringing women more closely in touch with the principles of unionism, and so help the labor movement as a whole."[27] The club proposed a membership drawn from "women trade unionists, self-supporting women, and the wives of trade-unionists." It would thus comprise a "women's auxiliary," a group typically consisting of the wives of union men, and would add to this women workers and women union members as well – making it almost a "One Big Women's Union" – and her method was explicitly social. The club doesn't seem to have had the follow-up success of the Evening Work Committee, but it demonstrates the link that some, like Gutteridge, sought to develop between women's social and political organizing.

Early on in a strike that seemed destined for success, the laundry workers' first dance was something of a coup: "Fifteen hundred tickets sold, $600 added to the local treasury, and a record breaking crowd in attendance briefly sums up the whist drive and dance given by the Laundry Workers Union, Local 37, in aid of the strike fund ... At 11 o'clock crowds were certainly pouring in, and it was necessary to call in a second orchestra in order to accommodate the great throng. In less time than it takes to tell, a second dance was in progress in the hall previously used by the whist drive." The reporter sees in this event not merely a simple social gathering but a strong affirmation of the labour movement itself: "Every branch of organized labor turned out in great style and numbers. It did one's heart good to witness such a feeling of fellowship that existed in that hall. It might have been that Labor was celebrating some great victory. In fact that is just what it was. An overwhelming proof of unionism."[28] Women union members, often new to the labour movement and to its established "brotherhoods," were seldom recognized for their political activism, and perhaps part of the problem had to do with men's and women's different styles of organizing and participation. Women may not have felt welcome in the smoke-filled rooms thick with Marxist male bonding, but they did know how to organize a dance. And while this form of political expression may have appeared frivolous to an established male leadership, some observers, such as this reporter, seem to have recognized a lively new kind of union spirit. In many ways, recognizing the political merit in dances would have been more challenging for union men than accepting women's picket-line violence, for clashing with strike-breakers and police was, after all, a standard aspect of strike activity. That a dance could so powerfully signify union solidarity suggests that the social bent characteristic of women's union involvement was a valuable unifying force. And insofar as dances provided an important source of income for strike funds, the material connection between social pursuits and organized protest was quite direct. The dance was such a success that it was quickly followed up with a second event, with even greater attendance. Publicity noted that "the catering is in the able hands of the Cooks, Waiters and Waitresses Union, while the 'Good Time Department' will be handled by the laundry girls themselves."[29]

The laundry strike would last four months, and as the women settled in for the protracted dispute, they got imaginative about their picket-line schemes. They exerted some moral pressure by sending a "special picket" on Sunday to the church attended by Alderman Kirk, a laundry owner. His wife was so offended by this reminder of the strike that she fired one of her own employees for being the sister of a laundry worker.[30] As the strike dragged on and winter approached, the picketers built sheds near the laundries to shelter themselves from the rain, and their commitment garnered great respect from the *BC Federationist,* which declared, "they deserve all the praise that can be handed to them, for they are simply splendid. 'No faltering' is their motto."[31] In fact, things got somewhat out of hand. A story ran in the *Vancouver Sun* titled "Organized Crowd of 500 Attacks Laundry Workers," and another the next day in the *Province* titled "Pelted with Eggs and then Kicked" told of two events: one where a crowd of male unionists had thrown stones at female strike-breakers and another where a male picketer had allegedly pelted a female strike-breaker with eggs and then kicked her; she came to court with a visible limp. In her story, he had several girls hold her while he plastered her with eggs and then kicked her, whereas his story was that he never kicked her but rather had seen her fall onto a picket fence while the other girls were chasing her down the hill.[32] The union had to fund his defence, a significant drain on its resources as the strike dragged on, and ultimately he was convicted. Girl strikers, meanwhile, continued to earn a reputation for violence on the picket lines, notably aided and abetted by their male fellow unionists.

The laundry workers' strike was further influenced by the specificity of women's forms of labour activism, in that the settlement of the strike was arbitrated in part by the newly established Minimum Wage Board. Helena Gutteridge, Mary Ellen Smith, and Helen MacGill were the force behind this legislation in British Columbia, and the other western provinces were engaged in the same process. Alberta was the first to pass the legislation in 1917, British Columbia and Manitoba followed in 1918, and Saskatchewan in 1919.[33] Using the tactics of moral suasion, advocates of the minimum wage for women argued that young women, the most vulnerable of workers, were the nation's future mothers and needed a basic subsistence wage to protect their health and prevent them from turning to prostitution. These arguments positioned working girls as symbolic of the nation and its future, and as one writer for the women's column in the *BC Federationist* put it, "Women cannot be overworked and underpaid without being underfed and affecting the future race."[34] The Minimum Wage Board settled the wage dispute in the laundry workers' strike by establishing a minimum of $13.50 per week, actually slightly more than the union had at first demanded when the strike was declared, but this applied to women over the age of eighteen; for those under eighteen, the minimum was set at $8.00.[35] The union also remained on strike for a short while after the wage settlement to try to secure union recognition and a closed shop, but in this it was unsuccessful, and, with union resources strained by court cases, the laundry workers returned to work four months after the strike began.

The laundry workers' strike is a fascinating narrative of gender, for the female-dominated Laundry Workers' Union drew on a variety of cultural resources to make its protest a success. The strike came at a time when the labour movement at large was in a fighting mood, and the women involved seem to have enjoyed the opportunity to forsake conventional restraint in order to take up newly politicized identities as female strikers. Women's presence on public streets was challenging to many onlookers of the time, but to the striking women it would seem that the picket lines offered a new social space outside the bounds of traditional femininity – a setting where noisy protest and even violent confrontations could be valorized as political demonstrations of loyalty and spirit. At the same time, the young female strikers adapted their own popular youth culture to fit the setting and organized some of the most successful social events that the labour movement had ever seen. While the mainstream media focused on the violent side of the strike as well as on the playfulness and fun of picket-line activity, the labour press urged the union on and consistently praised its members' spirit and publicized the great success of their dances. Drawing on a vibrant youth culture and a highly energized labour movement, young working women seem to have fashioned a political identity for themselves that drew both on a valorized gender difference and on their roles as workers, and in many ways their social gatherings and celebrations could signify political solidarity as forcefully as any traditional union meeting.

In the Vancouver sympathy strikes of 1919, telephone operators were the last to return to the job, and the Laundry Workers' Union expressed its support by organizing a dance on the operators' behalf: "The proceeds will be devoted to the aid of the Telephone Operators, who are still on strike against discrimination. That the dance will be well attended, there is no doubt; apart from the desire to assist the Telephone Operators, the reputation of the laundry workers in running social affairs makes success a certainty."[36] Given the experience that it had gained in financing its own strike through dances, the reputation of the Laundry Workers' Union preceded it, and here, its members were able to contribute financially while also providing a venue for the expression of union sympathy and female solidarity. Notably, the BC Federationist commented on the operators' strike that "the girls are showing a remarkable spirit of solidarity, considering that it is the first strike that they have been involved in."[37] In this case, however, the paper had a short memory when it came to the operators, who had struck both in 1902 and 1906;[38] admittedly, given the time lapse, these specific women were striking for the first time, but the BC Federationist's comment erases the operators' history of union participation and strike experience, suppressing the representation of working women as active and ongoing members of the labour movement and demonstrating once again a kind of mental block regarding women's political contributions. The dancing continued apace, however, as the telephone operators followed up on the laundry workers' generosity with their own event, a moonlight cruise to Bowen Island with a dance and picnic: "And as for the dancing, well, anybody who tripped the light fantastic with them at their dances during the winter can vouch for the fairy stuff that these girls are made of."[39] The struggles faced by the telephone operators were quite serious as they fought for reinstatement after the strike, and the same article that promotes the dance also mentions the donations received from other unions to support the operators' cause. What role the dances played in the politics of these often bitter conflicts is hard to say; they did contribute to the strike fund and perhaps thus capitalized on the romantic depiction of these spirited young union women. The media representations, moreover, were part of the construction of the working girl as a new and significant figure in an urban scene of social unrest. Although often represented as vulnerable innocents in need of legislative protection from heartless industrialism, they were also clearly capable of highly organized and quite forcible resistance of their own to workplace exploitation, and the media showed itself very interested in observing and portraying this female figure of social protest.

## THE WINNIPEG GENERAL STRIKE, 1919

One similarity between Winnipeg and Vancouver at this time was the presence of a strong leader in the women's labour movement. Like Helena Gutteridge, Winnipeg's Helen Armstrong had taken part in the suffrage movement and had then concentrated her efforts on women's labour activism; as she put it, "women's vote had given us the club. Now we wanted women to use it."[40] Strongly committed to the unionization of women workers, she brought new life to the Women's Labor League, first established in 1910 and taken over by Armstrong in 1917. Under Armstrong's leadership this organization held regular meetings open to women workers and unionists, providing the important meeting ground for the city's disparate women workers, and it became a member organization of the Trades and Labor Council, with Armstrong and two other women as its delegates. Thus not only did Armstrong organize women into unions of their own, but she also gained a seat for them at the table of the male labour movement, demanding that women's voices be heard there too. In the years leading up to the 1919 conflict, she was extremely busy: in 1917 she organized the Retail Clerks' Union and led them out on strike; in 1918 it was the Hotel and Household Workers' Union and the Housemaid's Union, and in 1919 the biscuit-factory workers, laundry women, and knitting-machine operators. By the time of the general strike, she was the leading figure for a whole set of predominantly female unions, all affiliated through the Women's Labor League.[41] The press in 1919 called her the "business manager of the Women's Unions."[42]

An initial underestimation by historians of women's activities in and contributions to the 1919 strike effort has been corrected by women labour historians such as Mary Horodyski and Linda Kealey. Horodyski points out the census data revealing that in Winnipeg in 1919 almost one in every four workers was a woman; and Kealey observes that although the labour movement had not always extended its efforts to organizing women workers, the new "general trend was to reach out to the previously unorganized, a trend which peaked during the labour strife of 1919."[43] Early on, women played an important role; the strike began on 15 May as five hundred telephone operators walked out, pulling the switches as they left and leaving much of the city with no phone service. The operators were joining more than five hundred female bakery and confectionary workers who were already on strike because their employer would not negotiate with the union. By the end of that day, over 20,000 workers were on strike, a number that would swell to an estimated 30,000 in all. The Central Strike Committee urged strikers from the start to avoid violence and do nothing, assuring the city that "we have no other motive than to maintain peace and order in the community,"[44] but minor incidents were soon being reported, and Helen Armstrong, who would be arrested several times during the next six weeks, was regularly before the court: "The third day of the great strike saw several clashes between men and employers. Most of it was due to picketing carried on in various parts of the city. At the Smart Woods plant factory girls created a disturbance and attacked the place and some alleged non-unionists. The police were called but made no arrests ... Mrs. Helen Armstrong, business manager of the Women's Unions, was arraigned in the police court charged with disorderly conduct on the street ... The action followed trouble at the Canada Bread Company."[45]

Women strikers were given a certain amount of special attention by women's groups like the YWCA, by Armstrong's Women's Labor League, and by the press. The need for a living wage was the central issue of the strike, and women workers were known to make even less than their male fellow strikers, so the hardship of a prolonged strike would fall hard on them if they didn't receive necessary support. The YWCA initially announced that it would provide emergency accommodation to girls still working, but soon extended the invitation to strikers as well. And Armstrong devoted the efforts of the Women's Labor League to the operation of a dining hall that would provide free meals to women strikers and meals by donation to male strikers; it opened one week into the strike and was publicized in the *Strike Bulletin* of the *Western Labor News* under the heading "No Girl Need Want for Food."[46] The dining hall reportedly served 1,200 to 1,500 free meals daily, and the Women's Labor League also provided women with cash grants to meet their rent. These efforts needed funding, and there was a Central Strike Fund as well as a Relief Committee, both of which raised funds through donations at the Labor Church and through the social events so well directed by female unions. Just five days into the strike the *Strike Bulletin* reported a meeting of the "Hello Girls and the Electrical boys," where "Doris Meakin announced that a dance had been arranged for Monday night in the Manitoba Hall, the profits from which were to go into the Central Strike Fund. The meeting was full of enthusiasm and determination to stick."[47] The dining hall did well in its requests for donations, and the *Strike Bulletin* reported that at one meeting $1,540 was collected "to feed girl strikers": "The collection of $1,540 speaks volumes. It shows that the strikers are gaining ground. Persons who have previously been indifferent to the cause of labor are becoming vitally interested and in ever increasing numbers are putting their resources behind the strike."[48] The next day a dance was held by the Modern Dance Club "in aid of the girl's cafe."[49] Women's ways of organizing seem to have had a social as well as pragmatic bent, and although efforts such as the dining hall required significant funds to operate, women organizers proved able fundraisers too. Indeed, the coverage of the $1,540 raised at one meeting suggests that the girl striker held a certain symbolic force; to support her was to support the larger movement in principle.

An incident reported in the *Strike Bulletin* builds on this emblematic quality of the girl striker. It was a report about a female "newsie." Since the young men who usually sold the city's papers on the streets were out on strike, the *Winnipeg Evening Tribune* had temporarily replaced them with young women from the paper's staff. The *Western Labor News* meanwhile, lent support to girl strikers by having them distribute its free *Strike Bulletin*. The young women seem to have relished these public jobs and identified themselves with the ideologies of their respective papers: the *Strike Bulletin* was the voice of labour and the central source of information for strikers and sympathizers; the *Tribune* cast itself as neutral but drew ire from the *Strike Bulletin,* which claimed that the *Tribune*'s sometimes faulty coverage of events showed a bias against the strikers. The women distributing the *Strike Bulletin* felt deeply hostile toward the women selling the other papers, and indeed they were encouraged by

Helen Armstrong, who would later appear in court for inciting them to violence: "Mrs. Armstrong, according to the testimony of two witnesses, told girls on strike to take newspapers away from girls 'if they were not afraid of pins,' when they asked her if it was their duty to stop the sale of newspapers on the streets."[50]

The story below about one of the *Strike Bulletin*'s girl newsies has a meta-textual quality in the way that it reports on the reporting and deliberately imbues the distribution of newspapers with symbolic and ideological import. The report appeared on 9 June, the day that the city's regular police were dismissed for refusing to sign an oath not to participate in general strikes; they were replaced by the "special police" hired under the direction of the Citizens' Committee of One Thousand, a group (of much less than a thousand) formed by Winnipeg's business leaders to oppose the strike in principle and in practice. The very next day the special police would clash with strikers in the strike's first serious outbreak of violence. Appearing on the brink of this severe escalation in the conflict, this story renders through a small event the complex tensions of the strike and the significant parts played by the *Tribune*, the *Strike Bulletin*, the Citizen's Committee, and the striking women:

### Good for the Goose, Good for the Gander

The Tribune tells us that it persuaded its female employees to go on the street and sell their paper so as to get them to the people. This was a good thing. But, when the women of the strikers sell the Labor News to get "the truth" before the people, then that is a bad thing.

Since when was it a bad thing to face the truth? Has truth become heresy to the 1,000 self-appointed celebrities of the Board of Trade?

One of these self-appointed 1,000 said to one [of] our news girls: "Go home and rest, you poor, miserable, ignorant fool!" The girl immediately challenged him to withdraw his unchivalrous statement or she would slap his face.

Her blood was hot and she further challenged him to get out from behind his pleas of loyalty, and face the facts of the strike.

Labor has come to the place where insults such as the above are deeply resented, and will long be remembered against these men to embitter the future.

Let the fight be fair. What is good for the goose is good for the gander. Womanhood is womanhood whether in silks or gingham. Let us at least, on both sides, be men enough to respect worthy women.[51]

For such a short account, there are several phases to this story. It begins with the conflict between the *Tribune* and the *Labor News*'s *Strike Bulletin*, both of which were using women to distribute their papers while suggesting that the practice was undesirable in the other. But the writer quickly turns this conflict into a question of allowing truth to prevail – the women thus become symbolic not just of their respective sides in the dispute but also of the higher principles of truth and heresy. Returning to the street level, the report tells of the exchange between the male member of the Citizens' Committee and the hot-blooded newsie, who does two things: threatens to slap his face if he doesn't withdraw his insult and exhorts him to "face the facts of the strike" – to see the other side. Her appeals thus take the form both of persuasion and intimidation but with the added element that only a female figure can bring: the honour and respect that are due a woman. The account of the girl newsie standing up to the member of the Citizens' Committee is the kind of David-and-Goliath story that nicely fitted the representational needs of the labour press to depict its worthy battle. And the girl newsie becomes a symbol for the paper itself, pleading, as does the paper, that her opponent "face the facts." The member of the Citizen's Committee, meanwhile, is doubly vilified by virtue of his antistrike beliefs and his "unchivalrous" treatment of womanhood. But her threat to slap his face and even her "further challenge" that he see her side ran very much counter to the *Strike Bulletin*'s constant warnings to strikers to remain calm and nonviolent. Considering the urgency with which it had been discouraging any and all violence in strikers, the paper's tacit approval of the young woman's threats of violence seems a little contradictory.

And there is more context too. The *Strike Bulletin* just two days earlier had stressed the nonviolent position: "We want to advise our strikers and their wives and sympathisers in every part of this city to maintain as they have done over three weeks, perfect law and order in every way. The strike committee ask that no rigs be at any time molested in any way, that the strikers do not argue with others on the streets, and that disorder of all kinds be continuously refrained from."[52] This warning appeals explicitly to both men and women, but given recent events, it was undoubtedly the wives to whom it was directed – for they had just been written up in the *Tribune*:

Women of Brooklands and Weston Thursday wrecked three delivery rigs owned by local department stores and assaulted the drivers and special policemen who accompanied to protect them ...

"We will murder you if you attempt to make deliveries in this district again," one woman warned a driver from a department store ...

A detective dispatched to find out who wrecked the rig, was unsuccessful. Women made the investigation impossible, he said.

"I wouldn't advise any man to go out there," he reported upon his return to central station. "His life is in danger, if these women find out that he is at work, or had been working during the strike," he said.

"They don't respect police officers, and apparently do anything that pleases them," he asserted.[53]

These recent events showed the violent side of women's strike activities, and the labour press, although it seldom dwelled on violence from its own strikers, clearly felt the need to gently remind its readership of the nonviolent position. So why, then, does it make a heroine of the girl newsie, whose "blood was hot" and who threatened to slap her opponent in the face? I would suggest that the story demonstrates an ambivalence in the labour press about women strikers' violence – that even though extreme acts like those of the Weston and Brooklands women needed to be checked, it found in the righteous indignation of the insulted girl striker a fitting symbol for the embattled virtue of the strike itself. A slap in the face, moreover, can be construed as a gesture of moral indignation rather than of truly destructive violence – although it is undeniably a violent act. In a way, the story of the newsie allows violence to be written and expressed and even validated, without its being coded as the "real" violent attack that typically takes place between men. The language of the article is itself markedly violent: apart from the threatened slap on the face, the girl twice "challenges" the man, "her blood was hot," the insults to labour are "deeply resented" and will "embitter the future," and the writer demands that "the fight be fair." By the end of the article, the fight has indeed returned to one between men: "Let us at least, on both sides, be men enough to respect worthy women." The story of the girl newsie thus allows for the use of violently charged rhetoric and the suggestion of violent male conflict, but it masks its combative intent by choosing to report the actions of a girl striker, whose threatened slap to the businessman's face is violence of a symbolic kind – moral rather than brutal in nature.

The conflict between business and labour suggested by the end of the article has meanwhile become a battle over manhood, with the noble voice of labour admonishing the unchivalrous business class to maintain a modicum of manly dignity in a "fair fight." Todd McCallum explores how these competing versions of manhood and masculinity became central to the rhetoric of the One Big Union: "For these men to make a claim about class was also, usually in a subtle fashion, to deploy working-class masculinities in a political manner."[54] This story clearly deploys particular constructions of both masculinity and femininity as part of its expression of political dissent. It would seem that insofar as women personified an honourable cause, those women who resorted to violence found, if not approval, at least a rhetorical esteem in the labour press. The overt violence of the Weston and Brooklands women, among others, was meanwhile covered only in the mainstream press, which registered the fierceness of the women's acts with noticeable shock and surprise.

The following day saw the first major clash between strikers and police. Mounted officers of the city's "special police" charged into the crowd of strikers and sympathizers at the corner of Portage Avenue and Main Street, and the *Tribune* reported that "some of the most troublesome members of the crowd were women."[55] A detailed account of the conflict reported that as the first horsemen were being thrown, "a woman seized the lid of a garbage can and hurled it at a horseman. Several others followed suit. The men soon joined in."[56] The paper also made mention of a woman on the scene whose "language was more expressive than elegant" and noted that "women gathered about the streets took the matters coolly, being interested spectators to the various and many fights that occurred, some of them going so far as to give advice as to further treatment."[57] The mainstream press here, as in Vancouver, was very interested in covering the women's participation in the strike, especially when it turned violent; reporters were evidently surprised by the degree of female violence that they witnessed. Occasionally, a more traditional female frailty also made its way into reports – "'They're shooting,' gasped a woman and fainted"[58] – but reports of strikers' courtroom appearances routinely included women charged with intimidation, assault, and as in Armstrong's case, inciting violence. By late June women's participation in street riots was predictable enough that the mayor issued a warning prior to the anticipated conflict at a "silent parade" of returned soldiers in support of the strike: "Any women taking part in a parade do so at their own risk."[59] The warning seems not to have been heeded. In the ensuing riot, known as Bloody Saturday, mounted police charged into the crowds, firing; one man was killed instantly, another died later of his injuries, and thirty others were seriously injured. The *Tribune* placed women at the centre of the action and wrote them into the headlines: "Isolated 'Cop' Fighting Off Crowd Is Run Down from behind by a Motor – Reporter in Thick of Fray Gives Detailed Story of the Battle – Women Are Prominent as Leaders of Belligerents."[60] The account that follows points out that "several women" had babies with them, and the shock value of the account thus comes from seeing this image of traditional motherhood on the streets in a riot. The women are further vilified as having "foreign accents," a standard refrain in the press coverage of the strike, which commonly depicted strikers as foreign radicals and "alien enemies." The incongruous coupling of familiar motherhood with dangerous otherness thus structures the account:

> There was a liberal sprinkling of women in the crowds on Main St. about the city hall. Several women with babes in their arms, refused to budge when warned off the streets. One woman with an infant which could not have been more than nine months old, advised by a male pedestrian to seek a place of safety, retorted with such a vile outburst of profanity, that the well-intentioned man turned about and beat a hasty retreat. The woman had a pronounced foreign accent.
>
> It was a woman who rushed into the street and set fire to the street car, marooned in front of the city hall. She appeared to be a foreigner. Many women of this ilk refused to budge when the special constables were clearing the streets, until they were forcibly pushed down side streets. Profanity from these women was not unusual in these cases.[61]

Profanity seems to be something that only reaches the press when women are the speakers. There is a clear shock value in the image of the cursing mother with babe in arms, and the repeated mention of the women being "foreign" further implies that such behaviour is either unacceptable or impossible in members of the "true" local community. It would seem that the image of the striking woman willing to resort to violence both verbal and physical was something deeply disturbing to reporters and observers, and this particular press representation highlights how threatening and how far outside the bounds of acceptability she was.

These profane mothers and pyromaniacs seem to inhabit an almost unthinkable space of riot and revolt, the corner of Portage and Main being the site of a battle as much over gender norms as over class warfare. But during quieter times in the strike, the same space was written of in the tame columns of the *Tribune*'s "Society Section and Woman's Magazine."

This section seldom touched on the strike, focusing instead on society ladies holding events, returning from abroad, and attending weddings as though untouched by a six-week general shut-down in the city. But one day in early June brought even the society reporters to the street, specifically to the corner of Portage and Main, to investigate the pressing question, "Who Do the Most Flirting in Winnipeg, Men or Women?" Although such a question could, presumably, be posed at any time, with or without a strike taking place, it was the presence of so many young men and women on the streets that gave the two reporters on the story (he said, she said) the perfect theatre for observation: "With so many men and girls thrown out of employment by the strike, and standing about the streets, shares in the 'Coquetry Company' have soared way above par. Knots of giggling girls and men decorate the office door-ways and curb-stones every hour of the day, and incredulous 'oh say's' and 'aw, kiddo's' reach passers-by."[62] This light piece provides a worthwhile sidelight on the strike, for indeed violence did not reign on a day-to-day basis, and although it is fascinating to follow Helen Armstrong in and out of jail and courtroom as she galvanized a new female activism, there were thousands of women on strike who were never arrested, who didn't throw bricks or garbage-can lids, but who were nonetheless participating in their own ways and perhaps even enjoying the chance to spend some time away from work in a city whose day-to-day routine was for a time suspended. The report on flirting shows a desire to observe the city's young women and to delve for a moment into the street-level youth culture of flirtation and fun that was also part of the culture of the strike. The male reporter doesn't mention the strike in his piece, but the female reporter acknowledges its role in populating the streets, and she works the language of the strike playfully into her rhetoric: "Consider the male flirt. He toileth not, neither doth he strike. He simply loiters along the curb stone watching for the first girl who looks as though she might be 'picked up.' He lifts his hat, smiles, and if the girl has the come-hither in her eye, they stroll off together in the direction of an ice-cream store."[63] Both articles investigate whether it is men or women who are the active initiators of flirtations, and although both observe that men are ready participants and that "the flirting game is 50-50,"[64] they both interest themselves more in the advances initiated by women, and the woman reporter asserts that "although Winnipeg men flirt, they do not flirt first." Both reporters thus demonstrate an interest in young women as active initiators, and their articles suggest a curiosity about how women's newfound self-assertion — so evident in the strike activity that placed them on the streets – might take effect in their personal lives as well.

. This woman's-page account uses the rhetoric of the strike for utterly different purposes than does the riot coverage, but the use of the strike rhetoric in this article about gender relations suggests the more subtle influence that the conflict may have had on everyday discourse and even in personal encounters. The media's interest in how the girl strikers were conducting their love lives on the picket line signals the curiosity aroused by this new terrain for gender relations. Courtship rituals are deeply important factors in the structuring of gender norms and behaviours, and this article suggests that it wasn't only setting fire to streetcars in front of city hall that made strikes an important space in the negotiation of gender; it could also be the day-to-day interactions made possible in the street life of picketing, protest, and indeed flirtation. Note the use of incendiary metaphor to enliven this description: "This is a typical flirtation witnessed on Broadway: A girl with enough powder on her face to blow up the city hall was waiting for a street car Wednesday. A man in a run-about Ford passed by. He looked back at the girl standing on the curb. She smiled. He stopped the car, and the girl got in. It was evident that the two had never met before."[65] This light-hearted figurative use of the language of revolt does lend a certain rebellious quality to the girl whose smile effectively stops traffic. The reporter seems to see the potential for the girl striker to signal defiance not just of the employers' rules but also of gender codes more generally, and she thus employs metaphors of social destruction – blowing up city hall – to describe that all-important item of feminine selfhood: makeup. It is almost as though the girl's attractiveness stems from and is heightened by the aura of rebellion – the explosive makeup – that she uses to face down city traffic.

It is difficult to make sense of the extreme variance in media accounts and representations of women's strike activities; one woman faints in horror, while another sets fire to street cars; girls flirt on the street by day, organize dances by night, and beat up other girls for selling the wrong newspaper in between; and even leadership figure Helen Armstrong organizes to feed the needy on a mass scale while getting thrown in and out of jail regularly for disorderly conduct and inciting violence. The media representations are of course mainly penned by men, the piece on flirtation being an exception, and one is reminded of Virginia Woolf's account of how the woman appears in the fiction of men: "one would imagine her a person of the utmost importance; very various; heroic and mean; splendid and sordid; infinitely beautiful and hideous in the extreme; as great as any man, some think even greater. But this is woman in fiction."[66] The newspapers at which I've looked are of course not fiction, although they employ representational strategies, tropes, and imagery that come from the same literary conventions. Taken together, the media coverage suggests that women, who participated in the labour activism of their day with great energy and determination, took seriously the licence to rebel that a strike granted them and used it not only in the context of their employment situation but also in regard to the constraints of gender more generally, challenging such limits in some cases with violence. Yet they also took what they were traditionally familiar with and known for – conducting social occasions – and found ways to imbue these talents with new political import and effect. Socializing and fundraising were a good match and undoubtedly strengthened strikes in concrete financial ways, while at the same time providing a space for men and women alike to experience and celebrate the feeling of solidarity. The working girl on strike was fascinating to her contemporaries, for she added an element of rebellion and revolt to this already contentious female figure of social turbulence. Through her labour activism – sometimes rowdy and violent, sometimes light-hearted and fun – the working girl was forcefully contesting and transforming the gender expectations of her day, and I would suggest that this struggle was taking place as much on the front cover of the newspaper as it was in the workplace and on the picket lines themselves.

## chapter 5

# White Working Girls and the Mixed-Race Workplace

Went to Vancouver Hotel to hear the speakers of the
Provincial Party, but found it terribly dull, so went
to a dance.

– JANET SMITH, "NO FEAR OF CHINESE BOY IS RECORDED,"
*Vancouver Sun,* 8 SEPTEMBER 1924

I n 1924 the *Vancouver Star,* one of the city's more sensationalist papers,
was especially concerned with the perceived danger posed to white
women in the mixed-race workplace: "A contemporary has just made
disclosures about the debauchery of a 17-year-old white girl by Chinese
patrons of a Granville Street Chinese restaurant. Enquiries indicate that
the facts are too unpleasant for public print. But white girls continue to
serve under these vile conditions of near-intimacy with Chinese employers
and patrons."[1] This story followed up on a murder investigation of great
public interest that featured a mixed-race domestic workplace; Scottish
nursemaid Janet Smith was found dead in the basement of the Vancouver
home where she had worked alongside the Chinese houseboy, the only
suspect in the case. This chapter examines narratives of the mixed-race
workplace as they affected the working girl in the West. I have chosen
once again to focus specifically on Vancouver, where the racial tensions
regarding Asian immigration felt throughout the West were especially
intense. Labour and the workplace proved productive sites in the
activation of race and gender ideologies, for the personal and cultural
encounters that took place there could both challenge preconceptions and
ignite deeply felt prejudices. While the working girl became iconic in
her figuration of the social changes brought about by urban development
and the world of work, another stereotypical figure familiar to western

Canadians was the Chinese bachelor, a target of acute racist hostility.

At the same time that white women from the British Isles were sought via Bride Ship campaigns and immigration societies, Chinese immigrants were subject to the most exclusionary immigration practices in the country's history. The story of their exclusion, moreover, is linked directly to the development of the West. Brought to Canada to help build the Canadian Pacific Railway, a vital link between East and West, the Chinese supplied some of this undertaking's most necessary and dangerous labour; in 1885, the same year that the railway was completed, all immigrants of Chinese origin became subject to a Head Tax of fifty dollars. This was raised to one hundred dollars in 1900 and to five hundred in 1903, and it is estimated that the Canadian government collected $23 million in all. In 1923 the Chinese Exclusion Act barred Chinese immigration altogether, a ban that was not lifted until 1947. It is important to note that British Columbia was especially insistent that the federal government enact these measures; in the western provinces, where Asian immigration was more visibly apparent, anti-Asian sentiment was substantially more intense.

At first glance, it might seem that these two groups – white working girls and Chinese men – had little, if anything, in common. In fact, they came to be intimately associated in the popular imagination through their shared workplaces, for as two of the cheapest sources of waged labour, they often competed for the same jobs and worked in the same environments. Domestic work is perhaps the most obvious example; controversy surrounded the choice by middle-class households to employ either Chinese houseboys or white female servants or both. Restaurants and rooming houses, meanwhile, often paired Chinese employers with white waitresses and chambermaids, and the *Vancouver Star* story cited above is typical of attitudes about white waitresses in Chinese restaurants. Alicja Muszynski has documented how British Columbia's salmon canneries drew on both Native women workers and Chinese labourers, and these low-paying jobs were also sometimes filled by white women workers.[2] A 1913 headline in the *BC Federationist* read "Scotch Girls Cheaper than Chinamen."[3] Young women from Scotland had been brought to Vancouver specifically to replace Chinese cannery workers. The white manager of one Vancouver cannery felt that his control over the Chinese workers was compromised by a system where he communicated only with Chinese foremen who were in charge of their own sets of workers; the Scottish women were expected to prove less expensive and more tractable. Their shared space in the labour market thus placed Chinese men and white working women in a specific kind of proximity, characterized in the *Vancouver Star* as "these vile conditions of near-intimacy," and this had a strong effect on how the working girl came to be represented – in the West more than elsewhere in Canada – as a symbol of imperilled whiteness.

In this chapter I examine in depth the story of Janet Smith's death and its investigation, for it highlights the special concern that was felt for the white working girl in the mixed-race workplace of the West. As discussed in Chapter 1, white women in the West were considered especially important to the young nation as cultural carriers and as future mothers who would assure the continuation of a white settler society of primarily British extraction. Yet the representational strategies involved in the construction of an iconic white womanhood lend themselves more easily to a middle-class ideal of wives and mothers in a white domestic haven than to working-class women whose morally and racially suspect workplaces might sully their spotless whiteness. For this reason, the rhetoric of protection for the working girl often concerned itself with her whiteness, and indeed when whiteness itself was under discussion, the image of the young working-class woman was invoked to embody a whiteness imperilled by contemporary immigration patterns.

## RACIAL DISCOURSE AND WORKING-CLASS WOMEN

The preoccupation with the mixed-race workplace and the need to separate white women from Asian men fuelled debates on women's labour in the West. Reformers suspected Asian men of playing a part in the white-slave trade, and middle-class women's groups felt that young working women were in need of careful protection and guidance. In fact, initial recommendations to safeguard white working women extended beyond Asian men and sought to ban women from working with Greeks and Italians as well. In 1911 the Local Council of Women submitted recommendations on women's working conditions to the BC Commission on Labour, advocating that "in no case shall Caucasians be permitted to work together [with] or be employed by Asiatics, Greeks, Italians." As council member Janet Kemp explained, "Regarding employment with Greeks, Italians, etc. that is a very urgent point because it is a matter in which real injury is being done our girls."[4] It is interesting that Greeks and Italians are grouped with "Asiatics" here, for it highlights the preoccupation at this time with a wide array of complex "racial" distinctions. Constance Backhouse examines in depth Canada's legal history of racism, and she notes the malleable nature of racial categories that shift over time: "'Racial' distinctions have historically been drawn among Saxon, Celtic, Norman, Irish, Scottish, and English communities. Immigrants from southern and eastern Europe, Syria, Armenia, Arabia, India, and the Philippines often found their claim to 'whiteness' contested in North America."[5]

Backhouse pays special attention to the "white women's labour laws" and to the court cases that arose from their enforcement. The first such legislation was passed in Saskatchewan in 1912, making it a criminal offence for Chinese men to employ white women; she notes that "the provinces of Manitoba, Ontario, and British Columbia were so impressed by the Saskatchewan initiative that they adopted identical or similar statutes over the next seven years."[6] In Saskatchewan two Chinese men, owners of two restaurants and a rooming house, were prosecuted for employing two waitresses and a chambermaid who were white. Backhouse examines the court proceedings, and her description of the female employees' testimony suggests that the women themselves were less than grateful for this legislative attempt to protect them: "The three working-class women who testified at the trials were indignant over the occupational constraints presented by the 'white women's labour bill.' While white middle- and upper-class social reformers sought to 'protect' them from perceived danger, the waitresses and chambermaid just wanted to hold on to their jobs. Indeed, they resented the aspersions cast upon their character by wealthier women who advocated that 'nice girls did not work for Orientals.'"[7] It is significant that "protecting" the working girl in this case actually meant depriving her of her job, and it is not surprising that such protection met with resentment. But this case would seem to be typical of the debate about white women working with Chinese men in that the moral imperative to guard white women from interracial contact utterly eclipsed the reality of the women's need for employment.

British Columbia passed its own white women's labour law in 1919, and the Women and Girls Protection Act, which replaced it in 1923, similarly grew out of a desire to separate white women from Chinese men, but both laws applied to Chinese-owned businesses, particularly restaurants and laundries, making it an offence for Chinese employers to hire white women. This excluded cases where white employers hired both white women and Asian men, such as private households with white maids and Chinese houseboys as well as other white-run businesses such as canneries, hotels, restaurants, and so on. This omission, along with the fact that these laws were seldom enforced, fuelled the controversy created by the alleged murder of Janet Smith by her Chinese co-worker, and led to MLA Mary Ellen Smith's campaign in 1924 to extend the law to private households. The most frequently stated reasons for racial segregation in the workplace were the Chinese opium trade and, subsequent to the Janet Smith case, the possibility that Asian men might assault white women. Drug deals, sexual harassment, and even violence did and still do occur in workplaces from time to time, but there was very little evidence that Asian men had a monopoly on such abuses. As Mary Ellen Smith sought support for the "Janet Smith" bill in 1924, the *Vancouver Province* noted that in crimes committed against women in the previous year, English, Scottish, and Irish men led the way with 40 percent, whereas not a single Asian man had been prosecuted in such a matter.[8] Yet a great deal of energy went into elaborating narratives of the Asian menace; they were highly instrumental in the political agenda of many members of the white majority, and the figure of the vulnerable white working girl was here, as elsewhere, a cypher for anxieties about the modern urban scene – which was an increasingly multicultural sphere.

How, then, did racist ideology inform the debates about and representations of the working girl? With the West already known for its preponderantly male population, young women were subject to a certain popular interest, their choice among marriage prospects reputedly ample. But the bachelor scene was always markedly multicultural, and the Chinese population was known to be almost exclusively male, due to the immigration restrictions that severed them from their families in China. These demographics, in concert with a segmented labour market placing women and Asian men at the bottom of the wage scale, meant that for British Columbians the mixed-race workplace referred quite specifically to white women mixed with Asian men. And since young working women on their own in the city were already thought to occupy a position of some moral ambiguity, the added element of close working associations with Asian men seemed further to undermine the social order, violating traditional boundaries meant to segregate genders and races. In British Columbia and in prairie cities, social divisions based on race found spatial expression in the delineation of separate and identifiable Chinatowns sequestered from exclusively white neighbourhoods for the respectable middle classes, and these neighbourhood divisions reflected the more fundamental desire to ensure the physical separation of bodies; but among the working classes, such clean divisions were not easily maintained. Many downtown workplaces brought young women into proximity with Chinatowns and into association with co-workers who lived there. Working women were thus leaving the sequestered private sphere for a racialized public sphere de-void of traditional markers of respectability. In the case of young working women, moreover, issues of sexual downfall and prostitution were always of concern. As Kay Anderson points out, for moral reformists, "the anx-iety was heightened in Vancouver by the location of its 'restricted area' (where prostitution was tolerated by the police) right next to the predomi-nantly male Chinese quarter from the time the city was incorporated."[9] This seeming conflation of racial and sexual otherness suggested to some a cause-and-effect relationship, as though interracial encounters might go hand in hand with sexual downfall and so lead to the associated danger of miscegenation. Because whiteness and purity share such an intimate con-ceptual space, especially for women, the idea that young working women were in danger of having their whiteness compromised by mixed-race workplaces fuelled a protective impulse to redraw racial lines and rid the workplace of one group or the other. Once again, working women were in danger of losing their jobs to a moral imperative.

In the early 1920s anxieties about race and gender in the workplace became particularly intense. In 1922 a prolonged debate took place in the House of Commons regarding legislation to put an end to Chinese immigration, which ultimately took effect in 1923. It was the following year that the Janet Smith case would take over the headlines in British Columbia, prompting debate over the "Janet Smith" bill to prohibit white women and Asian men from working as co-domestics in private homes.

British Columbia had long sought to enact a ban on Asian immigration, but only the federal government had the authority to do so, and it struck down the province's attempts until 1923, when the Exclusion Act finally went through. The debate included a litany of racial stereotypes that were endemic to British Columbia from the 1880s on. Robert McDonald outlines the four dominant racial stereotypes through which the white population viewed the Asian community, all of which were evident in the political debate:

> One stereotype is the perception at the time that hordes of Asian immigrants might inundate British Columbia and destroy its collective character as a land of White, European-based settlers. The second is an emphasis on the vastly different cultures and institutions of Asians, which, it was believed, insulated them from the influence of White society and made them inassimilable. The third is a focus on the willingness of Asians to work for less than what White workers considered a "fair" wage, thus lowering

the European community's standard of living. The fourth stereotype is the assertion that Asians, especially Chinese and Sikhs, were "unclean, diseased, and a threat to public health."[10]

The House of Commons debate returned many times to the inassimilable nature of the Asian community, and McDonald further points out that assimilation in the early twentieth century often referred not only to the adoption of customs and language but also specifically to marriage with white Canadians. This degree of assimilation, however, was wholly unpalatable to the majority of white Canadians, and the dominant attitude of the day held that, apart from being undesirable, such marriages would produce so-called degenerate progeny. As one speaker in the House stated, "The real test of assimilation is intermarriage. The divergences of the two races is so marked that intermarriage does not tend to perpetuate the good qualities of either race."[11] This preoccupation with marriage and the threat of miscegenation suggested the need for a degree of sexual surveillance that would cordon off white women from Asian men. One symptom of this urge to contain white women's sexuality was manifested in the intolerance shown to mixed-race couples, although only to those including a white woman. In fact, as Robert Campbell argues, in the context of public spaces such as beer parlours, the category of the mixed-race couple existed only when a white woman was involved – other combinations were a nonissue: "A mixed-race couple was a white woman with a man of colour, especially a black man. As categories of official and popular concern, women of colour with white men and mixed-race couples that included no white member simply did not exist."[12] A white woman with a man of colour, meanwhile, provoked instant disapproval because such a couple represented the disruption of racial codes and social hierarchies: "The reaction that they provoked emphasized the racial norms of decency. A man of colour 'racialized' himself – that is, engaged in indecent behaviour – if he was in the company of a white woman. Yet the woman also became less white, or pure, because of her behaviour. The potential for miscegenation threatened the dominance of white men and ultimately destabilized the category of 'white.'"[13] Even though efforts were made to foster assimilation – for instance, through the education system – the idea of mixed-race marriages involving white women continued to be totally unacceptable to the white majority, which subscribed, in this sense, to a racialized patriarchy.

Hilda Glynn-Ward, author of the intensely racist novel *The Writing on the Wall* (1921), was quoted in the assimilation debate as saying, "Marriage between orientals and whites has never been known to produce anything but degradation for both because it is an unnatural thing,"[14] and her comment highlights that the debate on the impossibility of Asians assimilating into Canadian society was also influenced by the discourse on eugenics. Eugenics was a pseudo-medical discourse that asserted a racial hierarchy with white English-speaking Anglo-Saxons at the top and all other ethnicities and nationalities ranged below. Eugenicists interested themselves in a wide range of national reforms, including highly selective immigration, birth control for the working classes, and sterilization of the mentally unfit. Angus McLaren points out that the movement was a convenient way to impose a veneer of authority on long-held prejudices: "eugenic arguments provided apparently new, objective scientific justifications for old, deep-seated racial and class assumptions."[15] The discourse of eugenics often drew on metaphors concerning the national body politic, warning that the wrong kind of immigration would undermine the purity of the nation and "the race": "It is desirable that we should have a white Canada and that we should not become a yellow or mongrel nation."[16] Thus both on the individual level of marriage and on the national level of immigration policy, the mixing of Asians and whites represented for many a kind of racial contagion. And while exclusionist legislation sought to protect Canada on a national level from unwanted immigrants, on an individual level, racial divisions and the preservation of whiteness were enforced through strict attention to moral codes and sexual proscriptions. Both of these racist agendas drew on representations of white femininity to signify an often sexualized racial threat.

One speaker appealed to the House on just these grounds when he gestured to the idea of white and Asian men being part of a human brotherhood but then qualified such notions by asking, "'what about these people for brothers-in-law?' It is all very well to refer to them as brothers; but would any honourable gentleman of this House consider an alliance between a sister or a daughter of his and a Chinaman or a Japanese? Is there an honourable member to whom such an alliance would appeal?"[17] That his questions were meant to be purely rhetorical signals the unthinkable quality of assimilation through marriage in the view of the white majority. But an appeal to the members of the House that draws in their daughters and sisters signals something more as well. In her book on white women and racism, *Beyond the Pale*, Vron Ware explains how familial representations of white women could take on an important racial symbolism in imperial or national contexts: "Whether as Mothers of the Empire or Britannia's Daughters, women were able to symbolize the idea of moral strength that bound the great imperial family together. In their name, men could defend the family in the same spirit as they would defend their own wives, daughters or sisters if they were under attack."[18] The idea of Asian men marrying into the families of Canada's political representatives was calculated to elicit a paternal and brotherly interest in young womanhood that was both protectionist and proprietorial while at the same time operating on a symbolic level to elicit a specifically masculine and racist patriotism. Wives and mothers had related roles to play in the service of a white Canada, but in this instance it is young white women of marriageable age who embody an endangered whiteness in need of careful guardianship.

Although the sisters to be sheltered from interracial contact were not, in this instance, identified according to any particular class position, young working women occupied the same field of representation, defined by a protectionist impulse and a feeling of sexualized racial threat. Added to this, however, were the more materialist concerns of the labour movement, for whom the Asian threat was as much economic as it was moral or cultural. Labour activists opposed Asian immigration on the grounds that it created unfair labour competition that drove down the standard of living for the white community, and while labour unions usually invoked this argument in order to protect their predominantly male membership, in the House of Commons debate Vancouver's embattled white working class was represented through depictions of young working women:

> When there are so many young women out of employment, the oriental problem becomes a serious affair. One young woman said "I have two bits left." I have lived for the last two weeks on two pints of milk and two doughnuts a day, and when I go to look for a job I mostly meet a Chinaman at the door and am told that I am not wanted." It is pretty hard for these young women that we have allowed into our country orientals to fill the jobs that our own people should fill. Another young woman said "I am supposed to be good, I have got 75 cents left, I am two weeks behind in my rent. The landlady says I must pay the rent or she will take my clothes. I have to earn the money some way." And yet the Chinamen are taking the jobs those women ought to have and want to fill.[19]

This speaker draws on the familiar figure of the lone working girl living on the brink of poverty and every day in danger of either starving or turning to prostitution despite her best efforts to "be good." And while utterly conventional, this representation of the working girl is interesting in that it demonstrates the flexibility of the figure: where white slavery is at issue, she embodies innocence endangered; where labour reform is needed, she is evidence of inadequate wages; where the city is criticized, she warns of a heartless modernity; and here she is the victim of unchecked Asian immigration. What is also interesting about this example is that whereas the first story addresses the material and economic issues of a labour market segmented by race and gender, the second story quickly returns us to the realm of morality, where the working girl's imperilled virtue is the primary concern. Indeed, this concern is the advantage here in persuasive effect. If one used a male subject to represent competition in the labour market, this story would stop at the unemployment of whites who compete with Asians for jobs, but with the destitute working girl, one can bring in the added pathos of innocence lost and so twist the knife that much further. The same speaker claimed that "the young girl, who, through lack of employment is forced to work in the restaurant with some of these orientals, is eagerly looking to see what the members of this House are going to do on this question,"[20] hinting once more that the difficult labour market would push young working women into ever-more-compromising positions if Asian immigration was not halted.

In the anecdote about the starving girl unable to find work because of Asian competition, the Chinese are only indirectly to blame – by saturating the labour market – for the young woman's potential downfall, but more extreme racist narratives depicted Chinese men as procurers of women for prostitution and as drug dealers deliberately victimizing young white women, who were sometimes their employees:

What is known as "snow parties" are held. Chinamen of great wealth, engaged in this odious practice, and living in expensive, luxurious quarters, give parties at which white women, whom they employ, act as hostesses. Young girls are invited from about the city to take part in these so-called social functions – perhaps at a dance, perhaps at a card party; something of that kind. Interspersed among these young people are two or three addicts who are trained and whose business it is to inveigle other people into the use of narcotics ... A girl of twenty-three, through the use of morphine and cocaine, had a child by a Chinaman named Pete Kong, a notorious Chinese drug peddler. She injected morphine into the infant with a hypo needle until it died – her mind being so distorted.[21]

This latter story about the baby is almost certainly either a fabrication or an urban myth, given its lurid details and its too-easy conflation of white female downfall, miscegenation, and drug-induced crime, all of which form elements of the speaker's argument to ban Asian immigration. It also seems to suggest that you can get pregnant by taking drugs, creating a link between drug abuse and the corruption of whiteness. Indeed, in the thinking of the white majority, the opium trade was so firmly associated with Chinatown and the Chinese population that a white person's drug use was perceived as compromising his or her white racial status. Young working-class women were thought to be particularly susceptible to drug addiction because of their mixed-race workplaces and because leisure pursuits such as dances were considered dangerously unregulated. The *Beacon*, a monthly Vancouver paper, took great interest in the drug traffic and warned of the dangers for young people of Chinatown's opium dens: "These conditions exist right here in Vancouver. Many shop girls are said to be addicted to a mild use of the drug as a stimulant. This mild use grows to very serious proportions. In dance halls in the city of Vancouver the use of 'snow' or white stuff is common."[22] The shop girl was a frequent figure of pathos because she was publicly visible in a way that most young working women were not, and because it was known that she worked for long hours on her feet; the idea that she might resort to stimulants may have seemed plausible to many readers and was likely meant to evoke their sympathies. But, as with the girl whose drug use led directly to a mixed-race baby, there is a feeling of whiteness compromised in the young white girl dependent on illicit Asian-supplied drugs.

Racial discourse in Canada drew on a litany of stereotypes that shaped popular perceptions of both Asian and white populations. And the figure of the white working girl often functioned as a trope within national narratives, embodying, on the one hand, the promise of white nationalism and, on the other, the vulnerability of white purity to impending racial contamination. Representations of the working girl thus informed certain threads of the debate on Asian immigration and served a rhetorical function in an argumentative strategy: to invoke to the figure of the single white working girl was to elicit a specific protectionist response to the idea of whiteness under threat. Whether the context was drug traffic, the flooded labour market, the possibility of assimilation, or miscegenation, the white working girl became a touchstone for debates on racial exclusion. But despite this popular interest in working women and the maintenance of their pristine whiteness, the pragmatics of women's position in the working world vis-à-vis the labour market, unequal wage scales, and the value of their work both to themselves (earning a living) and to the community (providing necessary services and functions) were never addressed. On the contrary, the emphasis on women's roles as vessels of whiteness deflected attention away from their needs and rights as workers. Thus middle-class administrators moved forward with plans to police the mixed-race workplace and even to eliminate women's jobs therein, without ever considering the financial implications that this could have for self-supporting women.

### ATTRACTION AND REPULSION: GENDER AND IMMIGRATION POLICIES FOR A WHITE CANADA

At the time of the Janet Smith case, anti-Asian feeling had hit a new height, culminating just the year before in the Exclusion Act, which essentially put a stop to Chinese immigration. The immigration of white women from the British Isles to work as domestic servants, by comparison, was still considered highly desirable and had passed from the hands of individual women's societies to be administered instead by a government bureau: the Women's Division of the Department of Immigration and Colonization, established in 1920. Both Asian immigrants and white domestic servants were thus objects of great interest in Canada's national narrative, one representing a figure of threat and the other a figure of promise.

In 1922 Canada and Britain made an arrangement with a decidedly imperial ring to it: the Empire Settlement Agreement provided assistance for agricultural workers, juvenile immigrants, and female domestics. The Women's Bureau concerned itself with the selection, transport, and placement of unaccompanied women immigrants, and while its work was mainly helpful and well intentioned, its brand of maternal feminist philanthropy could be highly prescriptive as well. In her 1924 annual report the head of the Women's Bureau pointed out that "it is necessary that all women coming to this country should be most carefully interviewed by a Canadian woman in order that we may secure a type of woman who will settle down in Canada and become good citizens; also, there are certain classes, such as factory workers, that must be discouraged because we already have an adequate supply of these workers in Canada."[23] The Empire Settlement Agreement was strongly biased in favour of those who would settle in rural communities, so factory workers were ruled out as a "class," even though women domestics and female factory workers would have occupied the same economic class. Also, by entering the public arena of work and money, factory workers challenged traditional gender roles in a way that domestic servants did not. Follow-up reports were administered by the bureau to confirm that women who came to Canada to work as domestics stayed in these positions. Such strict selection criteria and follow-up surveillance demonstrate the very precise kind of social engineering that underwrote female immigration policies: female domestic servants came the closest to fulfilling both the labour demands of the growing country and the ideological requirements of visibly traditional gender norms. Striking such a balance was a challenge, however, given that these two criteria were in certain ways antithetical: traditional ideals of femininity and the cult of domesticity sought to remove women from the realm of paid work and to render their unpaid work invisible, whereas the constant demand for domestic servants to do this very necessary work belied visions of domestic ease. This paradox was reflected in the ambivalence concerning women's paid employment and in the unwillingness to acknowledge its true value. Female immigrant domestics were thus subject to precise but conflicting agendas related to labour demands, gender norms, and racial preferences. For the Women's Bureau, making its charges meet these many demands was no small task.

The Empire Settlement Agreement applied to immigrants from the British Isles, but many of the women immigrants bound for domestic-service positions also came from eastern and southern Europe. The Women's Bureau took charge of all unaccompanied women immigrants – meeting them upon arrival, escorting them to women's hostels, supervising them in groups on westbound trains, and arranging for their placement in private homes. But some of these new arrivals were less than eager to make it to their final destinations; train conductresses seem to have been part chaperone and part warden in their mission to safeguard women immigrants: "The greatest vigilance has been necessary, day and night, by railroad officials and conductresses to guard these girls to their destination. Foreign girls have at times jumped from the windows of the train, not wishing to proceed to their destination. These girls are liable to leave without a moment's warning, so that constant supervision is essential."[24] Single female immigrants, then, although desirable, were an unruly group who needed almost constant supervision from the time they left Europe through to their placement in service, and even then, keeping them in service required further vigilance. Julia Bush analyzes female immigration schemes and points out that "moral surveillance was integral to a philosophy of female emigration which, despite its sometimes

emancipatory aura, stood rooted in a class-bound patriarchal society and a
racist imperialism. Servant girls were believed by the emigrators to be far
more prone to kick over the traces both in their work and in their general
behaviour."[25] And in their history of Canadian immigration policy,
Ninette Kelley and Michael Trebilcock note that many British female
domestics were deported in the 1920s because their behaviour transgressed
moral codes: "Departmental records reveal that offending public mores,
such as bearing an illegitimate child, contracting venereal disease, living
with a man out of wedlock, and having more than one sexual partner,
were often the underlying cause for expulsion."[26] In a national narrative
that espoused a white ideal complemented by largely traditional gender
roles, servant girls occupied an important but precarious position. Asked
to embody the promise of a racially and morally pure society, they were
actually deeply distrusted, subject to vigilant surveillance, and suspected
of imminent betrayal of national ideals.

It is interesting to note that while sporadic panics would break out about
working women – especially domestic workers – being in some form of
danger because of their Asian co-workers, no similar concerns applied
to the white mistresses in houses employing Asian help, even though
the spatial proximity of the shared house was presumably identical. It
is as though the class distinction formed an impervious barrier not only
between the white mistress and the Asian houseboy but also against the
very thought that any danger could exist in this context. That the Asian
houseboy's presence is a complete nonissue in the case of the middle-class
housewife but a supposedly tangible and significant danger to the white
female servant is a contradiction that signals the already-compromised
nature of the working woman's perceived position. As a single working-
class woman, she was inherently vulnerable to social and moral threats in
a way that middle-class women never were. Anne McClintock explains
how female servants in the context of empire, partly because they blurred
the boundaries between home and workplace, occupied a socially
ambiguous and morally uncertain position: "Like prostitutes and female
miners, servants stood on the dangerous threshold of normal work,
normal money and normal sexuality, and came to be figured increasingly
in the iconography of 'pollution,' 'disorder,' 'plagues,' 'moral contagion'
and 'racial degeneration.'"[27] This suspicion of the purity of female servants
appeared in the Janet Smith case when Smith's "character" came under
intense scrutiny, as though the victim's sexual purity were a factor in the
crime; such a consideration is common in a rape case but wouldn't seem

immediately relevant in a murder. With the Chinese houseboy as the main suspect, however, attention quickly fixed on the nature of the relationship between the two servants in a way that it never would have if Smith had been the mistress of the house, not a servant. At a time when the country was deeply invested in the idea of nation building, then, working-class women in particular tended to awaken anxieties concerning the fragility of the social and moral landscape, especially in its racial dimension.

## JANET SMITH AND DOMESTIC INTIMACIES

Vancouver's downtown core signified for many an unregulated territory of racial otherness, sexual vice, and lower-class dissipation – this in contrast to the quiet domesticity of the Tudor-style homes in respectable Kitsilano and well-to-do Shaughnessy. But in 1924 these preconceptions were overturned when the cheerful and popular young nanny of a Shaughnessy home was found apparently shot to death, and the Chinese houseboy was the only one on the scene. The many details of the Janet Smith case have been dwelt on at length in Edward Starkins's *Who Killed Janet Smith?* and in Ian Macdonald and Betty O'Keefe's *Canadian Holy War*, so I will only briefly summarize the major events.[28] Janet Smith worked as a nanny and domestic servant in the home of F.L. Baker on Osler Street in Shaughnessy, near a circular crescent where nannies were known to exchange pleasantries while strolling with their charges. On 26 July 1924 she was found dead in the basement by the Chinese houseboy, Wong Foon Sing, and the police were called. Seeing that she had a gunshot wound to the head and the gun by her hand, they assumed that it was a suicide and didn't bother to preserve or fully detail the crime scene, thereby destroying potentially vital evidence. The suicide theory quickly came under attack, but a coroner's inquest ruled the death accidental, and Janet Smith was buried. By this time, however, suspicion had fallen on Wong Foon Sing, in part because of the claims of a close friend of Smith named Cissie Jones, also a domestic worker, who said that Smith had been afraid of Wong. Wong was kidnapped, held overnight, and beaten by investigators associated with the police, but their attempts to force a confession were fruitless. The murder theory gained credence, however, and the body was exhumed for autopsy, whereupon a second inquest ruled that Smith had been murdered. By the end of the year MLA Mary Ellen Smith responded to public pressure by proposing the "Janet Smith" bill to prevent white women and Asian men from working together in private homes. But the bill was never passed because it was ruled unconstitutional. The case stayed in the papers for another year, as a clairvoyant came forward with evidence drawn from the mystical sphere, and Wong was kidnapped again, this time held for over a month, beaten, and tortured, then released and charged with murder. With no evidence to speak of, however, he eventually went free, and his captors, all affiliated with the police, were brought to justice. The Janet Smith case had many sensational elements, and narratives seemed to grow up like weeds at every turn. Had there been an unrequited mixed-race romance between the two co-workers? Was F.L. Baker a drug dealer trying to cover his tracks? Had there been a decadent party at the home where upper-class debauchery had gone awry? Was it a case of police corruption? What would Smith's secret diary reveal? The Janet Smith case played on fears and prejudices that were ever just below the surface of Vancouver's pleasant self-image, and in its rise to the level of urban myth, it represents an important formative narrative in the city's social history.

The second inquest regarding Janet Smith's death, which concluded that she was murdered, was held about a month after her death, and during this time Vancouver's Scottish societies had taken up the case, urged by Cissie Jones. At this point, competing representations of Smith began to take on great importance in the various scenarios thought to lead up to the death. Was she a devoted servant, an embodiment of pure white femininity defiled? Or was her death tied to working-class moral laxity and a too-active social life in the day's libertine youth culture? The Janet Smith mystery began to function as a cautionary narrative about women in the mixed-race workplace and in the unsupervised leisure sphere. Cissie Jones strongly asserted Wong's guilt, claiming that Smith had told her she feared him: "She was very very nervous. Terribly nervous of the Chinaman day after day. For the last three days before her death she was afraid to go into the kitchen for her meals ... I told her to go into the kitchen and get something in spite of him, and if he laid a hand on her to pick up something and hit him with it."[29] Jones was an outspoken young woman who resented the snobbery of the upper classes toward domestic servants, and she was determined to see justice done for her friend. She figured prominently in the second inquest, where Wong's lawyer, Harry Senkler, questioned her closely concerning Smith's feelings toward Wong. His main piece of evidence was Smith's diary, which, he asserted, showed no evidence that Smith feared Wong in the least. But rather than sticking to the two or three entries in the diary where Smith mentioned Wong, Senkler read from many portions, thereby revealing much more about

Smith's personal life than would seem immediately relevant to the case. Smith had a very active social life and was going out with three or four men in addition to her fiancé: "He says I must love him alone and have nothing else to do with any other man, but I like them all, Arthur, Steve, Carl and John. I suppose folks will think I am a terrible flirt."[30] Indeed, Smith's employer did get a little ruffled on account of her maid's many admirers, especially when they all phoned the house in one day: "All the boys phoned me. Mistress doesn't like it, but I do."[31] Senkler dwelt at length on Smith's romances and her leisure pursuits, all the time challenging Jones that if Smith had truly been in fear for her life she would surely have mentioned it in her diary, especially since she went into such detail about other aspects of her personal life. But by dwelling at such length on Smith's various flirtations, Senkler began to paint her as a not entirely innocent victim. Jones objected to insinuations regarding Smith's virtue and went out of her way to counter Senkler's representation of Smith as an untamed flirt. Vouching for Smith's good nature, she said, "Janet always helped her mother by sending money to her."[32] And using an odd combination of facts, she stated, "She complained to me often about being nervous of being left so much alone with a Chinaman and when she did get a Sunday off she went to church."[33] For Jones, establishing that Smith was killed by Wong went hand in hand with establishing Smith's good character and working-class honour. The last entry in Smith's diary told of an evening out where "Hall provided me with drinks until I feared catastrophe," but the "witness explained that they were soft drinks, and Miss Smith feared stomach troubles from it."[34] Finally, when Senkler asked her whether the extracts of the diary had changed her opinion of Smith, Jones replied, "No, I don't take any notice of it. She did not run after men."[35] Reporters noted that those in the courtroom took great interest in the cross-examination and were vocal in their support of Jones: "The crowd, patiently hostile at the cross-examination, muttered again and again in approval as the girl refused to read anything into the diary entries but what would bear out the character she had given her dead friend."[36] The use of the word "character" is replete with meaning here, for the contest between Jones and Senkler was essentially a battle over representation. Jones, full of spirit and deeply loyal to her friend, was heavily invested in Smith's female working-class honour, and she refused to see her represented in any other light. Senkler, on the other hand, drew on carefully selected excerpts from the diary to represent Smith as an uninhibited and carefree romantic. He may have had several reasons for doing this. In many legal cases, the victim's degree of innocence influences the severity of judgment against the culprit: killing a prostitute, for instance, has traditionally incurred less condemnation than killing a so-called "good" woman. Enumerating Smith's many admirers might also have served to spread suspicion beyond the houseboy. Janet Smith thus began to represent different things to different people: spotless white innocence defiled by the Asian threat for some, servant-girl romanticism run wild for others.

One theory that sprang from the diary entries detailing Smith's complicated love life suggested that the killer was a woman who sought revenge against Smith for stealing her boyfriend: "Was Janet Smith the victim of a jealous quarrel? ... the latest suggestion is that the unfortunate girl, who according to testimony at the previous inquest and entries said to have been found in her diary was fond of the company of the opposite sex, died as a result of her friendship for some male friend."[37] This theory was short-lived but demonstrates the remarkable capacity of the case to generate narratives, this one stemming from what some believed to be Smith's too-active and unsupervised love life.

Whether a romance might have existed between Janet Smith and Wong Foon Sing was soon a question of considerable interest. The urge to view the young woman's workplace as a site of sexual intrigue or moral downfall was perhaps even more powerful here than elsewhere, as the Smith murder stood to confirm society's worst fears about the female work environment. Smith made very few references to Wong in her diary, but two stand out. One was written quite soon before her death and read, "Sing is awfully devoted: gave me two rolls of film for my camera, also sweets, and does all my washing and ironing,"[38] and the other, an earlier entry, seems even more suggestive: "Poor Wong must be in love. He has just given me a silk nightie and two camisoles."[39] This latter quotation, however, is ambiguous because there is evidence that it refers to a different Wong – also a domestic worker but in a different house – probably F.L. Baker's mother's house;[40] the newspapers, nevertheless, either failed to pick up on this distinction or left it vague. More ambiguity surrounded an anecdote reported in the *Vancouver Star,* to the effect that Smith "had been on a visit to the McRae home and the Chinaman had resented her absence, retaliating by locking her out."[41] F.L. Baker later explained that Wong had Sundays off and that Smith was out when he left and locked the house after him. She had her own key but had forgotten it, so she was locked out on her return.[42] The tendency to misread events or to impose certain readings onto the events was pervasive in this case, demonstrating its power to ignite the popular imagination. Establishing whether Wong had had feelings for Smith was of particular interest to the newspapers and the public because sexual advances made by Wong would confirm widespread fears about the mixed-race workplace and, by extension, about race and gender relations in general. A sexual threat to white women from Asian men had a symbolic dimension that inflamed a masculinist racism. As Vron Ware argues, "One of the recurring themes in the history of colonial repression is the way in which the threat of real or imagined violence towards white women became a symbol of the most dangerous form of insubordination."[43] The rage that stemmed from this alleged dual assault on Smith herself and the unassailable whiteness that she represented likely motivated the intense desire for revenge against Wong, which culminated in his repeated kidnapping and torture by the police's henchmen. By operating on this symbolic level, the Janet Smith mystery played to deep-seated racial hatreds, revealing how powerful representations of Smith and Wong were in illuminating and shaping the attitudes of the day.

Rather than treat the case as an individual or isolated event, people sought to generalize from it regarding domestic workers, mixed-race workplaces, immigration policies, and so on. They therefore needed Janet Smith to represent all servant girls and Wong Foon Sing all Chinese men. The Janet Smith story thus tapped into the working girl's already-established ability to symbolize larger social ills and transcend any individual case. The Scottish societies, for instance, used the case to criticize schemes to import domestic servants:

> Last night caustic comments were made as to the manner in which the investigation has been handled so far, while the practice of bringing young girls out from the Old Country and leaving them alone in isolated houses with Orientals was roundly condemned ... "People bring these girls out from their homes and they should look after them. They are morally and legally responsible for the well-being of these girls, and they should be prepared either to keep all white help or all Oriental help if they cannot guarantee their proper protection," was the loudly applauded statement of a member of the council [of the United Scottish Societies].[44]

The Scottish societies took a special interest in the case because Smith had been one of their own, and they paint a picture here of young girls torn from their homeland and left all alone with no one but sinister Asian co-workers.

This emphasis on the women being alone and isolated suggests the anxiety that surrounded the single status of the typical young working woman, particularly in domestic service. The separation from family, homeland, and any sort of male guardian seemed to compound the problem of the mixed-race workplace: "The tragedy of Janet K. Smith, the lone Scotch girl who appears for some time before her tragic death in a Shaughnessy Heights home to have lived in terror of her Chinese fellow domestic, forces the question as to whether or not white girls and Orientals shall be allowed to share common employment."[45] Smith may have been "lone" in the sense of being single and having no family members in Vancouver, but according to her diary, she was hardly lonely; rather, the "lone" here signifies the supposed vulnerability of the unattached, self-supporting young woman who has stepped outside the protective and possessive influence of the family. That this emphasis on the "lone" working girl appears in connection with a patriotic impulse suggests that the threat of interracial contact raised an indignation that was protectionist toward young womanhood but also proprietorial concerning available female nationals. It was the combination of conventional fears about single women in the workplace and racist desires to secure an allegedly threatened white womanhood that made the Janet Smith mystery so compelling and so worrying as a narrative of race and gender in British Columbia.

Obviously, no one cared much about the "lone" loggers and miners who had to work with all kinds of people under all kinds of conditions. But according at least to the *Vancouver Star,* this had less to do with gender difference than with the supposed nature of the workplaces:

> It is a case of race psychology. The white and yellow races, while they may be able to work together in mills, trade, or in connection with railroading or as producer and consumer, cannot assimilate when it comes to domestic association.
>
> In the situation under consideration, that of domestic help, the problem of propinquity enters into the question. It is not morally in the eternal fitness of things that a white girl or woman should be placed in a position where she is constantly coming into daily personal touch with a Chinaman under the same roof. Such a measure as that proposed would render this impossible.[46]

The editor of the *Star*, Victor Odlum, had taken a strong interest in the Janet Smith case from the start, and several pieces that he wrote objecting to white women working with Asian men were part of the public pressure for legislation on the issue. Here, he makes an interesting distinction between sites where Asians can supposedly assimilate and where they cannot: in the public sphere of male labour the mixed-race workplace is acceptable, but as soon as one enters the domestic workplace the opposite is true because of the "eternal fitness of things." As in other contexts where the female workplace is at issue, male and female workplaces are believed to be inherently different because moral imperatives overshadow the women's roles as workers and the economic pragmatics of the situation. For Odlum, the domestic workplace does not operate according to the same rules or norms as other workplaces, perhaps because it blurs the divide between the public sphere of labour and capital and the private sphere of family and procreation. To the white majority, so hostile to mixed-race marriages, the idea of assimilation in the domestic sphere – even as a workplace – was still deeply disturbing. Thus Victor Odlum could gesture to supposedly universal absolutes as reasons for segregation in the domestic workplace, even though other (male-dominated) workplaces were not an issue.

It is unlikely that female servants would have described their work as involving "daily personal touch" – indeed, they would likely have been insulted – but the conceptual association between the domestic sphere and sexual reproduction was such that within this space male and female workers appeared intimate in a way that co-workers in other settings did not:

> Following a scandal or a tragedy, it is easily possible for a community to be stampeded into the adoption of hasty and foolish measures.
>
> But the matter under consideration is a psychological one. There can be no question that the intimacy which such a condition as the employment of white girls and Chinamen in the same home brings about leaves the door open to all sorts of possibilities. It is a racial as well as a moral question.[47]

According to a domestic worker who wrote an article for the *BC Federationist* just two months before Janet Smith's death, the most pressing problems with working conditions for servants included poor wages, no fixed hours, the monotony and loneliness of the work, and the snobbery of employers.[48] With the Janet Smith case came a sudden surge in interest among the general public in the daily lives of servants, yet none of these practical concerns were addressed. Instead, everything turned on the dangers of interracial contact between co-workers. The total elision of domestic workers' practical concerns in favour of the moral imperative to segregate the races was fully manifested when resulting legislation stood to deprive large numbers of women of their positions. Most employers, they had reason to believe, would keep their Asian workers and dismiss the white women.

In fact, the opinion of white female domestic servants seems to have been split on the issue. Mary Ellen Smith's campaign for her Janet Smith bill received a boost when twenty-eight white female servants quit their jobs rather than work alongside Asian male co-workers:

> "I do not know whether it is a panic among them or not but I have learned of twenty-eight girls who have quit their jobs in Vancouver because they refused to work with Orientals," Mrs. Smith said. "This movement would seem to indicate that their employers prefer to keep the Chinese rather than the white girls. If such discrimination were pushed to extremes it would be serious for our own white women indeed."[49]

Given that the policy sought by Smith would seem to be not only "discrimination pushed to extremes" but also discrimination legislated, there is an irony to her comments. But the fact that she had initiated and campaigned for this legislation without ever considering that it would endanger the women's jobs shows an utter lack of forethought as well as a fundamental disregard both for the importance of these jobs to the women and for the value of the work that they did. By privileging the moral aspect of women's working conditions and ignoring the material ramifications of her legislation, Smith participated in the consistent devaluation of female labour. Despite the twenty-eight women who walked off their jobs, a different delegation intent on safeguarding their jobs organized to protest against Smith's bill:

> Opposition to the "Janet Smith" bill, now before the Victoria legislature, sponsored by Mary Ellen Smith, is to be voiced by groups of girls representing the sisterhood of housemaids in Vancouver, it was learned through the Trades and Labour Council today.
>
> When the bill is pressed in the house a delegation is expected to speak on behalf of the girls, who fear that passage of the bill will throw large numbers of them out of employment. Employers prefer all Chinese to all white girls, they will contend.[50]

The bill also faced opposition from the Chinese community, which sent a delegate to oppose it on the grounds that it was discriminatory and baseless – the Janet Smith mystery, after all, was unsolved and so proved nothing about alleged dangers posed to white women by Asian workers. For the moment, white working women and their Asian co-workers had similar interests in resisting the prejudicial legislation and asserting instead their rights as workers. Ruled unconstitutional, the Janet Smith bill was never passed. That the female domestic workers themselves were split on the issue, however, demonstrates the ambivalence that permeated the issue of gender in the mixed-race workplace: the twenty-eight women who quit their jobs presumably did feel threatened in the workplace, either because of the panic surrounding the Janet Smith case or from experiences of their own that are not recorded. Those women who protested the legislation, by comparison, were motivated by the prospect of unemployment and saw the need to assert their own rights as workers to protect a needed source of employment for women. It is an interesting case where the subjects of a virulent ideological discourse themselves enact the split in opinion – one group confirming the supposed dangers of their racialized workplaces and the other refuting the threat by resisting any interference in their workplaces.

The Janet Smith mystery and the ongoing attempts to legislate a racially segregated workplace for women influenced the debates about the working girl in the West and exacerbated the tendency to magnify moral concerns and overlook practical matters. With whiteness a principal marker of their identities, women workers were subject to the vigilant surveillance thought necessary for the nation's single white womanhood. Often believed to be sexually vulnerable by nature of their unchaperoned presence in the realm of paid labour, young working women seemed doubly at risk of succumbing to a sexualized racial threat, especially when western workplaces came under attack as danger zones of racial mixing. When everyone jumped to the conclusion that Janet Smith's Chinese co-worker had made advances toward her before murdering her, the case seemed to confirm people's worst fears about women in the mixed-race workplace. And by foregrounding the all-important whiteness of working women, politicians such as Mary Ellen Smith came close to legislating women right out of their jobs. Racial tensions thus exacerbated the perception of women's workplaces as moral and sexual danger zones, allowing the actual work itself and its value to the women and to the community to be rendered practically invisible.

# Conclusion: Just Girls

"I've done it! ... Let's celebrate! ... I've got a place, a position, a job, a 'sit'! I'm an independent working person. Votes for women!"[1] So says the heroine of Isabel Ecclestone Mackay's *House of Windows* when she secures her first job as a shop girl; employment, independence, and women's rights are all united in a moment of unqualified delight. And in this narrative, which blends social realism and sensationalism, the job is the first step on a path to adventure, intrigue, romance, and moral triumph. A Calgary stenographer who wrote a series of articles in 1914 for the *Morning Albertan* also took an almost rebellious pleasure in her decision to join the working world: "I cannot remember when the idea of becoming a stenographer first found a perch in my rebellious female brain."[2] She recounts the joys and also the loneliness of supporting herself and living on her own in the city, and at one point she actually turns to her typewriter – the symbol of her work – and finds it to be, for the moment, as good a companion as she needs: "I looked down at my little Underwood, which so faithfully helps me earn my bread and butter, and I whispered to its staring keys, 'You are a good enough partner for me, little typewriter.'"[3] Like the Vancouver schoolteacher who couldn't see the sense in "giving up a sixty dollar school for a forty dollar man,"[4] the Calgary stenographer finds an independence in her work that she can weigh against the traditional option of marriage. Although long hours, low wages, and harsh working conditions were typical of almost all the female-defined workplaces of the early twentieth century, representations of the working girl do suggest that a certain degree of freedom was being found as women carved out their new identities as workers.

Interestingly, the Calgary stenographer's affectionate partnership with her typewriter is echoed in J.G. Sime's epilogue to *Sister Woman*. It hardly seems likely that Sime would have read the *Morning Albertan*, but her fictional speaker, who frames the collection of stories as a response to the "woman question," exactly duplicates the gesture. In Sime's prologue and epilogue, a frame narrative features a man and a woman who try to discuss what women want. They begin on good terms, and the woman sits down before her typewriter with great energy. But the epilogue suggests that the man has utterly failed to understand: "'Then that's the lot!' – relief was in his voice. 'That's all you have to say,' he said complacently."[5] The woman writer is appalled to find that nothing has gotten through, and faced with nothing but vacuous male condescension, she turns to a different kind of partnership: "I ran my fingers over the typewriter keys – and felt them lovingly."[6] Sime foregrounds modern technologies throughout her stories, and it is significant here that her writer figure is able to type, a skill that in this period was fairly specialized to women who worked as trained stenographers; indeed, the word "typewriter" could refer equally to the machine itself and to its female operator. Sime uses the typing skill to connect her writer figure to the wage-earning women on whom the stories centre, and as the technology of a specific kind of female-identified work, the typewriter symbolizes both work itself and the writing that is produced by the woman artist. The woman who turns away from male incomprehension and turns instead to her typewriter thus symbolizes at once the committed female writer and the skilled female worker. In both the autobiographical mode of the Calgary stenographer and the fictional mode of Sime, then, the working girl discovers possibilities in her work that make traditional avenues and traditional endings a little less mandatory.

In *A Room of One's Own*, Virginia Woolf recommends that in order to appreciate women's neglected roles in history, we must learn to think "poetically and prosaically at one and the same moment, thus keeping in touch with fact – that she is Mrs. Martin, aged thirty-six, dressed in blue, wearing a black hat and brown shoes; but not losing sight of fiction either – that she is a vessel in which all sorts of spirits and forces are irritating and flashing perpetually."[7] With her everyday struggles and independent spirit, the figure of the working girl seems uniquely equipped to elicit just this kind of dual perception. On the one hand, working women struggled for all the usual daily necessities, such as earning enough to pay the rent and managing day-to-day workplace strife. But on a more symbolic level, the working girl also attracted great interest from her contemporaries, who saw her significance as figuring a profound social transformation. Writers of socially engaged fiction especially seem to have been eager to explore not only the social implications of women's entrance into the public arena of work but also the individual dilemmas of young women who were gaining a new kind of independence as self-supporting wage earners in the city. In the West, moreover, the feeling of a society actually in the process of creation lent added resonance to the idea of the working girl as a social pioneer, a feeling certainly played upon by Bertrand Sinclair, whose working girl dreams of going West "for a measure of freedom from petty restraints."[8]

Even in the prostitute writer's account, the Canadian West holds a promise of freedom and possibility that she cannot find elsewhere. In Madeleine Blair's chronicle of work as a prostitute and madam, the West actually becomes a motif for her sense of self-discovery and self-assertion: "It was the lure of the 'Just Beyond' which caused my vagrant feet to turn in a northerly direction. To my mind, the Canadian Northwest represented a land of great adventure, an unexplored country in which there was something hidden from me; when once I had heard the call of it my restless heart could know no peace until I had gone 'to search beyond the ranges.'"[9] Madeleine has a strong reaction to the landscape in the West and describes in detail an almost spiritual awakening that takes place upon her arrival in Canada. Sinclair suggests the same experience in his heroine Hazel as she looks at a photograph of the snow-clad Rockies: "She had never seen a greater height of land than the rolling hills of Ontario. Here was a frontier, big and new and raw, holding out to her as she stared at the print a promise – of what? She did not know."[10] Hazel moves west because of the many openings for teachers, and although Madeleine's world is the illicit one of prostitution, workers in her industry were similarly in high demand in the West. She finds more opportunity for financial return there, and in Alberta she successfully starts her own business. But she also reveals that the West offers her greater scope for her own individual development; she walks the prairie in the early morning hours and is able suddenly to imagine a whole new phase to her existence: "My thwarted girlhood was behind me, and in my dawning womanhood I felt that somewhere and somehow I should demand from life the things that had been denied me."[11] Both of these fictional and autobiographical accounts carry their own representational complexities in how they romanticize their heroines and imbue them with this deep aesthetic sensitivity, but one nevertheless suspects that the working girls – even the prostitutes – who moved west for work were likely also inspired by the new landscapes around them, and that their pioneer efforts in the female workforce may have found a fitting backdrop in the Rockies and the Prairies.

In the Canadian West rapid industrialism and exponential population growth in the cities accounted for the steady growth in the female workforce, and women began to define a great deal of the service work necessary in these growing centres. Progress was on everyone's mind, and the towns and cities of the West, so visibly under construction, seemed to hold great promise as a place where the ideals of nationhood and imperial progress might be borne out by the right kind of woman settler. As Ella Sykes put it, "I consider it is an Imperial work to help girls of a high stamp to seek their fortunes beyond the seas – women who will care for our glorious Flag and what it signifies, who will stand for higher ideals than the worship of the 'almighty dollar,' and who will do their part in the land that their brothers are developing so splendidly."[12] It is interesting here that despite her desire to see women "seek their fortunes," Sykes expects them to militate against the materialism of the West – its worship of the "almighty dollar" – and to uphold the purer ideals of the glorious Union Jack. This points to the important tension between women's symbolic role in the West as agents of social uplift and the more concrete reason for their presence, which was to earn a living and to fill a labour shortage. At the turn of the century and following, the West was hungry for workers of both genders; and women's employment agencies helped employers to find domestic workers, waitresses, chambermaids, telephone operators, laundry workers, seamstresses, stenographers, teachers, nurses, sales and retail workers, and factory and food-processing workers. Yet rather than simply adding women's jobs to the help-wanted list and representing the economic incentives available to them, narratives of female migration to the West tended, like Sykes, to add a rhetorical gloss of imperial uplift and romantic fulfilment for this new society's brides-to-be. And as Sykes reports, some women believed so heartily in the West's mythic bachelors that they left rejected husbands in England to find Canadian upgrades or wept upon arriving at a train station where no kneeling bachelors awaited their hands. The working girl and the narratives that thus choreographed her entrance on the western scene are worthy of our attention because they help us to understand the gender history of the West and how the specific elements of the local scene and the narratives that it embraced helped to shape the society that was under such furious construction at the time.

This book has focused on the representation and portrayal of the working girl because it would seem that through representational efforts the working girl became a symbolic figure of social transformation. The intense interest in the working girl – in her morality, her working conditions, her love life – signals the urge of her contemporaries to understand what the rise of the working girl meant and to see in her the social upheavals of the day. This representational work was taking place in a wide range of texts, and I've referenced a sampling of them here to suggest the different kinds of attention that the working girl received from reformers, travel writers, newspapers, and especially authors of fiction. All these were interested in the degree to which the working girl was bucking convention – by entering the public waged workforce, by weighing work against marriage, by supporting herself and living on her own, by inhabiting the dubious venues of the industrializing city, by joining the West's radicalized labour movement, and by mixing with co-workers of heterogeneous origins. Because morality became such a central theme in understandings of the working girl's plight, the actual value and importance of the work that she was doing, her contribution to the workforce and to the economy, tended to be elided and forgotten. But the fictional and nonfictional versions of her to be found in print sources suggest that she was recognized in other ways, especially by creative writers who saw their working-girl heroines as cultural pacesetters through whom to explore the new themes of modern city life.

I have placed these historically specific narratives and historical documents alongside the literary productions of the day, for I believe that the creative portrayals of the working girl help us to understand the imaginative resonance that this figure had in her time. Although the examples are too few to generalize about a pattern, it is worth noting one difference between the eastern and western writers. Eastern writers J.G. Sime and Agnes Maule Machar are committed to social realism in their works, their projects placing the struggles and hardships faced by self-supporting women at centre stage. Western writers Bertrand Sinclair and Isabel Ecclestone Mackay, on the other hand, though both socially engaged writers, include prominent elements of sensationalism and romance in their novels, perhaps reflecting the popular culture that promised adventure and romantic fulfilment for women in the West, with the workplace as a stage on the journey. Sinclair in particular adapts the popular narrative of the working girl who moves west for work and finds herself whisked away by one of the rough-and-tumble backwoods bachelors reputedly endemic to the West.

One aspect of the attitudes toward the working girl that comes out in the sources is a difficulty that many observers had taking her seriously and taking her problems and concerns seriously. One laundry owner who was interviewed by the British Columbia Commission on Labour in 1912 defended the low wages that he paid female employees by stating that "they are girls, mind you. They are not women. You can't class these girls that get $1.25 a day as women."[13] This feeling that they were "just girls" and that their concerns – even about wages – were not a serious matter had subtle but perhaps far-reaching effects. A newspaper article following a highly effective strike by Vancouver telephone operators and linemen took a fly-on-the-wall perspective on the operators' return to work:

> The central exchange office of the telephone company is once more cheerful with the sounds of the dropping drops and the pretty voices of the still prettier hello girls … "I don't care," said the curly-headed little girl as she climbed up on her chair and felt again to ascertain if her earpiece was still on straight, "It was just too mean for anything. In the first place, when we asked for more money we should have got it, and now, when I was having just the loveliest time doing nothing and having a splendid chance to meet Charlie every day, they go and stop it and I have to come back to work." … "This work at the switchboard is really harder than lots of people think. Just imagine the other day before the strike that nice looking boy in the drug store sent me a box of chocolates in the morning and though I was just dying to have one I could not eat any until the afternoon, for you know," she said explainingly, "you just cannot answer calls and eat chocolates. Wasn't that a shame?"[14]

Girlishness here is the central theme, with the "curly-headed little girl" actually having to "climb up on her chair" as though she is truly child-sized. Though the strike in which they had just participated was successful and though this newspaper, the *Vancouver Province*, had largely supported the strikers claims, the portrayal here emphasizes the operators' flippant girlishness, suggesting that the strike was nothing but a pleasant holiday for them and that the hardship of their work consists merely of the inconvenience that one can't work and eat chocolates at the same time. Still, the end of the article grudgingly admits the women's accomplishment: "There they were all working away, long and short, slender and otherwise, and they did really seem to be somewhat weak in numbers and in strength to have put the entire business of a city out of joint for so many days and to have made a wealthy corporation come to terms."[15] The writer of this piece plays on the incongruity of these apparently frivolous "hello girls" wielding such power over business and industry. The media often seems to have struggled to understand the many characteristics of the working girl, particularly when involved in organized labour disputes. This story, like other media portrayals in this period, highlights the social events that union women were known for: "'You just see,' said a vivacious one, 'if we girls can't get up a union ball for them and you just won't be in it, that is unless you belong to a union, and I think,' she added musingly, 'that I'll go in white.'"[16] Suggesting that unionized girl workers simply saw strikes as an excuse to put on a dance and wear a new dress seems an almost calculated attempt to deny political agency to young women who were otherwise showing themselves more than capable of determined and organized protest. What may have been missed was the possibility that dances – key to the youth culture of the day – could perhaps signal political solidarity and provide concrete financial support to a strike and thus have political meaning even while affording an occasion for a white dress. The desire to see wage-earning women for their girlishness could override a serious estimation of their claims and contributions. And this representational dismissal of them as "just girls" likely influenced the culture at large, including the organized labour movement, the middle-class feminist movement, and even early labour historians.

The working girl and the representational complexities surrounding her, then, are important to our understanding of Canada's past, for they show how constructions and representations of gender powerfully shape our understanding of historical circumstances. When she entered the workplace, the working girl stepped into a whirlwind of contradiction about women's place, the perils of the city, and the meaning of work, and she foreshadowed much about women's changing roles in the twentieth century.

# Notes

## INTRODUCTION

1 Alice Barrett Parke, *Hobnobbing with a Countess and other Okanagan Adventures: The Diaries of Alice Barrett Parke, 1891-1900,* ed. Jo Fraser Jones (Vancouver: University of British Columbia Press, 2001), 44.

2 Carolyn Strange, *Toronto's Girl Problem: The Perils and Pleasures of the City, 1880-1930* (Toronto: University of Toronto Press, 1995).

3 Ella Sykes, *A Home-Help in Canada* (London: G. Bell, 1912).

4 Anne McClintock, *Imperial Leather: Race, Gender and Sexuality in the Colonial Contest* (New York: Routledge, 1995), 35.

5 R.G. Moyles and Douglas Owram, *Imperial Dreams and Colonial Realities: British Views of Canada, 1880-1914* (Toronto: University of Toronto Press, 1988), 239.

6 Linda Kealey, *Enlisting Women for the Cause: Women, Labour, and the Left in Canada, 1890-1920* (Toronto: University of Toronto Press, 1998), 16.

7 Canada, *Census,* vol. 7 (1931), 3.

8 Gillian Creese, "The Politics of Dependence: Women, Work, and Unemployment in the Vancouver Labour Movement before World War II," in *British Columbia Reconsidered: Essays on Women*, ed. Gillian Creese and Veronica Strong-Boag (Vancouver: Press Gang, 1992), 370.

9 Melanie Buddle, "The Business of Women: Female Entrepreneurship in British Columbia, 1901-1941," *Journal of the West* 43, 2 (2004): 44-53.

10 Genevieve Lesley, "Domestic Service in Canada, 1880-1920," in *Women at Work: Ontario, 1850-1930,* ed. Janice Acton, Penny Goldsmith, and Bonnie Shepard (Toronto: Canadian Women's Educational Press, 1974), 96.

11 Mary Quayle Innis, *Unfold the Years: A History of the Young Women's Christian Association in Canada* (Toronto: McClelland and Stewart, 1949), 45, 48.

12 Paul Voisey, "The Urbanization of the Canadian Prairies, 1871-1916," in *The Prairie West: Historical Readings*, ed. R. Douglas Francis and Howard Palmer (Edmonton:

Pica Pica Press, 1985), 383.

13 Hugh Dempsey, ed., "Confessions of a Calgary Stenographer" (1914), *Alberta History* 36, 2 (1988): 4.

14 Madeleine Blair [pseud.], *Madeleine: An Autobiography* (1919; reprint, New York: Persea, 1986).


## CHAPTER 1:
## WORKING WOMEN IN THE WEST
## AT THE TURN OF THE CENTURY


1 Keith Grint, *The Sociology of Work: An Introduction* (Cambridge: Polity, 1991), 7.

2 Ella Sykes, *A Home-Help in Canada* (London: G. Bell, 1912), 304.

3 Carolyn Strange and Tina Loo, *Making Good: Law and Moral Regulation in Canada, 1876-1939* (Toronto: University of Toronto Press, 1997).

4 Robert A.J. McDonald, "Working," in *Working Lives: Vancouver, 1886-1986,* ed. Working Lives Collective (Vancouver: New Star, 1985), 28.

5 Jessie M. Saxby, "Women Wanted," in *West Nor'West* (London: James Nisbet and Co., 1890), reprinted in *A Flannel Shirt and Liberty: British Emigrant Gentlewomen in the Canadian West,* ed. Susan Jackel (Vancouver: University of British Columbia Press, 1982), 69.

6 Cited in Susan Jackel, "Introduction," in *A Flannel Shirt and Liberty: British Emigrant Gentlewomen in the Canadian West, 1880-1914,* ed. Susan Jackel (Vancouver: University of British Columbia Press, 1982), plate 1 (following p. 28).

7 Sylvia Van Kirk, *Many Tender Ties: Women in Fur-Trade Society, 1670-1870* (Winnipeg: Watson and Dwyer, 1999), 54.

8 Cynthia Comacchio, *The Infinite Bonds of Family: Domesticity in Canada, 1850-1940* (Toronto: University of Toronto Press, 1999), 46.

9 Jackie Lay, "To Columbia on the Tynemouth: The Emigration of Single Women and Girls in 1862," in *In Her Own Right: Selected Essays on Women's History in B.C.,* ed. Barbara Latham and Cathy Kess (Victoria: Camosun College, 1980), 23.

10 Jackel, "Introduction," xiv.

11 Marion Cran (Mrs. George Cran), *A Woman in Canada* (Toronto: Musson, 1908), 247.

12 Frederick Whymper, *Travel and Adventure in the Territory of Alaska* (New York: Harper and Brothers, 1871), 23.

13 N. de Bertrand Lugrin, *The Pioneer Women of Vancouver Island* (Victoria: Women's Canadian Club, 1928), 147.

14 Whymper, *Travel and Adventure,* 25.

15 Marilyn Barber, "The Gentlewomen of Queen Mary's Coronation Hostel," in *Not Just Pin Money: Selected Essays on the History of Women's Work in British Columbia,* ed. Barbara K. Latham and Roberta J. Pazdro (Victoria: Camosun College, 1984), 145.

16 Adele Perry, *On the Edge of Empire: Gender, Race, and the Making of British Columbia, 1849-1871* (Toronto: University of Toronto Press, 2001), 141.

17 Sykes, *Home-Help,* 5.

18 Ibid., 98.

19 Lugrin, *Pioneer Women,* 156.

20 Sykes, *Home-Help,* 10.

21 Ibid., 28.

22 Ibid.

23 Jean Barman, *The West beyond the West: A History of British Columbia,* rev. ed. (Toronto: University of Toronto Press, 1998), 139-40.

24 Cole Harris, *The Resettlement of British Columbia* (Vancouver: University of British Columbia Press, 1997), 263.

25 George Godwin, *The Eternal Forest* (1929; reprint, Vancouver: Godwin, 1994), 119.

26 Daiva Stasiulus and Radha Jhappan, "The Fractious Politics of a Settler Society: Canada," in *Unsettling Settler Societies: Articulations of Gender, Race, and Class,* ed. Daiva Stasiulus and Nira Yuval-Davis (London: Sage, 1995), 98.

27 Adele Perry, "Interlocuting Empire: Colonial Womanhood, Settler Identity, and Frances Herring," in *Rediscovering the British World,* ed. Phillip A. Buckner and R.D. Francis (Calgary: University of Calgary Press, 2003), 159.

28 Sykes, *Home-Help,* 145.

29 Whymper, *Travel and Adventure,* 23.

30 Elizabeth Lewthwaite, "Women's Work in Western Canada," *Fortnightly Review,* October 1901, reprinted in *A Flannel Shirt and Liberty: British Emigrant Gentlewomen in the Canadian West,* ed. Susan Jackel (Vancouver: University of British Columbia Press, 1982), 118.

31 Ibid.

32 Ibid., 113.

33 Barbara Roberts, "'A Work of Empire': Canadian Reformers and British Female Immigration," in *A Not Unreasonable Claim: Women and Reform in Canada, 1880s-1920s,* ed. Linda Kealey (Toronto: Women's Press, 1979), 186.

34 Carol Fairbanks, *Prairie Women: Images in American and Canadian Fiction* (New Haven: Yale University Press, 1986).

35 Cran, *Woman in Canada,* 109.

36 Robert A.J. McDonald, *Making Vancouver: Class, Status, and Social Boundaries, 1863-1913* (Vancouver: University of British Columbia Press, 1996), 189.

37 Sykes, *Home-Help,* 24.

38 Lugrin, *Pioneer Women,* 150.

39 Sara Jeanette Duncan, *Selected Journalism*, ed. T.E. Tausky (Ottawa: Tecumseh, 1978), 30.

40 Mrs. Mitchell, "Address," in British Columbia Commission on Labour (1912-14), Transcripts of Proceedings, box 2, file 1, 313-17, quote at 317, BC Archives.

41 Helena Gutteridge, "Woman's Work," *BC Federationist,* 16 January 1914, 5.

42 Paul Voisey, "The Urbanization of the Canadian Prairies, 1871-1916," in *The Prairie West: Historical Readings*, ed. R. Douglas Francis and Howard Palmer (Edmonton: Pica Pica Press, 1985), 390.

43 Sykes, *Home-Help,* 22.

44 "The City and the School," *Vancouver Province,* 6 March 1915, 9.

45 Mary Ann Doane, *Femmes Fatales: Feminism, Film Theory, Psychoanalysis* (New York: Routledge, 1991), 263.

46 J.S. Woodsworth, *My Neighbor: A Study of City Conditions, A Plea for Social Service* (1911; reprint, Toronto: University of Toronto Press, 1972), 11.

47 Ibid., 63.

48 Moral and Social Reform Council of British Columbia, "Social Vice in Vancouver," report (Vancouver: James F. Morris, 1912), 3.

49 Linda Kealey, *Enlisting Women for the Cause: Women, Labour, and the Left in Canada, 1890-1920* (Toronto: University of Toronto Press, 1998), 34.

50 Christine Smillie, "The Invisible Workforce: Women Workers in Saskatchewan from 1905 to World War II," *Saskatchewan History* 39, 2 (1986): 62-80.

51 Gutteridge, "Woman's Work," 5.

52 British Columbia Commission on Labour (1912-14), Transcripts of Proceedings, box 1, file 8, 105-6, BC Archives.

53 Strange and Loo, *Making Good,* 214.

54 Mrs. Mitchell, "Address," in British Columbia Commission on Labour (1912-14), Transcripts of Proceedings, box 2, file 1, 313, BC Archives.

55 C.M. Bayfield, "Paper on Home-Making as a Profession," in *Report of the 14th Annual Meeting of the National Council of Women of Canada,* proceedings of meeting held in Vancouver, 1907 (Toronto: G. Parker and Sons, 1907), 67-68, original emphasis.

56 "Wage Slaves in Hotels," *Woman Worker,* November 1927, 8-9.

57 Maude Pettit ("Videre"), "There Is the Light of Love and Romance in Her Life, Too: Life Stories of Girl Workers in Toronto Factories," *Toronto Star,* 17 June 1912, 14.

58 Kathy Peiss, "'Charity Girls' and City Pleasures: Historical Notes on Working-Class Sexuality, 1880-1920," in *Passion and Power: Sexuality in History*, ed. Kathy Peiss and Christina Simmons (Philadelphia: Temple University Press, 1987), 63.

59 Maude Pettit ("Videre"), "We Had Spare Ribs, Potatoes, and Some Tapioca Pudding: Life Stories of Girl Workers in Toronto Factories," *Toronto Star,* 6 June 1912, 1.

CHAPTER 2:
THE URBAN WORKING GIRL IN
TURN-OF-THE-CENTURY CANADIAN LITERATURE

1 Carole Gerson, "Marie Joussaye Fotheringham: Canada's First Woman Labour Poet," *Canadian Notes and Queries* 44 (Spring 1991): 21-23.

2 Marie Joussaye, quoted in ibid., 22.

3 Wayne Roberts, *Honest Womanhood: Feminism, Femininity and Class Consciousness among Toronto Working Women, 1893-1914* (Toronto: University of Toronto Press, 1986); Linda Kealey, *Enlisting Women for the Cause: Women, Labour, and the Left in Canada, 1890-1920* (Toronto: University of Toronto Press, 1998).

4 Marie Joussaye, "Only a Working Girl," in *The Songs that Quinte Sang* (Belleville, ON: Sun Printing and Publishing Company, 1895), 66-67.

5 Peter Donovan ("Tom Folio"), review of *Sister Woman, Saturday Night,* 28 February 1920, 9.

6 "A Montreal Woman on Women," *Canadian Bookman,* April 1920, 57.

7 Carole Gerson, "Introduction," in *Roland Graeme, Knight: A Novel of Our Time,* by Agnes Maule Machar (Ottawa: Tecumseh, 1996), xiii.

8 W.H. New, *A History of Canadian Literature* (London: Macmillan, 1991), 140.

9 Ibid., 140.

10 Isabel Ecclestone Mackay, *House of Windows* (Toronto: Cassel and Co., 1912), 66.

11 Bertrand Sinclair, *North of Fifty-Three* (New York: Grosset and Dunlap, 1914), 158.

12 Ibid., 161.

13 Ibid., 276.

14 Sandra Campbell, "Introduction: Biocritical Context for J.G. Sime and *Sister Woman,*" in *Sister Woman,* by J.G. Sime, Canadian critical ed., ed. Sandra Campbell (Ottawa: Tecumseh, 2004), 212.

15 J.G. Sime, quoted in ibid., 214.

16 Annie Merrill, "The Woman in Business," *Canadian Magazine* 21 (1903): 409.

17 Ibid.

18 Ibid.

19 Agnes Maule Machar, *Roland Graeme, Knight: A Novel of Our Time* (1892; reprint, Ottawa: Tecumseh, 1996), 66.

20 Sinclair, *North of Fifty-Three,* 52.

21 Ibid., 55.

22 J.G. Sime, *Sister Woman* (1919), Canadian critical ed., ed. Sandra Campbell (Ottawa: Tecumseh, 2004), 27, 31.

23 "A Montreal Woman on Women," *Canadian Bookman,* April 1920, 58.

24 Merrill, "Woman in Business," 408.

25 Sime, *Sister Woman,* 26.

26 Anne McClintock, *Imperial Leather: Race, Gender and Sexuality in the Colonial Contest* (New York: Routledge, 1995), 172.

27 Sinclair, *North of Fifty-Three,* 14.

28 Ibid., 21.

29 Ibid., 53.

30 Ibid., 55.

31 Ibid., 65.

32 Ibid., 79.

33 Ibid., 186.
34 Ibid., 213.
35 Nan Enstad, *Ladies of Labour, Girls of Adventure: Working Women, Popular Culture, and Labor Politics at the Turn of the Twentieth Century* (New York: Columbia University Press, 1999), 19.
36 Michael Denning, *Mechanic Accents: Dime Novels and Working-Class Culture in America* (New York: Verso, 1987), 196.
37 Ibid., 192.
38 Mackay, *House of Windows,* 151.
39 Denning, *Mechanic Accents,* 191.
40 Enstad, *Ladies of Labour,* 74.
41 Merrill, "Woman in Business," 408.
42 Enstad, *Ladies of Labour,* 78.
43 Mackay, *House of Windows,* 123.
44 Hugh Dempsey, ed., "Confessions of a Calgary Stenographer" (1914), *Alberta History* 36, 2 (1988): 4.
45 Susan Porter Benson, *Counter Cultures: Saleswomen, Managers, and Customers in American Department Stores, 1890-1940* (Chicago: University of Illinois Press, 1986), 235.
46 Mackay, *House of Windows,* 75.
47 Sime, *Sister Woman,* 85.
48 Mariana Valverde, "The Love of Finery: Fashion and the Fallen Woman in Nineteenth-Century Social Discourse," *Victorian Studies* 32 (Winter 1989): 169.
49 Miss Philips, "Paper on Home Arts and Handicrafts," in *Report of the 8th Annual Meeting of the National Council of Women of Canada,* proceedings of meeting held in London, Ontario, 1901 (Ottawa: Taylor and Clarke, 1901), 138.
50 Machar, *Roland Graeme, Knight,* 283.
51 Mackay, *House of Windows,* 144.
52 Ibid.
53 Linda Kealey, *Enlisting Women for the Cause: Women, Labour, and the Left in Canada, 1890-1920* (Toronto: University of Toronto Press, 1998), 36.
54 Benson, *Counter Cultures,* 210.
55 Ibid., 181.
56 Ibid., 233.
57 Mackay, *House of Windows,* 125.
58 Ibid., 35.
59 Ibid., 195.
60 Ibid., 65.
61 Ibid., 138.
62 Ibid., 66.
63 Merrill, "Woman in Business," 408.
64 Sime, *Sister Woman,* 191.

65 Ibid., 65-66.

66 Ibid., 55.

67 Ibid., 143.

68 Ibid., 192.

69 Ibid., 193-94.

70 Ibid., 195.

71 Carolyn Strange, *Toronto's Girl Problem: The Perils and Pleasures of the City, 1880-1930* (Toronto: University of Toronto Press, 1995), 22.

## CHAPTER 3:
## WHITE SLAVES, PROSTITUTES, AND DELINQUENTS

1 Mary Odem, *Delinquent Daughters: Protecting and Policing Adolescent Female Sexuality in the United States, 1885-1920* (Chapel Hill: University of North Carolina Press, 1995), 95.

2 Barbara Meil Hobson, *Uneasy Virtue: The Politics of Prostitution and the American Reform Tradition* (New York: Basic Books, 1987), 189.

3 Joan Sangster, *Regulating Girls and Women: Sexuality, Family and the Law in Ontario, 1920-1960* (Don Mills: Oxford University Press, 2001), 88.

4 Ibid., 89.

5 W.T. Stead, "The Maiden Tribute of Modern Babylon," *Pall Mall Gazette* (London), 4 July 1885: 1; 6 July 1885: 1-6; 7 July 1885:1-6; 8 July 1885: 1-5; 10 July 1885: 1-9.

6 Cecily Devereux, "'A Strange, Inverted World': Interpreting 'The Maiden Tribute of Modern Babylon' in English Canada," *Essays on Canadian Writing* 62 (Fall 1997): 51.

7 Ruth Rosen, *The Lost Sisterhood: Prostitution in America, 1900-1918* (Baltimore: Johns Hopkins Universtiy Press, 1982) 115-16.

8 Ibid., 153.

9 Hilda Glynn-Ward [pseud.], *The Writing on the Wall* (1921; reprint, Toronto: University of Toronto Press, 1974), 83.

10 Ibid., 84.

11 Ibid., 83.

12 Mariana Valverde, *The Age of Light, Soap, and Water: Moral Reform in English Canada, 1885-1925* (Toronto: McClelland and Stewart, 1991), 79.

13 Deborah Nilson, "The 'Social Evil': Prostitution in Vancouver, 1900-1920," in *In Her Own Right: Selected Essays on Women's History in BC,* ed. Barbara Latham and Cathy Kess (Victoria: Camosun College, 1980), 206.

14 John G. Shearer, *Canada's War on the White Slave Trade* (Toronto: Board of Moral and Social Reform, 1912), 8.

15 Ibid., 10.

16 Rosen, *Lost Sisterhood,* 132.

17 Gary Kinsman, *The Regulation of Desire: Homo and Hetero Sexualities*, rev. 2nd ed. (Montreal: Black Rose, 1996), 57.

18 Shearer, *Canada's War,* 11.

19 Bessie Pullen-Burry, *From Halifax to Vancouver* (London: Mills and Boon, 1912), 324, original emphasis.

20 Nellie McClung, quoted in David Jones, "There Is Some Power about the Land: The Western Canadian Agrarian Press and Country Life Ideology," *Journal of Canadian Studies* 17, 3 (1982): 102.

21 Nellie McClung, *Sowing Seeds in Danny* (New York: Doubleday, Page and Company, 1908); Nellie McClung, *The Second Chance* (Toronto: Ryerson Press, 1910); Nellie McClung, *Purple Springs* (Toronto: T. Allen, 1921).

22 Shearer, *Canada's War,* 4.

23 B.G. Jefferis, *Search lights on health, light on dark corners: A complete sexual science and a guide to purity and physical manhood, advice to maiden, wife and mother, love, courtship and marriage* (Toronto: J.L. Nichols, 1894), 382.

24 Kathy Peiss, *Cheap Amusements: Working Women and Leisure in Turn-of-the-Century New York* (Philadelphia: Temple University Press, 1986), 382.

25 Valverde, *Age of Light,* 83.

26 Nilson, "'Social Evil,'" 213; John McLaren, "White Slavers: The Reform of Canada's Prostitution Law and Patterns of Enforcement, 1900-1920," *Criminal Justice History* 8 (1987): 125.

27 Charlene P. Smith, "Boomtown Brothels in the Kootenays, 1895-1905," in *People and Place: Historical Influences on Legal Culture*, ed. Jonathan Swainger and Constance Backhouse (Vancouver: University of British Columbia Press, 2003), 146.

28 Greg Marquis, "Vancouver Vice: The Police and the Negotiation of Morality, 1904-1935," in *Essays in the History of Canadian Law VI: British Columbia and the Yukon*, ed. Hamar Foster and John McLaren (Toronto: University of Toronto Press, 1995), 243.

29 Lori Rotenberg, "The Wayward Worker: Toronto's Prostitute at the Turn of the Century," in *Women at Work: Ontario, 1850-1930,* ed. Janice Acton, Penny Goldsmith, and Bonnie Shepard (Toronto: Canadian Women's Educational Press, 1974), 33.

30 Madeleine Blair [pseud.], *Madeleine: An Autobiography* (1919; reprint, New York: Persea, 1986), 254.

31 Ibid., 255.

32 Ibid., 282.

33 Marcia Carlisle, "Introduction," in *Madeleine: An Autobiography,* by Madeleine Blair [pseud.] (New York: Persea, 1986), xxii.

34 Sidonie Smith, *A Poetics of Women's Autobiography: Marginality and the Fictions of Self-Representation* (Bloomington: Indiana University Press, 1987), 48-49.

35 Blair, *Madeleine,* 326.

36 Sidonie Smith and Julia Watson, *Autobiography: A Guide for Interpreting Life Narratives* (Minneapolis: University of Minnesota Press, 2001), 10.

37 Blair, *Madeleine,* 176-77.

38 Ibid., 179-80.

39 Ibid., 178-79.

40 Ibid., 252.

41 Ibid., 247.

42 Ibid., 266.

43 Ibid., 327.

44 Ibid., 321.

45 Ibid., 322.

46 Ibid., 164.

47 Ibid., 324.

48 Marquis, "Vancouver Vice," 267.

49 McLaren, "White Slavers."

50 Moral and Social Reform Council of British Columbia, "Social Vice in Vancouver," report (Vancouver: James F. Morris, 1912), 5

51 Ibid., 6.

52 Carolyn Strange and Tina Loo, *Making Good: Law and Moral Regulation in Canada, 1876-1939* (Toronto: University of Toronto Press, 1997), 95-96.

53 Indiana Matters, "Sinners or Sinned Against?: Historical Aspects of Female Juvenile Delinquency in British Columbia," in *Not Just Pin Money: Selected Essays on the History of Women's Work in British Columbia,* ed. Barbara K. Latham and Roberta J. Pazdro (Victoria: Camosun College, 1980), 270.

54 Ibid.

55 Lucy Brooking, "A Study of the Delinquent Girl," *Social Welfare,* 1 April 1921, 182.

56 Ibid.

## CHAPTER 4:
### GIRLS ON STRIKE

1 "Albert Goodwin Shot and Killed by Police Officer Near Comox Lake," *BC Federationist,* 2 August 1918, 1.

2 Irene Howard, *The Struggle for Social Justice in British Columbia: Helena Gutteridge, the Unknown Reformer* (Vancouver: University of British Columbia Press, 1992), 95.

3 Harry Gutkin and Mildred Gutkin, *Profiles in Dissent: The Shaping of Radical Thought in the Canadian West* (Edmonton: NeWest, 1997); Howard, *Struggle for Social Justice.*

4 Todd McCallum, "'Not a Sex Question'? The One Big Union and the Politics of Radical Manhood," *Labour/Le Travail* 42 (Fall 1998): 32.

5 Ruth Frager, "No Proper Deal: Women Workers and the Canadian Labour Movement, 1870-1940," in *Union Sisters: Women in the Labour Movement,* ed. Linda

Briskin and Lynda Yanz (Toronto: Women's Press, 1983), 50.

6 Janice Newton, *The Feminist Challenge to the Canadian Left, 1900-1918* (Montreal and Kingston: McGill-Queen's University Press, 1995), 41-42.

7 Gillian Creese, "The Politics of Dependence: Women, Work, and Unemployment in the Vancouver Labour Movement before World War II," in *British Columbia Reconsidered: Essays on Women*, ed. Gillian Creese and Veronica Strong-Boag (Vancouver: Press Gang, 1992), 370.

8 Helena Gutteridge, "A Minimum Wage," *BC Federationist*, 16 January 1914, 3.

9 Frager, "No Proper Deal," 54.

10 Star Rosenthal, "Union Maids: Organized Women Workers in Vancouver, 1900-1915," *BC Studies* 41 (Spring 1979): 36-55.

11 Christine Smillie, "The Invisible Workforce: Women Workers in Saskatchewan from 1905 to World War II," *Saskatchewan History* 39, 2 (1986): 62-80.

12 Mary Horodyski, "Women and the Winnipeg General Strike of 1919," *Manitoba History* 11 (Spring 1986): 28-37.

13 Helena Gutteridge, "Votes for Women and Trade Unions," *BC Federationist*, 17 October 1913, 5.

14 Howard, *Struggle for Social Justice*, 100.

15 "Chambermaids Back To Work," *BC Federationist*, 9 August 1918, 1; "Laundry Workers Still on Strike," *BC Federationist*, 20 September 1918, 1.

16 "Strike Ties Up Laundries," *Vancouver Daily World*, 10 September 1918, 15.

17 "They Demand Protection," *Vancouver Province*, 19 September 1918, 17.

18 Ibid.

19 "Chief of Police to Take Hand in Laundry Strike," *Vancouver Daily World*, 19 September 1918, 1.

20 Ibid.

21 "Laundry Workers Still on Strike," *BC Federationist*, 20 September 1919, 1.

22 Linda Kealey, "No Special Protection -- No Sympathy: Women's Activism in the Canadian Labour Revolt of 1919," in *Class, Community and the Labour Movement: Wales and Canada, 1850-1930*, ed. Deian R. Hopkin and Gregory Kealey (Wales: Society for Welsh Labour History and the Committee on Canadian Labour History, 1989), 152, 136.

23 Howard, *Struggle for Social Justice*, 61-2.

24 "Home and Domestic Employees' Union," *BC Federationist*, 28 March 1913, 1.

25 Rosenthal, "Union Maid"; "Home and Domestic Employees' Union," 1.

26 "Home and Domestic Employees' Union," 4.

27 "Union Women's Social Club," *BC Federationist*, 5 March 1915, 1.

28 "Laundry Workers Have Good Time," *BC Federationist*, 27 September 1918, 5.

29 "Second Laundry Workers Dance," *BC Federationist*, 11 October 1918, 1.

30 "Laundry Workers Still Carrying On Strike," *BC Federationist*, 29 November 1918, 1.

31 "Laundry Strikers Cause Unrest," *BC Federationist*, 1 November 1918, 1.

32 "Pelted with Eggs and Then Kicked," *Vancouver Province*, 11 December 1918, 21.

33 Smillie, "Invisible Workforce," 71.

34 "Some Reasons Why," *BC Federationist,* 10 October 1913, 5.

35 The union would go on to dispute the wage scale for women under eighteen; see "Minimum Wage and Laundry Workers," *BC Federationist,* 20 June 1919, 2.

36 "Laundry Workers to Hold Dance," *BC Federationist,* 11 July 1919, 1.

37 "'Hello' Girls Are Not Easily Beaten," *BC Federationist,* 11 July 1919, 1.

38 Elaine Bernard, *The Long Distance Feeling: A History of the Telecommunications Workers Union* (Vancouver: New Star, 1982).

39 "This Will Be Some Affair," *BC Federationist,* 1 August 1919, 1.

40 Helen Armstrong, quoted in *Western Labor News,* 12 September 1919, 8.

41 Gutkin and Gutkin, *Profiles in Dissent.*

42 "Winnipeg Is Isolated, Channels Are Blocked," *Toronto Star,* 17 May 1919, 1.

43 Horodyski, "Women and the Winnipeg General Strike"; Kealey, "No Special Protection," 135.

44 "Strike Committee Issues Statement," *Winnipeg Evening Tribune,* 15 May 1919, 2.

45 "Winnipeg Is Isolated, Channels Are Blocked," *Toronto Star,* 17 May 1919, 1.

46 "No Girl Need Want for Food," *Western Labor News, Strike Bulletin,* 26 May 1919, 3; "Women Open Eating House in Strathcona Hotel," *Western Labor News, Strike Bulletin,* 23 May 1919, 1.

47 "Hello Girls!" *Western Labor News, Strike Bulletin,* 20 May 1919, 2.

48 "Multitudes Flock to Labor Church," *Western Labor News, Strike Bulletin,* 10 June 1919, 1.

49 "The Dance," *Western Labor News, Strike Bulletin,* 11 June 1919, 4.

50 "Mrs. Armstrong to Stand Trial," *Winnipeg Evening Tribune,* 25 June 1919, 5.

51 "Good for the Goose, Good for the Gander," *Western Labor News, Strike Bulletin,* 9 June 1919, 2.

52 "A Word to the Wise," *Western Labor News, Strike Bulletin,* 7 June 1919, 4.

53 "Weston Women Wreck Stores' Delivery Rigs - Threaten to Murder Drivers and Special Policemen Sent as Guards," *Winnipeg Evening Tribune,* 6 June 1919, 2.

54 McCallum, "'Not a Sex Question'?" 53.

55 "Mounted Policemen Charge Huge Crowd at Portage and Main," *Winnipeg Evening Tribune,* 10 June 1919, 1.

56 "Police Kept off Streets after Fighting," *Winnipeg Evening Tribune,* 11 June 1919, 2.

57 "Sidelights on the Riot," *Winnipeg Evening Tribune,* 11 June 1919, 5.

58 "1 Killed, Many Hurt in Winnipeg Riots," *Toronto Star,* 23 June 1919, 8.

59 "Gray Blames Leaders of Soldier-Strikers for Inciting Mob to Riot," *Winnipeg Evening Tribune,* 23 June 1919, 3.

60 "Isolated 'Cop' Fighting Off Crowd Is Run Down from behind by a Motor," *Winnipeg Evening Tribune,* 23 June 1919, 3.

61 Ibid.

62 Ethelwyn Ellis, "Who Do the Most Flirting in Winnipeg, Men or Women? Reporter of Gentler Sex Blames Girls," *Winnipeg Evening Tribune,* 7 June 1919, 5.

63 Ibid.

64 Roy Buckingham, "Bow-Legged Scribe Sallies Forth to Find Romance; Says

Coquetting is Fifty-Fifty," *Winnipeg Evening Tribune,* 7 June 1919, 5.

65 Ellis, "Who Do the Most Flirting," 5.

66 Virginia Woolf, *A Room of One's Own* (1929; reprint, London: Grafton, 1977), 49.

## CHAPTER 5:
## WHITE WORKING GIRLS AND THE
## MIXED-RACE WORKPLACE

1 "Should Chinese Work with White Girls?" *Vancouver Star,* 8 August 1924, 4.

2 Alicja Muszynski, "Race and Gender: Structural Determinants in the Formation of British Columbia"s Salmon Cannery Labour Force," in *Class, Gender, and Region: Essays in Canadian Historical Sociology,* ed. Gregory S. Kealey (St. John's, NF: Committee on Canadian Labour History, 1988).

3 "Scotch Girls Cheaper than Chinamen," *BC Federationist,* 18 April 1913, 1.

4 Local Council of Women, "Recommendations for Changes or Additions to the 'Factory, Shops and Offices Act,'" in British Columbia Commission on Labour (1912-14), Transcripts of Proceedings, box 2, file 1, 9, BC Archives.

5 Constance Backhouse, *Colour-Coded: A Legal History of Racism in Canada, 1900-1950* (Toronto: Published for the Osgoode Society for Canadian Legal History by University of Toronto Press, 1999), 6.

6 Constance Backhouse, "The White Women's Labour Laws: Anti-Chinese Racism in Early Twentieth-Century Canada," *Law and History Review* 14, 2 (Autumn 1996): 346.

7 Ibid., 362.

8 "Domestics Bill in the House," *Vancouver Province,* 5 December 1924, 7.

9 Kay Anderson, *Vancouver's Chinatown: Racial Discourse in Canada, 1875-1980* (Montreal and Kingston: McGill-Queen's University Press, 1991), 97.

10 Robert A.J. McDonald, *Making Vancouver: Class, Status, and Social Boundaries, 1863-1913* (Vancouver: University of British Columbia Press, 1996), 206.

11 Canada, *House of Commons Debates* (8 May 1922), 1516.

12 Robert A. Campbell, *Sit Down and Drink Your Beer: Regulating Vancouver's Beer Parlours, 1925-1954* (Toronto: University of Toronto Press, 2001), 85.

13 Ibid., 81.

14 Canada, *House of Commons Debates* (8 May 1922), 1516.

15 Angus McLaren, *Our Own Master Race: Eugenics in Canada, 1885-1945* (Toronto: Oxford University Press, 1990), 49

16 Canada, *House of Commons Debates* (8 May 1922), 1516.

17 Ibid., 1521.

18 Vron Ware, *Beyond the Pale: White Women, Racism and History* (London: Verso, 1992), 162.

19 Canada, *House of Commons Debates* (8 May 1922), 1533.

20 Ibid.

21 Ibid., 1529-30.

22 "Editorial," *Vancouver Beacon,* December 1925, 5.

23 "Report of the Supervisor of the Women's Branch, Miss M.V. Burnham," in Canada, *Report of the Department of Immigration and Colonization,* Annual Departmental Reports, 1927-28 (Ottawa: Government of Canada, 1927), 52.

24 Ibid., 81.

25 Julia Bush, "'The Right Sort of Woman': Female Emigrators and Emigration to the British Empire, 1890-1910," *Women's History Review* 313 (1994): 396.

26 Ninette Kelley and Michael Trebilcock, *The Making of the Mosaic: A History of Canadian Immigration Policy* (Toronto: University of Toronto Press, 1998), 192.

27 Anne McClintock, *Imperial Leather: Race, Gender and Sexuality in the Colonial Contest* (New York: Routledge, 1995), 154.

28 Edward Starkins, *Who Killed Janet Smith?* (Toronto: Macmillan, 1984); Ian MacDonald and Betty O'Keefe, *Canadian Holy War: A Story of Clans, Tongs, Murder, and Bigotry* (Surrey, BC: Heritage House, 2000).

29 "Girl Witness Is Cheered by Court Crowd," *Vancouver Star,* 8 September 1924, 1.

30 Ibid.

31 Ibid.

32 Ibid.

33 "City Scots Probe Death of Nurse," *Vancouver Star,* 29 July 1924, 1.

34 "No Fear of Chinese Boy Is Recorded," *Vancouver Sun,* 8 September 1924, 4.

35 Ibid., 4.

36 "Girl Witness Is Cheered by Court Crowd," *Vancouver Star,* 8 September 1924, 1.

37 "Woman May Be Killer," *Vancouver Sun,* 30 August 1924, 1.

38 "No Fear of Chinese Boy Is Recorded," *Vancouver Sun,* 8 September 1924, 4.

39 Ibid., 1.

40 Ibid., 1.

41 "Janet Smith Feared Chinese Friends State," *Vancouver Star,* 2 August 1924, 1.

42 "Janet Smith Case," *Vancouver Star,* 11 August 1924, 1.

43 Ware, *Beyond the Pale,* 38.

44 "Scots Demand Inquiry into Tragedy," *Vancouver Star,* 7 August 1924, 1.

45 "Should Chinese Work with White Girls?" *Vancouver Star,* 8 August 1924, 4.

46 "Chinese and White Girls," *Vancouver Star,* 13 November 1924, 4.

47 "Chinese and White Girls," *Vancouver Star,* 9 October 1924, 4.

48 "Domestic Servants," *BC Federationist,* 16 May 1924, 1.

49 "Servant Girls Quit Homes, Refusing to Work with Chinese," *Victoria Daily Times,* 24 November 1924, 1.

50 "Housemaids Opposed to Oriental Ban Act," *Vancouver Star,* 29 November 1924, 1.

## CONCLUSION:
## JUST GIRLS

1 Isabel Ecclestone Mackay, *House of Windows* (Toronto: Cassel and Co., 1912) 111.

2 Hugh Dempsey, ed., "Confessions of a Calgary Stenographer" (1914), *Alberta History* 36, 2 (1988): 2.

3 Ibid., 14.

4 Alice Barrett Parke, *Hobnobbing with a Countess and Other Okanagan Adventures: The Diaries of Alice Barrett Parke, 1891-1900*, ed. Jo Fraser Jones (Vancouver: University of British Columbia Press, 2001), 44.

5 J.G. Sime, *Sister Woman* (1919), Canadian critical ed., ed. Sandra Campbell (Ottawa: Tecumseh, 2004), 205.

6 Ibid.

7 Virginia Woolf, *A Room of One's Own* (1929; reprint, London: Grafton, 1977), 50.

8 Bertrand Sinclair, *North of Fifty-Three* (New York: Grosset and Dunlap, 1914), 55.

9 Madeleine Blair [pseud.], *Madeleine: An Autobiography* (1919; reprint, New York: Persea, 1986), 243.

10 Sinclair, *North of Fifty-Three,* 55.

11 Blair, *Madeleine,* 180.

12 Ella Sykes, *A Home-Help in Canada* (London: G. Bell, 1912), 304.

13 British Columbia Commission on Labour (1912-14), Transcripts of Proceedings, box 1, file 8, 105-6, BC Archives.

14 "Union Telephone Girls Resume Their Places at the Switchboard," *Vancouver Province,* 15 December 1902, 1.

15 Ibid.

16 Ibid.

# Bibliography

"Albert Goodwin Shot and Killed by Police Officer Near Comox Lake." *BC Federationist,* 2 August 1918, 1.

Anderson, Kay. *Vancouver's Chinatown: Racial Discourse in Canada, 1875-1980.* Montreal and Kingston: McGill-Queen's University Press, 1991.

Backhouse, Constance. *Colour-Coded: A Legal History of Racism in Canada, 1900-1950.* Toronto: Published for the Osgoode Society for Canadian Legal History by University of Toronto Press, 1999.

–. "The White Women's Labour Laws: Anti-Chinese Racism in Early Twentieth-Century Canada." *Law and History Review* 14, 2 (Autumn 1996): 315-68.

Barber, Marilyn. "The Gentlewomen of Queen Mary's Coronation Hostel." In *Not Just Pin Money: Selected Essays on the History of Women's Work in British Columbia,* ed. Barbara K. Latham and Roberta J. Pazdro, 141-58. Victoria: Camosun College, 1984.

Barman, Jean. *The West Beyond the West: A History of British Columbia.* Rev. ed. Toronto: University of Toronto Press, 1998.

Bayfield, C.M. "Paper on Home-Making as a Profession." In *Report of the 14th Annual Meeting of the National Council of Women of Canada,* 67-68. Proceedings of meeting held in Vancouver, 1907. Toronto: G. Parker and Sons, 1907.

Benson, Susan Porter. *Counter Cultures: Saleswomen, Managers, and Customers in American Department Stores, 1890-1940.* Chicago: University of Illinois Press, 1986.

Bernard, Elaine. *The Long Distance Feeling: A History of The Telecommunications Workers Union.* Vancouver: New Star, 1982.

–. "Last Back: Folklore and the Telephone Operators in the 1919 Vancouver General Strike." In *Not Just Pin Money: Selected Essays on the History of Women's Work in British Columbia,* ed. Barbara K. Latham and Roberta J. Pazdro, 279-86. Victoria: Camosun College, 1984.

Blair, Madeleine [pseud.]. *Madeleine: An Autobiography.* 1919. Reprint, New York: Persea, 1986.

British Columbia Commission on Labour (1912-14). Transcripts of Proceedings. Box
    1, file 8. BC Archives.

Brooking, Lucy. "A Study of the Delinquent Girl." *Social Welfare* 1 (April 1921): 181-84.

Buckingham, Roy. "Bow-Legged Scribe Sallies Forth to Find Romance; Says
    Coquetting is Fifty-Fifty." *Winnipeg Evening Tribune,* 7 June 1919, 5.

Buddle, Melanie. "The Business of Women: Female Entrepreneurship in British
    Columbia, 1901-1941." *Journal of the West* 43, 2 (2004): 44-53.

Bush, Julia. "'The Right Sort of Woman': Female Emigrators and Emigration to the
    British Empire, 1890-1910." *Women's History Review* 313 (1994): 385-409.

Campbell, Robert A. *Sit Down and Drink Your Beer: Regulating Vancouver's Beer
    Parlours, 1925-1954.* Toronto: University of Toronto Press, 2001.

Campbell, Sandra. "'Gently Scan': Theme and Technique in J.G. Sime's 'Sister
    Woman' (1919)." *Canadian Literature* 133 (Summer 1992): 40-55.

—. "Introduction: Biocritical Context for J.G. Sime and *Sister Woman.*" In *Sister
    Woman,* by J.G. Sime, Canadian critical ed., ed. Sandra Campbell. Ottawa:
    Tecumseh, 2004.

Canada. *Census*. Vol. 7. 1931.

Canada. *House of Commons Debates*. 8 May 1922.

Carlisle, Marcia. "Introduction." In *Madeleine: An Autobiography,* by Madeleine Blair
    [pseud.], v-xxviii. New York: Persea, 1986.

"Chambermaids Back to Work." *BC Federationist,* 9 August 1918, 1.

"Chief of Police to Take Hand in Laundry Strike." *Vancouver Daily World,* 19
    September 1918, 1.

"Chinese and White Girls." *Vancouver Star,* 9 October 1924, 4.

"Chinese and White Girls." *Vancouver Star,* 13 November 1924, 4.

"The City and the School." *Vancouver Province,* 6 March 1915, 9.

"City Scots Probe Death of Nurse." *Vancouver Star,* 29 July 1924, 1.

Comacchio, Cynthia. *The Infinite Bonds of Family: Domesticity in Canada, 1850-1940.*
    Toronto: University of Toronto Press, 1999.

Coote, Lillian. "Home and Domestic Employees' Union." *BC Federationist,* 28 March
    1913, 1, 4.

—. "Home and Domestic Employees' Union." *BC Federationist,* 11 April 1913, 2.

Cran, Marion (Mrs. George Cran). *A Woman in Canada*. Toronto: Musson, 1908.

Creese, Gillian. "The Politics of Dependence: Women, Work, and Unemployment
    in the Vancouver Labour Movement before World War II." In *British Columbia
    Reconsidered: Essays on Women,* ed. Gillian Creese and Veronica Strong-Boag,
    364-90. Vancouver: Press Gang, 1992.

"The Dance." *Western Labor News, Strike Bulletin,* 11 June 1919, 4.

Dempsey, Hugh, ed., "Confessions of a Calgary Stenographer." *Alberta History* 36, 2
    (1988): 1-15.

Denning, Michael. *Mechanic Accents: Dime Novels and Working-Class Culture in
    America.* New York: Verso, 1987.

Devereux, Cecily. "'A Strange, Inverted World': Interpreting 'The Maiden Tribute of Modern Babylon' in English Canada." *Essays on Canadian Writing* 62 (Fall 1997): 46-64.

Doane, Mary Ann. *Femmes Fatales: Feminism, Film Theory, Psychoanalysis*. New York: Routledge, 1991.

"Domestics Bill in the House." *Vancouver Province,* 5 December 1924, 7.

"Domestic Servants." *BC Federationist,* 16 May 1924, 1.

Donovan, Peter ("Tom Folio"). Review of *Sister Woman. Saturday Night,* 28 February 1920, 9.

Dreiser, Theodore. *Sister Carrie*. 1900. Reprint, Oxford: Oxford University Press, 1999.

Duncan, Sara Jeanette. *Selected Journalism*. Ed. T.E. Tausky. Ottawa: Tecumseh, 1978.

"Editorial." *Vancouver Beacon,* December 1925, 5.

Ellis, Ethelwyn. "Who Do the Most Flirting in Winnipeg, Men or Women? Reporter of Gentler Sex Blames Girls." *Winnipeg Evening Tribune,* 7 June 1919, 5.

Enstad, Nan. *Ladies of Labour, Girls of Adventure: Working Women, Popular Culture, and Labor Politics at the Turn of the Twentieth Century*. New York: Columbia University Press, 1999.

Fairbanks, Carol. *Prairie Women: Images in American and Canadian Fiction*. New Haven: Yale University Press, 1986.

Frager, Ruth. "No Proper Deal: Women Workers and the Canadian Labour Movement, 1870-1940." In *Union Sisters: Women in the Labour Movement,* ed. Linda Briskin and Lynda Yanz, 44-66. Toronto: Women's Press, 1983.

Gerson, Carole. "Introduction." In *Roland Graeme, Knight: A Novel of Our Time*, by Agnes Maule Machar, vii-xx. Ottawa: Tecumseh, 1996.

–. "Marie Joussaye Fotheringham: Canada's First Woman Labour Poet." *Canadian Notes and Queries* 44 (Spring 1991): 21-23.

"Girl Witness Is Cheered by Court Crowd." *Vancouver Star,* 8 September 1924, 1.

Glynn-Ward, Hilda. *The Writing on the Wall*. 1921. Reprint, Toronto: University of Toronto Press, 1974.

Godwin, George. *The Eternal Forest*. 1929. Reprint, Vancouver: Godwin, 1994.

"Good for the Goose, Good for the Gander." *Western Labor News, Strike Bulletin,* 9 June 1919, 5.

"Gray Blames Leaders of Soldier-Strikers for Inciting Mob to Riot." *Winnipeg Evening Tribune,* 23 June 1919, 3.

Grint, Keith. *The Sociology of Work: An Introduction*. Cambridge: Polity, 1991.

Gutkin, Harry, and Mildred Gutkin. *Profiles in Dissent: The Shaping of Radical Thought in the Canadian West*. Edmonton: NeWest, 1997.

Gutteridge, Helena. "B.C. Woman's Suffrage League." *BC Federationist,* 3 October 1913, 8.

–. "How Men Protect Women in the Labor Market." *BC Federationist,* 9 January 1914, 1.

–. "A Minimum Wage." *BC Federationist,* 16 January 1914, 5.

–. "Votes for Women and Trade Unions." *BC Federationist,* 17 October 1913, 5.

—. "Woman's Work." *BC Federationist,* 16 January 1914, 5.

Harris, Cole. *The Resettlement of British Columbia.* Vancouver: University of British Columbia Press, 1997.

"Hello Girls!" *Western Labor News, Strike Bulletin,* 20 May 1919, 2.

"'Hello' Girls Are Not Easily Beaten." *BC Federationist,* 11 July 1919, 1.

Hobson, Barbara Meil. *Uneasy Virtue: The Politics of Prostitution and the American Reform Tradition.* New York: Basic Books, 1987.

"Home and Domestic Employees Union." *BC Federationist,* 18 April 1913, 1.

Horodyski, Mary. "Women and the Winnipeg General Strike of 1919." *Manitoba History* 11 (Spring 1986): 28-37.

"Housemaids Opposed to Oriental Ban Act." *Vancouver Star,* 29 November 1924, 1.

Howard, Irene. *The Struggle for Social Justice in British Columbia: Helena Gutteridge, the Unknown Reformer.* Vancouver: University of British Columbia Press, 1992.

Innis, Mary Quayle. *Unfold the Years: A History of the Young Women's Christian Association in Canada.* Toronto: McClelland and Stewart, 1949.

"Isolated 'Cop' Fighting Off Crowd Is Run Down from behind by a Motor." *Winnipeg Evening Tribune,* 23 June 1919, 3.

Jackel, Susan. "Introduction." In *A Flannel Shirt and Liberty: British Emigrant Gentlewomen in the Canadian West, 1880-1914,* ed. Susan Jackel, xiii-xxvii. Vancouver: University of British Columbia Press, 1982.

"Janet Smith Case." *Vancouver Star,* 11 August 1924, 1.

"Janet Smith Feared Chinese Friends State." *Vancouver Star,* 2 August 1924, 1.

Jefferis, B.G. *Search lights on health, light on dark corners: A complete sexual science and a guide to purity and physical manhood, advice to maiden, wife and mother, love, courtship and marriage.* Toronto: J.L. Nichols, 1894.

Jones, David. "There Is Some Power about the Land: The Western Canadian Agrarian Press and Country Life Ideology." *Journal of Canadian Studies* 17, 3 (1982): 96-108.

Joussaye, Marie. "Only a Working Girl." In *The Songs that Quinte Sang,* 66-67. Belleville, ON: Sun Printing and Publishing Company, 1895.

—. *Selections from Anglo-Saxon Songs.* Dawson, Yukon: Dawson News Publishing Company, 1918.

Kealey, Linda. *Enlisting Women for the Cause: Women, Labour, and the Left in Canada, 1890-1920.* Toronto: University of Toronto Press, 1998.

—. "No Special Protection – No Sympathy: Women's Activism in the Canadian Labour Revolt of 1919." In *Class, Community and the Labour Movement: Wales and Canada, 1850-1930,* ed. Deian R. Hopkin and Gregory Kealey, 134-59. Wales: Society for Welsh Labour History and the Committee on Canadian Labour History, 1989.

Kelley, Ninette, and Michael Trebilcock. *The Making of the Mosaic: A History of Canadian Immigration Policy.* Toronto: University of Toronto Press, 1998.

Kemp, Janet C. "Address." In British Columbia Commission on Labour (1912-14),

Transcripts of Proceedings. Box 2, file 1, 9-12. BC Archives

Kinsman, Gary. *The Regulation of Desire: Homo and Hetero Sexualities*. 2nd rev. ed. Montreal: Black Rose, 1996.

Klein, Alice, and Wayne Robers. "Besieged Innocence: The 'Problem' and Problems of Working Women, Toronto, 1896-1914. In *Women at Work: Ontario, 1850-1930,* ed. Janice Acton, Penny Goldsmith, and Bonnie Shepard, 211-60. Toronto: Canadian Women's Educational Press, 1974.

"Ladies Auxiliaries." *BC Federationist,* 11 October 1918, 3.

"Laundry Strikers Cause Unrest." *BC Federationist,* 1 November 1918, 1.

"Laundry Workers Are Standing Firm." *BC Federationist,* 11 October 1918, 1.

"Laundry Workers Have Good Time." *BC Federationist,* 27 September 1918, 5.

"Laundry Workers Still Carrying On Strike." *BC Federationist,* 29 November 1918, 1.

"Laundry Workers Still on Strike." *BC Federationist,* 29 September 1919, 1.

"Laundry Workers to Hold Dance." *BC Federationist,* 11 July 1919, 1.

Lay, Jackie. "To Columbia on the Tynemouth: The Emigration of Single Women and Girls in 1862." In *In Her Own Right: Selected Essays on Women's History in B.C.,* ed. Barbara Latham and Cathy Kess, 19-41. Victoria: Camosun College, 1980.

Lesley, Genevieve. "Domestic Service in Canada, 1880-1920." In *Women at Work: Ontario, 1850-1930,* ed. Janice Acton, Penny Goldsmith, and Bonnie Shepard, 71-125. Toronto: Canadian Women's Educational Press, 1974.

Lewthwaite, Elizabeth. "Women's Work in Western Canada." *Fortnightly Review,* October 1901. Reprinted in *A Flannel Shirt and Liberty: British Emigrant Gentlewomen in the Canadian West,* ed. Susan Jackel, 111-20. Vancouver: University of British Columbia Press, 1982.

Local Council of Women. "Recommendations for Changes or Additions to the 'Factory, Shops and Offices Act.'" In British Columbia Commission on Labour (1912-14), Transcripts of Proceedings. Box 2, file 1, p. 9. BC Archives.

Lugrin, N. de Bertrand. *The Pioneer Women of Vancouver Island.* Victoria: Women's Canadian Club, 1928.

Macdonald, Ian, and Betty O'Keefe. *Canadian Holy War: A Story of Clans, Tongs, Murder, and Bigotry.* Surrey, BC: Heritage House, 2000.

Machar, Agnes Maule. *Roland Graeme, Knight: A Novel of Our Time.* 1892. Reprint, Ottawa: Tecumseh, 1996.

Mackay, Isabel Ecclestone. *Blencarrow*. Toronto: T. Allen, 1926.

–. *House of Windows.* Toronto: Cassel and Co., 1912.

–. *The Shining Ship and Other Verse for Children*. Toronto: McClelland, Goodchild and Stewart, 1918.

Marquis, Greg. "Vancouver Vice: The Police and the Negotiation of Morality, 1904-1935." In *Essays in the History of Canadian Law VI: British Columbia and the Yukon,* ed. Hamar Foster and John McLaren, 242-73. Toronto: University of Toronto Press, 1995.

Matters, Indiana. "Sinners or Sinned Against? Historical Aspects of Female Juvenile

Delinquency in British Columbia." In *Not Just Pin Money: Selected Essays on the History of Women's Work in British Columbia,* ed. Barbara K. Latham and Roberta J. Pazdro, 265-77. Victoria: Camosun College, 1980.

McCallum, Todd. "'Not a Sex Question'? The One Big Union and the Politics of Radical Manhood." *Labour/Le Travail* 42 (Fall 1998): 15-54.

McClintock, Anne. *Imperial Leather: Race, Gender and Sexuality in the Colonial Contest.* New York: Routledge, 1995.

McClung, Nellie. *Purple Springs*. Toronto: T. Allen, 1921.

–. *The Second Chance*. Toronto: Ryerson Press, 1910.

–. *Sowing Seeds in Danny.* New York: Doubleday, Page and Company, 1908.

McDonald, Robert A.J. *Making Vancouver: Class, Status, and Social Boundaries, 1863-1913.* Vancouver: University of British Columbia Press, 1996.

–. "Working." In *Working Lives: Vancouver, 1886-1986,* ed. Working Lives Collective, 25-33. Vancouver: New Star, 1985.

McLaren, Angus. *Our Own Master Race: Eugenics in Canada, 1885-1945.* Toronto: Oxford University Press, 1990.

McLaren, John. "White Slavers: The Reform of Canada's Prostitution Law and Patterns of Enforcement, 1900-1920." *Criminal Justice History* 8 (1987): 125-65.

Merrill, Annie. "The Woman in Business." *Canadian Magazine* 21 (1903): 407-10.

"Minimum Wage and Laundry Workers." *BC Federationist,* 20 June 1919, 2.

Mitchell, Mrs. "Address." In British Columbia Commission on Labour (1912-14), Transcripts of Proceedings. Box 2, file 1, 313-17, BC Archives.

"A Montreal Woman on Women." *Canadian Bookman,* April 1920, 57-58.

Moral and Social Reform Council of British Columbia. "Social Vice in Vancouver." Report. Vancouver: James F. Morris, 1912.

"Mounted Policemen Charge Huge Crowd at Portage and Main." *Winnipeg Evening Tribune,* 10 June 1919, 1.

Moyles, R.G., and Douglas Owram. *Imperial Dreams and Colonial Realities: British Views of Canada, 1880-1914.* Toronto: University of Toronto Press, 1988.

"Mrs. Armstrong to Stand Trial." *Winnipeg Evening Tribune,* 25 June 1919, 5.

"Multitudes Flock to Labor Church." *Western Labor News, Strike Bulletin,* 10 June 1919, 1.

Muszynski, Alicja. "Race and Gender: Structural Determinants in the Formation of British Columbia's Salmon Cannery Labour Force." In *Class, Gender, and Region: Essays in Canadian Historical Sociology,* ed. Gregory S. Kealey, 103-20. St. John's, NF: Committee on Canadian Labour History, 1988.

New, W.H. *A History of Canadian Literature*. London: Macmillan, 1991.

Newton, Janice. *The Feminist Challenge to the Canadian Left, 1900-1918.* Montreal and Kingston: McGill-Queen's University Press, 1995.

Nilson, Deborah. "The 'Social Evil': Prostitution in Vancouver, 1900-1920." In *In Her Own Right: Selected Essays on Women's History in BC,* ed. Barbara Latham and Cathy Kess, 205-28. Victoria: Camosun College, 1980.

"No Fear of Chinese Boy Is Recorded." *Vancouver Sun,* 8 September 1924, 1, 4, 13.

"No Girl Need Want for Food." *Western Labor News, Strike Bulletin,* 26 May 1919, 3.

Odem, Mary. *Delinquent Daughters: Protecting and Policing Adolescent Female Sexuality in the United States, 1885-1920.* Chapel Hill: University of North Carolina Press, 1995.

"1 Killed, Many Hurt in Winnipeg Riots." *Toronto Star,* 23 June 1919, 8.

Parke, Alice Barrett. *Hobnobbing with a Countess and Other Okanagan Adventures: The Diaries of Alice Barrett Parke, 1891-1900.* Ed. Jo Fraser Jones. Vancouver: University of British Columbia Press, 2001.

Peiss, Kathy. "'Charity Girls' and City Pleasures: Historical Notes on Working-Class Sexuality, 1880-1920." In *Passion and Power: Sexuality in History,* ed. Kathy Peiss and Christina Simmons, 57-69. Philadelphia: Temple University Press, 1987.

–. *Cheap Amusements: Working Women and Leisure in Turn-of-the-Century New York.* Philadelphia: Temple University Press, 1986.

"Pelted with Eggs and Then Kicked." *Vancouver Province,* 11 December 1918, 21.

Perry, Adele. "Interlocuting Empire: Colonial Womanhood, Settler Identity, and Frances Herring." In *Rediscovering the British World,* ed. Phillip A. Buckner and R.D. Francis, 159-180. Calgary: University of Calgary Press, 2003.

–. *On the Edge of Empire: Gender, Race, and the Making of British Columbia, 1849-1871.* Toronto: University of Toronto Press, 2001.

Pettit, Maude ("Videre"). "There Is the Light of Love and Romance in Her Life, Too: Life Stories of Girl Workers in Toronto Factories." *Toronto Star,* 17 June 1912, 14.

–. "We Had Spare Ribs, Potatoes, and Some Tapioca Pudding: Life Stories of Girl Workers in Toronto Factories." *Toronto Star,* 6 June 1912, 1, 4..

Philips, Miss. "Paper on Home Arts and Handicrafts." In *Report of the 8th Annual Meeting of the National Council of Women of Canada,* 138-41. Proceedings of meeting held in London, Ontario, 1901. Ottawa: Taylor and Clarke, 1901.

"Police Kept off Streets after Fighting." *Winnipeg Evening Tribune,* 11 June 1919, 2.

Pullen-Burry, Bessie. *From Halifax to Vancouver.* London: Mills and Boon, 1912.

"Report of the Supervisor of the Women's Branch, Miss M.V. Burnham." In Canada, *Report of the Department of Immigration and Colonization.* Annual Departmental Reports, 1927-28. Ottawa: Government of Canada, 1927.

Richardson, Dorothy. *The long day, the story of a New York working girl.* 1905. In *Women at Work, including The long day, the story of a New York working girl by Dorothy Richardson and Inside the New York Telephone Company by Elinor Langer,* ed. William L. O'Neill. Chicago: Quadrangle Books, 1972.

Roberts, Barbara. "'A Work of Empire': Canadian Reformers and British Female Immigration." In *A Not Unreasonable Claim: Women and Reform in Canada, 1880s-1920s,* ed. Linda Kealey, 185-201. Toronto: Women's Press, 1979.

Roberts, Wayne. *Honest Womanhood: Feminism, Femininity and Class Consciousness among Toronto Working Women, 1893-1914.* Toronto: University of Toronto Press, 1986.

Rosen, Ruth. *The Lost Sisterhood: Prostitution in America, 1900-1918.* Baltimore: Johns Hopkins University Press, 1982.

Rosenthal, Star. "Union Maids: Organized Women Workers in Vancouver 1900-1915." *BC Studies* 41 (Spring 1979): 36-55.

Rotenberg, Lori. "The Wayward Worker: Toronto's Prostitute at the Turn of the Century." In *Women at Work: Ontario, 1850-1930,* ed. Janice Acton, Penny Goldsmith, and Bonnie Shepard, 33-69. Toronto: Canadian Women's Educational Press, 1974.

Sangster, Joan. *Regulating Girls and Women: Sexuality, Family and the Law in Ontario, 1920-1960.* Don Mills: Oxford University Press, 2001.

Saxby, Jessie M. "Women Wanted." In *West Nor'West.* London: James Nisbet and Co., 1890. Reprinted in *A Flannel Shirt and Liberty: British Emigrant Gentlewomen in the Canadian West,* ed. Susan Jackel, 68-74. Vancouver: University of British Columbia Press, 1982.

"Scotch Girls Cheaper than Chinamen." *BC Federationist,* 18 April 1913, 1.

"Scots Demand Inquiry into Tragedy." *Vancouver Star,* 7 August 1924, 1.

"Second Laundry Workers Dance." *BC Federationist,* 11 October 1918, 1.

"Servant Girls Quit Homes, Refusing to Work with Chinese." *Victoria Daily Times,* 24 November 1924, 1.

Shearer, John G. *Canada's War on the White Slave Trade.* Toronto: Board of Moral and Social Reform, 1912.

"Should Chinese Work with White Girls?" *Vancouver Star,* 8 August 1924, 4.

"Sidelights on the Riot." *Winnipeg Evening Tribune,* 11 June 1919, 5.

Sime, J. G. *Canada Chaps.* London: J. Lane, 1917.

–. *The Mistress of All Work.* London: Methuen, 1916.

–. *Our Little Life: A Novel of To-day.* (1921). Canadian critical ed. Ed. K. Jane Watt. Ottawa: Tecumseh Press, 1994.

–. *Sister Woman* (1919). Canadian critical ed. Ed. Sandra Campbell. Ottawa: Tecumseh Press, 2004.

Sinclair, Bertrand. *North of Fifty-Three.* New York: Grosset and Dunlap, 1914.

Smillie, Christine. "The Invisible Workforce: Women Workers in Saskatchewan from 1905 to World War II." *Saskatchewan History* 39, 2 (1986): 62-80.

Smith, Charlene P. "Boomtown Brothels in the Kootenays, 1895-1905." In *People and Place: Historical Influences on Legal Culture,* ed. Jonathan Swainger and Constance Backhouse, 120-152. Vancouver: University of British Columbia Press, 2003.

Smith, Sidonie. *A Poetics of Women's Autobiography: Marginality and the Fictions of Self-Representation.* Bloomington: Indiana University Press, 1987.

–, and Julia Watson. *Autobiography: A Guide for Interpreting Life Narratives.* Minneapolis: University of Minnesota Press, 2001.

"Some Reasons Why." *BC Federationist,* 10 October 1913, 5.

Starkins, Edward. *Who Killed Janet Smith?* Toronto: Macmillan, 1984.

Stasiulus, Daiva, and Radha Jhappan. "The Fractious Politics of a Settler Society:

Canada." In *Unsettling Settler Societies: Articulations of Gender, Race, and Class,* ed. Daiva Stasiulus and Nira Yuval-Davis, 95-131. London: Sage, 1995.

Stead, W.T. "The Maiden Tribute of Modern Babylon." *Pall Mall Gazette* (London) 4 July 1885: 1; 6 July 1885: 1-6; 7 July 1885:1-6; 8 July 1885: 1-5; 10 July 1885: 1-9.

Strange, Carolyn. *Toronto's Girl Problem: The Perils and Pleasures of the City, 1880-1930.* Toronto: University of Toronto Press, 1995.

–, and Tina Loo. *Making Good: Law and Moral Regulation in Canada, 1876-1939.* Toronto: University of Toronto Press, 1997.

"Strike Committee Issues Statement." *Winnipeg Evening Tribune,* 15 May 1919, 2.

"Strike Ties Up Laundries." *Vancouver Daily World,* 10 September 1918, 15.

Sykes, Ella. *A Home-Help in Canada.* London: G. Bell, 1912.

"They Demand Protection." *Vancouver Province,* 19 September 1918, 17.

"This Will Be Some Affair." *BC Federationist,* 1 August 1919, 1.

"Union Telephone Girls Resume Their Places at the Switchboard." *Vancouver Province,* 15 December 1902, 1.

"Union Women's Social Club." *BC Federationist,* 5 March 1915, 1.

Valverde, Mariana. *The Age of Light, Soap, and Water: Moral Reform in English Canada, 1885-1925.* Toronto: McClelland and Stewart, 1991.

–. "The Love of Finery: Fashion and the Fallen Woman in Nineteenth-Century Social Discourse." *Victorian Studies* 32 (Winter 1989): 169-88.

Van Kirk, Sylvia. *Many Tender Ties: Women in Fur-Trade Society, 1670-1870.* Winnipeg: Watson and Dwyer, 1999.

Voisey, Paul. "The Urbanization of the Canadian Prairies, 1871-1916." In *The Prairie West: Historical Readings,* ed. R. Douglas Francis and Howard Palmer, 383-407. Edmonton: Pica Pica Press, 1985.

"Wage Slaves in Hotels." *Woman Worker,* November 1927, 8-9.

Ware, Vron. *Beyond the Pale: White Women, Racism and History.* London: Verso, 1992.

"Weston Women Wreck Stores' Delivery Rigs – Threaten to Murder Drivers and Special Policemen Sent as Guards." *Winnipeg Evening Tribune,* 6 June 1919, 2.

Whymper, Frederick. *Travel and Adventure in the Territory of Alaska.* New York: Harper and Brothers, 1871.

"Winnipeg Is Isolated, Channels Are Blocked." *Toronto Star,* 17 May 1919, 1.

"Woman May Be Killer." *Vancouver Sun,* 30 August 1924, 1.

"Women Open Eating House in Strathcona Hotel." *Western Labor News, Strike Bulletin,* 23 May 1919, 1.

Woodsworth, J.S. *My Neighbor: A Study of City Conditions, A Plea for Social Service.* 1911. Reprint, Toronto: University of Toronto Press, 1972.

Woolf, Virginia. *A Room of One's Own.* 1929. Reprint, London: Grafton, 1977.

# Index

Aboriginal women, 18-19, 146
activism. *See* labour movement
advice for working women: advice
    manuals, 59; fashion, 73-78, 81;
    sexual, 81-82; Sykes on, 23, 27;
    workplace etiquette, 60-61, 63-64
Alberta, 35, 105, 108, 112-13, 132
American Federation of Labor, 54
Anderson, Kay, 150
architecture, 64
Armstrong, Helen, 122, 123, 125, 134-44
Asian immigrant population: attitudes
    toward, 3, 14, 35, 93-95, 145-46, 148-
    59, 167; business ownership, 148;
    Chinese Exclusion Act, 146, 150, 152,
    156, 163; employment, 153; Janet
    Smith case, 145-46, 159-67; labour
    movement, 153; prostitution, 154;
    racism/racist narratives, 3, 14, 93-95,
    154, 156-57, 159-67
assimilation, 151-52, 165
autobiography, 13, 88, 90, 105, 107-13

"bachelor girls," 20, 82-83, 85. *See also*
    working women
bachelors: abundance of in Canadian
    West, 3-4, 10, 18-20, 24, 39, 71, 172-
    73; all-male households, 27-28; Asian

immigrants, 146, 149; sex industry,
    103
Backhouse, Constance, 147-48
Baker, F.L., 159, 160, 162
Banff/Banff Springs Hotel, 40, 42, 112
Barber, Marilyn, 22-23
Barman, Jean, 25
bars, 106
Bayfield, Mrs., address to National
    Council of Women, 40
*BC Federationist*: domestic workers,
    165-66; gender stereotypes, 36; low
    wages, 132; mixed-race workplace,
    146; telephone operators' strike, 133;
    Vancouver laundry workers' strike,
    127-28, 131
Benson, Susan Porter, 75, 78
Blair, Madeleine, 13, 88, 105-15, 171
Bloody Saturday, 140-41
boarding houses and hostels, 33, 34, 68,
    98-99, 101
bride ships, 19-26, 31, 56, 146
Britain, 19-26, 30-31, 146
British Columbia: bride ships, 19-26,
    31, 146; Commission on Labour,
    30, 38-39, 174; demographics, 10,
    18; economic base, 18, 32, 55; Janet
    Smith bill, 159-60, 166-67; labour

unrest, 121-34; Minimum Wage
Board, 132; Women and Girls
Protection Act, 148; works set in:
*North of Fifty-Three* (Sinclair), 53,
55-57; *Pioneer Women of Vancouver
Island* (Lugrin), 21-22, 24. *See also*
Vancouver
Brooking, Lucy, 118-19
brothels, 89, 92, 103-6, 109-11
Buddle, Melanie, 10
Bush, Julia, 157-58

Calgary, 11-12, 23, 32, 169-70
Campbell, Robert, 151
Campbell, Sandra, 52, 59
*Canadian Bookman,* 50-51
Canadian Emigration Society, 22-23
Canadian literature, 44-87; class cross-
dressing, 71-81; cult of domesticity,
60-65; geography and style, 53, 173;
recognition of women authors, 50-52;
sex and the city, 81-87; social realism,
50-60; working girl goes west, 65-71.
*See also* figure of working girl
*Canadian Magazine,* "The Woman in
Business," 60-63, 73-76, 81-82
Canadian Pacific Railway (CPR), 25,
26, 146
Canadian Women's Press Club, 57
canneries, 11, 146, 148
Catholicism, 50
Chinatown, 94-95, 116, 149-50, 155
Chinese population. *See* Asian
immigrant population
Chipman, Walter William, 59
chloroform, 92
civilization, white women and, 12, 16-
17, 19, 43
Clarke, C.K., 91, 92
class distinctions: class-based
institutions, 25, 49, 52-53, 61-62, 67,
74, 87; class cross-dressing, 71-81;
feminist movement, 46, 175; identity

and consumption, 79; middle-class
philanthropy, 7, 19, 42, 54, 72, 90,
156; "middle-class sympathy" novels,
72-73; prostitutes, 89-92, 97-103,
116, 119-20; sexuality, 73, 98, 115-20;
Victorian era, 29, 30, 92, 102, 153;
working women, 71-81. *See also*
working class
clerical work, 11-12
Columbia Female Emigration Society, 20
Comacchio, Cynthia, 19
Coote, Lillian, 129
country-to-city migration, 11, 96-101
Cran, Marion, 16, 20, 22, 29-30
Creese, Gillian, 124
crime: incorrigibility as, 118; Janet
Smith case, 159-67; sexual
delinquency, 91, 118
cult of domesticity: in Canadian
literature, 60-65; imperialism and,
7-8, 17, 23, 32, 43
cultural narratives: gender norms and
working women, 42-43, 83, 143-44,
158-59, 175; ideology of Empire, 4,
7-8, 16-17, 19, 29, 35; Janet Smith
case, 160-61; women and cultural
reproduction, 25-32, 147, 153, 172;
women's' voices in, 108. *See also*
figure of working girl; Victorian era

dance halls, 101-2, 119
dances, 14, 122, 128, 130-31, 133, 136,
144, 175
dating, 39, 60, 81-82, 84, 102-3
Deighton, "Gassy Jack," 88-89
delinquency, "fallen woman" and, 91-
92, 115-20
demographics: Britain, 19-20; British
Columbia, 10, 18; Toronto, 18, 116;
urban growth, 32, 172; western
Canada, 3-4, 9-10, 32, 172; workforce,
9-11, 172
Denning, Michael, 72, 73

Department of Immigration and
    Colonization, 156
department stores, 58, 78-79, 87, 138-39
Devereux, Cecily, 93
dime novelettes, 71-73, 84-85
Doane, Mary Ann, 33-34
Domestic Employees Union, 129
domestic service: attitudes toward, 29-
    32, 36, 40, 60-65, 156-59; employment
    in, 4, 10, 22-23, 25, 28, 35-36, 43;
    houseboys, 158-59; immigration
    policy, 156-59, 163; insanity rates,
    31; Janet Smith case, 145-46, 159-67;
    union organizing, 123-25, 129; wages
    and working conditions, 146, 165-66.
    See also mixed-race workplace
domesticity: cult of, 7-8, 17, 23, 32,
    43, 60-65, 157; female sexuality, 64;
    labour activism, 123-24; re-emphasis
    on, 3-9, 24, 27
Dreiser, Theodore, 52
drink, 88-89, 104-6
Duncan, Sara Jeannette, 31

economy: British Columbia industries,
    18, 32, 55; sex trade, 103-5, 107, 111-
    13, 120, 154. See also employment/
    employment opportunities;
    industrialization; urbanization;
    wages
Edmonton, 32
Empire, ideology of, 2-7, 16-17, 23, 26-
    29, 35, 42
Empire Settlement Agreement, 156-57
employment/employment opportunities:
    Asian immigrant population, 153;
    deceptive ads, 96-98, 100, 103;
    and delinquency, 119-20; gender-
    stereotyped occupations, 3-4, 8, 10-12,
    35-37, 55-57, 172; manufacturing, 11;
    nursing, 11, 99-100; service sector, 11,
    32-33, 35, 40-41; stenographers, 11-
    12, 65-66, 169-70; teachers, 11, 169,

171; white-slave trade conspiracies,
    90, 97, 98. See also domestic service;
    mixed-race workplace; wages
Enstad, Nan, 72, 74
ethnic neighbourhoods, 103
eugenics, 91-92, 152
Evening Work Committee, 129

factories/factory workers: employment
    in, 11, 33-35, 54, 77, 79, 81, 156-57,
    172; in fiction, 54, 60-63, 72, 77;
    labour activism, 125, 134-35; morality
    concerns, 79, 81, 87, 92, 96, 109
Fairbanks, Carole, 28
"fallen woman," Victorian notion of, 54,
    58, 72, 80, 88-92, 95-96, 115-20
family, Victorian ideal of, 28
fashion advice, 73-78, 81
feeblemindedness, 91, 92, 115-20
femininity/girlishness, 46, 73-76, 174-75
feminist movement, 175
figure of working girl: as cultural
    narrative, 45-60, 67, 87, 154, 173,
    175; formula fiction, 57-58, 72;
    industrialization, 12-13, 17, 173;
    labour movement, 46-48, 154; in
    literature of United States, 12-13, 52,
    71-72; poetry, 46-48; racist narratives,
    149, 155-56, 163; romances, 12-13, 51-
    58, 71-81, 173; serial fiction, 52-53, 71,
    72; sexuality, 13, 24; social realism,
    12-13, 50-60, 65-71, 85, 171, 173;
    urbanization, 33-34, 42, 57, 66-68,
    145-46; wages, 154; western Canada,
    24-25, 26, 27, 32, 42, 65-71
"finery-to-fall" narrative, 77-78
fish processing, 11, 36, 146, 148
Fleming, Mary Agnes, 71
flirting/flirtation, 60, 72, 77, 142-43, 161
formula fiction, 57-58, 72
Frager, Ruth, 123-24
frontier, iconic portrayals of pioneer
    women, 2-5, 7, 21-22, 24, 28-29

fundraising. *See under* labour movement

fur trade society, 18-19

Gananoque, 54

Gastown, 89

gender codes: gender-segregated employment, 35-37, 165; immigration policy, 156-59; imperial ideology, 7-8, 16-19, 35; industrialization, 2-4, 17; redefinition of, 12, 15-19, 66-68, 76, 82-89, 126; union movement, 123-25, 132-44, 153, 175; urbanization, 2-4, 35-37, 99-103; and working women, 42-43, 83, 143-44, 158-59, 175. *See also* mixed-race workplace

gender stereotypes: occupations, 3-4, 8, 10-12, 35-37, 55-57, 172; in press reports, 36; value of women's work, 30, 49-50, 64-65, 104, 107, 157; and white-slave narrative, 93; working women/prostitute linkage, 89-92, 97-103, 116, 119-20

genre: autobiography, 13, 88, 90, 105, 107-13; dime-novelettes, 71-73, 84-85; dominant forms of, 12-13, 45; formula fiction, 57-58, 72; urban social themes, 52-53; US working-girl fiction, 72. *See also* figure of working girl; white-slave narratives

Gerson, Carol, 45, 51

girlishness/femininity, 46, 73-76, 174-75

Glynn Howard, Hilda (Hilda Glynn-Ward), *The Writing on the Wall,* 93-95, 151-52

Godwin, George, 26

gold rush, 18

Goodwin, Albert "Ginger," 121

Grint, Keith, 16-17

Gutteridge, Helena, 15, 31, 36-37, 121-30, 132

hair styles, 74-75

Harris, Cole, 25-26

"hello girls," 8, 136, 174-75. *See also* telephone operators

historical romances. *See* romance narratives

Hobson, Barbara Meil, 91

home values, and industrialization, 28, 33, 34, 40-42

Horódyski, Mary, 125, 135

Hotel and Household Workers' Union, 134

Hotel Vancouver, 126

House of Commons, immigration debate, 150-51, 152

houseboys, 158-59

Housemaid's Union (Winnipeg), 134

Howard, Irene, 125-26

immigration: brides/bride ships, 19-26, 31, 146, 172; causes for expulsion, 158; Chinese Exclusion Act, 146, 150, 156, 163; female narratives of, 6; planned immigration, 29-31; policy initiatives, 146, 150, 152, 156-59; promotional campaigns, 3, 5, 16-25; working-class, 156-59. *See also* Asian immigrant population; whiteness

Imperial Order Daughters of the Empire, 7-8

imperialism: cult of domesticity, 7-8, 17, 23, 32, 43, 60-65, 153; racism, 156-59; women's responsibilities, 172

Industrial Home for Girls (Vancouver), 117-19

industrialization, 32-37; British Columbia industries, 18, 32, 55; delinquency linked to, 119; employment opportunities, 10-11, 172; figure of working girl, 12-13, 17, 173; gender roles transformed, 2-4, 17; home values, 28, 33-34, 34, 40-42; moral degradation attributed to, 95-96. *See also* urbanization

interracial marriage, 18-19, 151-53, 165

Janet Smith case, 145-46, 159-67
Jefferis, B.G., 101-2
Johnson, Pauline, 71
Jones, Cissie, 160
*Journal of United Labour,* 46
Joussaye, Marie, 45-46; "Only a
    Working Girl," 46-48, 67; *Selections
    from Anglo-Saxon Songs,* 46; *The
    Songs that Quinte Sang,* 45-50
Juvenile Delinquents Act, 117

Kealey, Linda, 9, 46, 128, 135
Kelley, Ninette, 158
Kemp, Janet, 147
Kinsman, Gary, 98
Knights of Labor, 54

labour movement, 121-44; American
    Federation of Labor, 54; Asian
    immigrant population, 153;
    Domestic Employees Union, 129;
    and domesticity, 123-25; figure of
    working girl, 46-48, 154; fundraising
    and social events, 14, 122, 128-33, 136,
    144, 175; gender behaviour, 132-44,
    175; Hotel and Household Workers'
    Union, 134; Housemaid's Union
    (Winnipeg), 134; Laundry Workers
    Union, 121-34; male-dominated,
    123-25, 139-40, 153; Retail Clerks'
    Union (Winnipeg), 134; Vancouver
    laundry workers' strike, 123, 125-34;
    Winnipeg General Strike, 134-44;
    women and union membership, 121-
    34; workers' rights, 54; and working
    women, 13-14, 43, 148, 173, 175. *See
    also* wages
laundry workers, 38, 121-44, 174
law enforcement, 105-6
leisure activities: dance halls and public
    balls, 101-2, 119; dating, 39, 60, 81-82,
    84, 102-3; flirting/flirtation, 60, 72,

77, 142-43, 161; labour strikes, 128;
    morality, 119, 142-43, 155, 160, 175;
    new forms of, 4, 160-62; working
    women's social life, 41-42, 81-87, 101-
    2, 160-62; youth culture, 39-40, 122,
    133, 142-43, 160, 175
Lewthwaite, Elizabeth, 27-28
Libbey, Laura Jean, 52-53, 71, 72
liquor, 104-6
London: Female Middle-Class
    Emigration Society, 19; white-slavery
    fears, 92-93. *See also* Britain
Loo, Tina, 117
Lugrin, N. de Bertrand, *The Pioneer
    Women of Vancouver Island,* 21-22, 24

MacDonald, Ian, 159
MacGill, Helen, 132
Machar, Agnes Maule (aka "Fidelis"),
    53-54, 173; *Roland Graeme, Knight,*
    50, 51-55, 60-61, 67, 72-73, 77
Mackay, Isabel Ecclestone, 57, 173;
    *Blencarrow,* 57; *House of Windows,* 55,
    57-58, 60, 71-81, 87, 169; *The Shining
    Ship and Other Verse for Children,* 57
MacMurchy, Helen, 91
makeup, 40-41, 143
Manitoba, 9, 132, 148
manual labour, 36
manufacturing, 11. *See also* factories/
    factory workers
Marquis, Greg, 105, 116
marriage: attitudes toward, 1-2, 20,
    39-40, 69-70, 100, 114, 169; Bride
    Ship initiative, 19-22, 24, 146;
    British Columbia marriage rates,
    10; interracial, 18-19, 151-53, 165; in
    romance narratives, 32
materialism, 172
Matters, Indiana, 117-18
McCallum, Todd, 123, 140
McClintock, Anne, 7, 64, 91-92, 158
McClung, Nellie, 99-100

McDonald, Robert A.J., 30, 150-51
McLaren, Angus, 152
McLaren, John, 116
McMullen, Lorraine, 52
men: all-male households, 27-28;
    autobiography and, 108; gender-
    stereotyped work, 36; male
    characters as social opposites of
    women, 68-69; sex industry, 154;
    union movement, 123-25, 139-40,
    153. See also bachelors; women
mercenary girls, 82
Merrickville, 54
Merrill, Annie, "The Woman in
    Business," 60-63, 73-76, 81-82
middle-class philanthropy, 7, 19, 42, 54,
    72, 90, 156
migration: country-to-city, 11, 96-97,
    99-101. See also immigration
Minimum Wage Board (British
    Columbia), 132, 186n35. See also
    wages
miscegenation, 151-52
Mitchell, Mrs., address to Vancouver
    Local Council of Women, 31, 39-40
mixed-race workplace, 145-67; domestic
    service, 146-47, 159-67; gender and
    immigration policies, 14, 150-51, 156-
    59; Janet Smith case, 145-46, 159-67;
    press reports, 145-47, 164-65; racial
    anxieties and working-class women,
    14, 147-56. See also race/racism;
    whiteness
mobility, 95-97
Montreal, 44, 50-51, 59
Moral and Social Reform Council of
    British Columbia, 35, 116-18
morality: boarding houses, 99; fashion,
    75-78; leisure activities, 142-43,
    160, 175; makeup, 40-41; moral
    protectionism, 14, 34-35, 40-42,
    116-18, 147-48, 164, 166; sexuality,
    87; technology, 84-85; urbanization,

95-96, 98, 149; working women, 173;
    workplace, 8-9, 13, 66-68, 84-87, 90,
    97-103, 173
Morning Albertan, "The Log of a
    Calgary Stenographer," 11-12, 169-70
motherhood, 86
Moyles, R.G., 7
multiculturalism, 3, 26
Muszynski, Alicja, 146

narrative style: geographical differences
    in, 53, 173; importance of social
    narratives, 6-7, 171; and working
    women, 6-7, 172-73. See also figure of
    working girl
National Council of Women, 40, 77
National Trades and Labour Council,
    54
New, William H., 51-52
New York City, 41
newspapers: news girls, 136-39. See also
    press reports
Newton, Janice, 124
Nilson, Deborah, 95
North of Fifty-Three (Sinclair), 55-57,
    65-66
nursing, 11, 99-100

Odem, Mary, 91
Odlum, Victor, 164-65
O'Keefe, Betty, 159
Old Maid stereotypes, 86
"Only a Working Girl" (Joussaye), 46-48
Ontario, 148
opium/opium trade, 149, 154-55
organized labour. See labour movement
otherness, sexual and racial, 150⁻
Owram, Doug, 7

Parke, Alice Barrett, 1-2
patriotism, 172
Peiss, Kathy, 41, 82, 102
Perry, Adele, 23, 26

Pettit, Maude ("Videre"), 41-42
philanthropy, 7, 42, 54, 72, 90, 156
picket-lines, 122, 126-28, 131-32
pioneer women, iconic portrayals of, 2-5, 7, 21-22, 24, 28-29
poetry, 46-48
policy initiatives: Asian immigrant population, 150, 152; Chinese Exclusion Act, 146, 150, 156, 163; immigration, 146, 150, 152, 156-59; Janet Smith bill, 159-60; minimum wage, 132; mixed-race workplace, 150-51; moral protectionism, 14, 34-35, 40-42, 116-18, 147-48, 164, 166; prostitution, 93, 95-97, 116, 117
prairie provinces: demographics, 3, 9, 11, 32, 135; iconic portrayals of pioneer women, 28-29; impact of railroads, 25; inspiration from, 88, 171-72; labour laws, 148; "Log of a Calgary Stenographer," 11-12, 169-70; population growth, 3, 11; sex trade, 105, 108-13; shortage of women, 18; union movement, 134; urban racism, 145-51; white-slave trade, 96; Winnipeg General Strike, 121, 123, 125, 134-44
premarital sex, 102, 118-19
Presbyterian Church, 96
press reports: domestic service, 31; gender stereotypes, 36; Janet Smith case, 161, 162-66; mixed-race workplace, 145-47, 164-65; telephone workers' strike, 174-75; Vancouver laundry workers' strike, 126-34; Winnipeg General Strike, 136-44
prison-brothel, 92
profanity, 40-41
Progressive movement, 91. See also Reform era
promiscuity, 118-19
prostitution, 88-120; Alberta, 105, 108, 112-13; Asian men as procurers,

154; dance halls, 101-2; deceptive employment ads as cover, 96-100, 103; economics, 103-5, 107, 111-13, 120; Madeleine Blair, 13, 107-15; public policy debates, 93, 95-97, 116-17; reasons for becoming a prostitute, 97, 104-5; suppression of, 103, 116; as symbol of sexual downfall, 88-89; working conditions, 110-11, 114; working women linked with, 89-92, 97-103, 116, 119-20, 153-54. See also white-slave narratives
pseudo-science, 91-92, 96-97, 115-20
public balls, 101-2
Pullen-Burry, Bessie, 98-99

race/racism: eugenics, 91-92, 152; immigration policies, 156-59, 163; interracial marriage, 18-19, 151-53, 165; labour laws, 148; mixed-race couples, 150-53; prairie provinces, 145-51; racial exclusion, 149, 155-56, 166-67; Victorian assumptions about, 92; and working-class women, 14, 147-56, 163, 167. See also mixed-race workplace; whiteness
racist narratives: Asian immigrants, 3, 14, 93-95, 154-67; context of racial symbolism, 152-53; figure of working girl, 149, 155-56, 163; Janet Smith case, 159-67; sexual and racial otherness, 150
railroads, 11, 25-26, 96, 105, 146, 157, 164
RCMP, 106
red-light districts, 98, 103, 109, 116
Reform era, 88-92, 96-97, 115-20
Regina, 32
Remington Typewriter Company, 12
Retail Clerks' Union (Winnipeg), 134
Richardson, Dorothy, 52
Roberts, Barbara, 28
Roberts, Wayne, 46

romance narratives: bride ships, 19-22, 24, 56; Cinderella narratives, 72, 79; figure of working girl, 51-58, 71-81, 173; historical romances, 12-13, 51-55; women immigrants, 28-29, 42
Rosen, Ruth, 93, 97
Rosenthal, Star, 125, 129
Rossland, British Columbia, 104
Rotenberg, Lori, 105

Sangster, Joan, 91-92
Saskatchewan, 32, 35, 125, 132, 148
Saskatoon, 32
Saxby, Jessie M., 18
Scott, Sir Walter, 51
Scottish societies, 163-64
segregation, 14, 35-37, 96, 149, 165-67
Senkler, Harry, 160-61
serial fiction, 52-53, 71, 72
servants. *See* domestic service
service sector, 11, 32-33, 35, 40-41
sex trade. *See* prostitution
sexual advice, 81-82
sexual downfall. *See* "fallen woman"
sexual harassment, 66-68
sexuality: attitudes toward, 91-92, 151; delinquency, 115-20; figure of working girl, 13, 24; identity, 86-87; illicit relationships, 83-87; sexual and racial otherness, 150; Sime's short stories, 59, 63-64; urbanization, 33-34, 63-64, 81-87, 115-20, 150; white women and racial threats, 152-56
Shearer, John G., "Canada's War on the White-slave Trade," 96-101
shop girls, 71, 74-79
short story, Sime's use of, 59
Sime, Jessie Georgina (J.G.), 8, 58-59, 63-65, 173; "A Woman of Business," 84-85; "An Irregular Woman," 83-84; "Bachelor Girl," 85-86; *Canada Chaps,* 59; *The Mistress of All Work,* 59; "Munitions," 62-63, 84; *Our Little Life,* 59; *Sister Woman,* 44, 50-51, 52, 58-59, 81-87, 170
Sinclair, Bertrand, 8, 55, 173; *North of Fifty-Three,* 53, 55-57, 60-62, 65-71, 72, 82, 171
Smillie, Christine, 125
Smith, Charlene P., 104
Smith, Janet, 145-46, 158-67
Smith, Mary Ellen, 132, 149, 159, 166, 167
Smith, Sidonie, 108, 109
snow parties, 154-55
social narratives, importance of, 6-7, 171
social realism, 12-13, 50-60, 65-71, 85, 171, 173
social reform movement, 91-97, 103, 115-19, 157
social science, rhetoric of, 91-92, 115-16
social transformation, working women and, 45, 85, 171-73, 175
society, moral breakdown of, 81-87, 95-96
Starkin, Edward, 159
Stead, William Thomas, "The Maiden Tribute of Modern Babylon," 92-93
stenographers, 11-12, 65-66, 169-70
stereotypes: Asian immigrants, 3, 14, 93-95, 145-46, 150-51; domestic service, 36; "Old Maid," 86; in racial discourse, 155-56; working women linked with prostitutes, 89-92, 97-103, 116, 119-20. *See also* gender stereotypes
Stockholm Syndrome, 69
Strange, Carolyn, 5, 39, 82, 87, 116-17
*Strike Bulletin (Western Labor News),* Winnipeg General Strike, 136-38
strikes: Gananoque, 54; picket lines, 122, 126-28, 131-32; Saskatchewan, 125; and social events, 128-31, 175; telephone operators' strike, 133-34, 174-75; Vancouver laundry workers' strike, 123, 125-34; Winnipeg General Strike, 123, 134-44
suffrage movement, 128-29, 129-30, 134

Sykes, Ella: advice for working women, 23; cultural responsibilities of women, 26-27, 172; on domestic service, 29, 31; "Log of a Calgary Stenographer," 11-12, 23, 169-70; voyage to Canada, 24-25; YWCA accommodations, 33

teachers, 11, 169, 171
technology, 84-85
telephone operators, 8, 124, 133, 135, 174
Toronto: demographics, 18, 116; non-domestic service employment, 35; prostitution, 105; sexual latitude, 41, 87; social reform movement, 103, 118-19; working girls as social problem, 5, 87, 116
Toronto Psychiatric Clinic, 91
Trades and Labor Council (Winnipeg), 134
Trades and Labour Congress, 54
travel accounts, 5, 18, 19-22, 20, 24
Trebilcock, Michael J., 158
Tynemouth (bride ship), 21-22
"typewriters," clerical workers as, 11-12, 169-70

unions. See under labour movement
United States, 12-13, 52, 71-72, 100, 107-8
urbanization: anxieties about sexuality, 33-34, 63-64, 81-87, 115-20, 150; corruption and moral degradation, 66-68, 88-89, 95-96, 98, 147, 149, 162-63; delinquency, 115-20; employment opportunities, 10-11, 172; figure of working girl as symbol of, 33-34, 42, 57, 66-68, 145-46; gender behaviour, 2-4, 35-37, 99-103; growth of cities, 32, 172; rejection of, 52-53; sex and the city, 81-87; in Sime's short stories, 59, 85; urban ghettos, 35; working girls as social problem, 5,

87, 116; working women and urban transformation, 35-37, 85, 115-20. See also industrialization; white-slave narratives
US Society for the Prevention of Vice, 107-8

Valverde, Mariana, 76-77, 95, 103
Van Kirk, Sylvia, 18-19
Vancouver: Chinatown, 94-95; demographics, 32; domestic service employment, 35; ghettos, 35; Industrial Home for Girls, 117-19; Janet Smith murder case, 145-46, 159-67; laundry workers' strike, 121-34; liminal quality, 3; opium trade, 154-55; as racial melting pot, 26, 145; telephone workers' strike, 174-75; union membership, 125; vice industry, 105; works set in: From Halifax to Vancouver (Pullen-Burry), 98-99; House of Windows (Mackay), 55, 57-58, 71-81; North of Fifty-Three (Sinclair), 53, 55-57, 61-62, 65-71; The Writing on the Wall (Howard), 93-95
Vancouver Daily World, and laundry workers' strike, 126-27
Vancouver Island, 121
Vancouver laundry workers, 123, 125-30, 132
Vancouver Local Council of Women, 31, 39-40, 147
Vancouver Province: on crimes against women, 149; laundry workers' strike, 126, 131-32; telephone workers' strike, 174-75
Vancouver Star: Janet Smith case, 162, 164-65; on mixed-race workplace, 145, 146-47, 164-65
Vancouver Sun: on mixed-race workplace, 145; Vancouver laundry workers' strike, 131
venereal disease, 92, 114

Victorian era: class- and race-based
hierarchies, 29, 30, 92, 102, 153;
ideal of family, 28; notion of "fallen
woman," 54, 58, 72, 80, 88-92, 95-
96, 115-20; societal expectations of
women, 1-4, 8-9, 12, 15-16, 19-20, 23,
91, 147
violence, strike actions, 122-27, 131-32,
135, 138-41
virginity, 90
Voisey, Paul, 11

wages: British Columbia Commission
on Labour report, 38-39, 174;
domestic service, 165; figure of
working girl, 154; justification for
lower wages, 36-39, 78, 117, 174;
Minimum Wage Board, 132, 186n35;
and prostitution, 97, 103-4, 154;
sexism in, 36-39, 83, 103-4; as strike
issue, 135; wage scales, 132, 149,
156, 186n35. See also employment/
employment opportunities
waitresses, 40-41
Ware, Vron, Beyond the Pale, 152-53, 163
western Canada: in Canadian fiction,
65-71; country-to-city migration, 11,
96-97, 99-101; demographics, 3-4, 9-
10, 32; domestic-service employment,
35; figure of working girl, 24-27,
32, 42, 65-71; gender-segregated
employment, 35-37, 165; inspiration
from, 88, 111-12, 171-72; pioneer
enthusiasm, 68; prostitution, 13, 88-
89, 103-15, 120, 171; reform rhetoric,
96-97, 116-18; shortage of women, 2,
16-20, 172; women's imagined space
in, 12-13, 16-17
Western Labor News, Winnipeg General
Strike, 136
white-slave narratives, 88-120; alarmist
notions, 6, 9, 98, 115; international
conspiracy, 89-92, 93-95; mobility, 95-

97; origins and conventions, 92-97;
prostitution, 13, 113-14; public balls,
101-2; as specific genre, 92-93, 96-97;
as urban legend, 95; and working
girls, 97-103, 119-20, 154
whiteness: desire for white Canada,
14, 25, 147-48, 156-59; gender and
immigration policies, 156-59; labour
laws, 148; and racial discourse, 147,
152-56, 163, 167; white women and
civilization, 12, 16-17, 19, 43; and
working women, 147-48, 163, 167.
See also race/racism
Whymper, Frederick, 21-23, 26-27
Winnipeg: Bloody Saturday, 140-41;
brothels, 109-10; demographics, 11,
32, 135; General Strike, 121, 123, 125,
134-44; union movement, 134; white-
slave trade, 96; "Women's Welcome
Home in Winnipeg" (Sykes), 24, 25
Winnipeg Evening Tribune: society
section, 141-42; Winnipeg General
Strike, 136-42
"woman adrift," 12, 36
women: Canadian recognition
of women authors, 50-52;
commodification of, 17-25;
conflicting narratives, 23-24, 29, 43,
172-73; and cultural reproduction,
25-32, 147, 153, 172; imperial
ideology, 2, 5, 7, 17, 23, 26-29, 42;
shortage of in Canadian West, 2, 16-
20, 18, 20; Victorian expectations of,
1-4, 8-9, 12, 15-16, 19-20, 23, 91, 147.
See also working women
Women's Bureau (Department of
Immigration and Colonization),
156-58
Women's Labor League, 134-35
Wong Foon Sing, 159-67
Woolf, Virginia, A Room of One's Own,
143-44, 170
workers' rights. See labour movement

workforce: demographics, 9-11; moral protectionism, 14, 34-35, 42, 147-48, 164, 166; stereotypes, 3-4, 8, 10-12, 35-37, 55-57, 172

working class: immigration, 156-59; racial discourse, 14, 147-56, 163, 167; sexuality, 98, 115-20

working conditions: department stores, 79-80; domestic servants, 165-66; prostitutes, 110-11; and Social Evil, 117

working women: advice for, 23, 27, 60-64; class distinctions, 71-81; definitions, 8-10, 50; demographics, 9-10; denigration of, 48-49; gender-stereotyped work, 36-37; labour activism, 121-44, 175; leisure activities/social life, 41-42, 81-87, 101-2, 160-62; literary representations, 12-13, 35-37, 42-43, 134, 161-62, 171-73; living conditions, 11, 33-34, 38-42, 99, 117; non-recognition of, 8-9, 16-17, 31, 35-37, 40-43, 64, 167, 173; "Only a Working Girl" (Joussaye), 46-48; perceptions of, 36, 41-42, 67, 82; and prostitution, 89-92, 97-103, 116, 119-20; single working girls/"bachelor girls," 20, 37-43, 82-83, 85, 122; and social transformation, 45, 85, 171-73, 175; symbolism and reputation, 2-8, 14, 30, 63-64, 72, 145, 163-64, 170-73; temporary status, 38-39; value of women's work, 30, 49-50, 64-65, 104, 107, 157. *See also* employment/employment opportunities; labour movement; women

workplace, 109-11; advice on etiquette for, 60-64; corruption, 66-68, 147, 150, 162-63, 167; gender roles, 2-4, 15, 17, 104, 107; gender-segregated employment, 35-37, 165; profanity, 40-41; workforce demographics, 9-10. *See also* mixed-race workplace; morality

youth culture, 39-40, 122, 133, 142-43, 160, 175

YWCA (Young Women's Christian Association), 11, 33-34, 67-68, 98-99, 101, 135-36

Printed and bound in Canada by Friesens
Set in Granjon and Bernhard by Blakeley
Copy editor: Robert Lewis
Proofreader: Anna Eberhard Friedlander
Indexer: Lillian Ashworth